Islamic Radicalism and Multicultural Politics

The British experience

Tahir Abbas

Routledge
Taylor & Francis Group

LONDON AND NEW YORK

First published 2011
by Routledge
2 Park Square, Milton Park, Abingdon, Oxon, OX14 4RN

Simultaneously published in the USA and Canada
by Routledge
711 Third Ave, New York, NY 10017

*Routledge is an imprint of the Taylor & Francis Group, an
informa business*

© 2011 Tahir Abbas

Typeset in Times New Roman by Glyph International Ltd

British Library Cataloguing in Publication Data
A catalogue record for this book is available from the British Library

Library of Congress Cataloging in Publication Data
A catalog record for this book has been requested.

ISBN 978-0-415-57224-8 (hbk)
ISBN 978-0-415-57225-5 (pbk)
ISBN 978-0-203-85004-6 (ebk)

Islamic Radicalism and Multicultural Politics

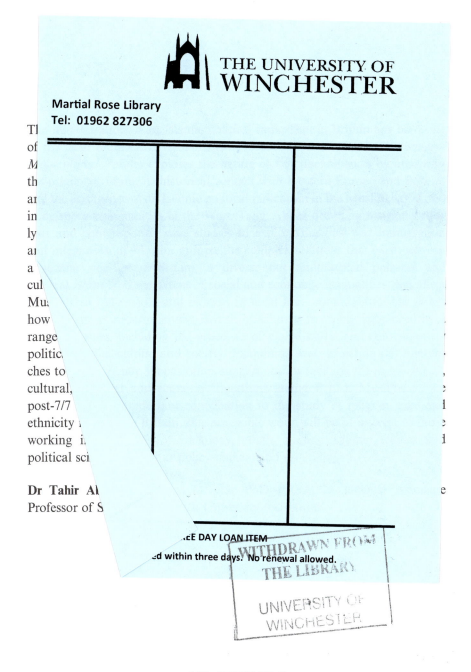

Tl
of
M
th
ar
in
ly
ar
a
cul
Mu
how
range
politic
ches to
cultural,
post-7/7
ethnicity
working i
political sci

Dr Tahir Al
Professor of S

To Mother and Father

Contents

Acknowledgements

The study of Muslims in Britain and in Western Europe is more significant and topical than ever. This is especially the case since the geopolitical developments at the end of the Cold War and the rise of 'Islamic fundamentalism' as a counter-hegemonic anti-capitalist discourse. Interest in Islam and Muslims has been compounded by the experience of violence, counter-ideology, misrepresentation and the misrecognition of the religion, culture, politics and its people. It has occurred in an increasingly interdependent world where negative media and political discourses are never far from the construction of this 'other', minority or majority, at home or abroad.

There has been considerable writing and commentary on the subject of Islam in the West, including the radicalisation of young Muslims, but there is a lack of study on the relations between Muslims and non-Muslims in Western European nation-states set in an economic, sociological and cultural context. The current project is not just about history, international relations, politics and theology (although they are an important part of the explanations behind the causes and solutions to radicalism), it relates also to aspects of the local, national and international that shape British Muslim experiences in the light of wider shifts to post-Cold War geopolitical and ethno-cultural relations between Islam and the West. After decades of research and writing there is a great deal that remains unclear about Muslims and Islam, especially in relation to social research and policy issues pertaining to minorities in Britain and in Western Europe. This book attempts to take the reader from the inception of a British Islamic community to current sociological, political and philosophical concerns that affect the understanding of Muslim minorities in Britain today. It is an analysis rooted in a study of the historical detail of the nature of Muslim minority communities as well as an evaluation of the economic, social, cultural and political dynamics of the lived experience in relation to issues of identity politics, radicalism, modernity, law, citizenship and multiculturalism.

I began writing the book in early 2005 as an analysis of the issues of identity and politics impacting on Muslims in Britain given the terrorist attacks in Madrid and the murder of Theo van Gogh in Amsterdam, both in 2004. With the events of 7/7 in London occurring soon after, there emerged a particular dimension to the study, one that invariably added considerable emphasis to the question of how it is possible to arrive at the phenomenon of the 'home-grown', 'made in Britain', 'Muslim terrorist'. Questions in relation to this event and subsequent issues of Muslim minority engagement, representation and participation have concerned academics, activists, think-tanks, policy-makers, theologians, community groups and political figures. Written by a social scientist educated within a secular liberal Western European scientific tradition, methodologically this analysis is historical and sociological. It incorporates a participant-observation and reflexive ethnographic account of the experiences of British Muslim minorities, combined with a detailed conceptual and theoretical analysis of the nature of communities in the light of the post-9/11 and post-7/7 social and political world using case studies.

To a significant degree, I have lived the experience of being a British Muslim and the challenges and opportunities that emerge as a second-generation minority stepping 'between cultures'. As to my ontological and epistemological position, as a social scientist and a British-born South Asian Muslim, I believe in a set of moral codes that dictate how I relate to others in any given context, and with any Muslim or non-Muslim. As a 'radical', I am a 'progressive liberal' who believes that religions are only relevant if they continue to advance their application to current social concerns, striving to make faith germane to the needs of the world today. Suffice to say, I have an appreciation of life in the West as well as of the religion of Islam, and this scholarly project is argued to be a logical and reasonable account, based on the use of social science tools of analysis and interpretation. I am not an Islamic scholar per se, rather I am a Muslim social scientist who studies individuals, groups, institutions and societies in context.[1] Readers are left to make up their own minds about its intellectual, political and spiritual impact.

Throughout the time I spent researching and writing this book, I was able to meet and engage with a number of highly regarded philosophers, scholars, researchers, mentors and friends, and they shaped my thinking and writing throughout, directly and indirectly. They include Muhammad Anwar, Ziauddin Sardar, Akbar S. Ahmed, Yasir Suleiman, Tariq Ramadan, Musharraf Hussain, Sheikh Ibrahim Mogra, Muhammad A.S. Abdel Haleem, John L. Esposito, Steven Vertovec, Jørgen S. Nielsen, Ceri Peach, James Piscatori, Carole Hillenbrand, John Rex, Frank Reeves, François Burgat, Nasr Abu Zayd, Jochen Blaschke, John R. Bowen, Yayha Michot, Sally Tomlinson, Máirtín Mac an Ghaill, David Marsh, Ash Amin,

---

1 Abbas, T. (2010) 'Muslim-on-Muslim Social Research: Knowledge, Power and Religio-cultural Identities', *Social Epistemology: A Journal of Knowledge, Culture and Policy*, 24(2): 123–36.

Stuart Croft, Scott Poynting Farhan Nizami, Waqar I.U. Ahmad, Samina Yasmin, Tariq Modood, Khurshid Ahmed, Anas Al Shaikh Ali, Mehri Niknam, Talip Küçükcan, Gareth Stansfield, Sajjad Rizvi, Salma Yaqoob, Nafeez Mosaddeq Ahmed, Sayyed Nadeem Kazmi, Arun Kundnani, H.E. Hellyer, Iftikhar Malik, Yunus Samad, Virinder Kalra, Humayun Ansari, Peter Sanghera, Aftab Ahmed Malik, Yayha Birt, Ed Hussain, Amir Saeed, Gabrielle Marranci, Mohammad M. Idriss, Ross Abbinnett, Rajinder Kumar Dudrah, Malcolm Dick and Jahan Mahmood. I also thank Nusrat Shaheen and Alex Hall for their support on a project on Islamophobia carried out at the University of Warwick in 1997. I am grateful to Baroness Kishwer Falkner of Margravine and Lord Nazir Ahmed of Rotherham for launching at the House of Lords my previous two edited collections in this area, as well as their continuous support (*Muslim Britain* in 2005 and *Islamic Political Radicalism* in 2007). I also thank the authors who made the two books possible, and those who made the trip to the Moses Room each time to speak about their contributions and to engage in lively debate. I thank Sir David Logan, former British Ambassador to Turkey, and Sir Francis Richards, former Governor of Gibraltar and former Head of Government Communications Headquarters, for the opportunities to work with them at the University of Birmingham. I also thank the many civil servants in Whitehall who were able to provide me with an insider perspective on policy. Dr Maleeha Lodhi, formerly High Commissioner for Pakistan in London, has remained an ardent supporter. Her ideas of 'enlightened moderation' remain important in defining the relations between Islam and the West.

I cordially thank the many other nameless people who took the time to speak with me about issues relating to Islam and Muslims in Britain, including many community elders, youths, students, politicians, writers, artists, activists, film-makers, journalists, theologians and historians from a range of different Muslim and non-Muslim communities across the globe. Invited seminar presentations, public lectures and conference papers given in USA, Europe and Asia provided me with a unique opportunity to present my ideas to a learned audience, and I am grateful for both the opportunity to travel and to meet and engage with interested individuals, groups and institutions, including universities, government departments and embassies. I must also thank my many diverse undergraduate and postgraduate students for the hours of stimulating discussion. Many of the issues explored in this book originate from the third-year course I taught at the University of Birmingham ('Islam, Multiculturalism and the State'). Invited speakers to seminars and conferences that the Centre for the Study of Ethnicity and Culture hosted on campus at the University (2004–7) were crucial in helping to give exposure to the sociological, political and social policy concerns facing British Muslims. Teaching in a social science faculty, many of students who took my course wanted to know about the issues behind radicalism and identity politics but had little, if any, independent knowledge of the religion of Islam or the nature of Muslim–West relations over the millennia. Thus, as with my former students, I start at the beginning of Islam itself. The usefulness of this book is that it ought to appeal to a range of readers – from the complete novice to the specialist looking for snippets of additional intellectual and policy insights.

I thank the Oxford Centre for Islamic Studies for granting me a timely visiting fellowship, permitting me to complete much of the book in the intellectual comforts of Oxford University. Last but not least, I thank Soni Diamond for reviewing my drafts, and James Whiting of Routledge for supporting the book project to its natural end.

Some of the original ideas in this book first appeared in my journal articles in this area to date, including *Journal of Muslim Minority Affairs* and *Journal of Intercultural Studies,* and opinion-editorials published in *Neue Zürcher Zeitung, Guardian Comment is Free, Birmingham Post* and *Muslim News.*

Any errors or omissions that remain are my own.

T.A.
April 2010

Preface and Introduction

The religion of Islam was founded in seventh-century Arabia. To be a Muslim is to submit to the one true God, Allah. Muslims believe that the message of Allah was revealed to Prophet Muhammad who was at the time of Revelation a successful Meccan trader, and the last of the great prophets of Islam. Islam has many facets, and even more descriptions; it is regarded as theology, culture, civilisation, empire, political ideology and a global economic system, and there are deep historical and contemporary intellectual discussions on these perspectives. Existence is predestined by Allah, but Muslims are free to exercise independent will. Spiritually and politically, if not culturally and intellectually, Muslims across the globe are united by the concept of the *ummah* (imagined and real global community).[1]

The unprecedented initial expansion of Islam led to half of the known world being conquered with huge swathes of territory continuing to be gained until the fifteenth century. The Crusades attempted to reclaim the 'Holy Lands', and Muslims lost and won them back, but parts of Africa, Central Asia, South Asia and South-East Asia have essentially remained under Islamic systems throughout their history. Contact with the West first took place during these battles for power and supremacy, and the view of the 'other' in starkly negative and oppositional terms was principally framed during this period. Nevertheless, the scientific, technological and philosophical advances of the 'Golden Age' (750–1250) of Islam had a tremendous role in the emergence of the European Renaissance, the Reformation and then the Enlightenment, as well as for subsequent political and cultural developments to Europe itself.[2]

England traded with Muslim entrepreneurs as early as the ninth century, and during the medieval period many attended the renowned institutions of higher learning in Fez, Cairo and Baghdad, bringing back an appreciation of the Arabic language, and knowledge of the intellectual and cultural

---

1 Watt, W.M. (1999) *Islam: A Short History*, second edition, Oxford: One World.
2 Sardar, Z. (2004) *Desperately Seeking Paradise: Journeys of a Sceptical Muslim*, London: Granta.

developments of Islam. What began with the Crusades and continued through the colonial encounters with Muslims between the sixteenth and twentieth centuries right through to the post-colonial nature of current relations characterises how Muslims regard 'the West' and how Britain and Western Europe regards Islam and Muslims today. During this time, sixteenth-century Ottoman and eighteenth-century Mughal rulers lived luxuriant lifestyles, while the Muslim masses remained subjugated and outside the spheres of economic and political influence. These inequalities in wealth distribution and the lack of democratic principles continue to plague many Muslim majority nations to this day. How colonials and nationalists were able to maintain age-old feudal systems of power and governance in the maintenance of underdeveloped social and political structures remains important to consider. This had an impact on how difference was conceptualised and understood, in particular in relation to those seen to have different religions and cultures, too. It had a role in racialising culture, and formalising hierarchical systems of domination and subordination.

It was after the end of the Second World War that Britain began to see significant waves of immigration from a range of once-colonised lands, and it is these Muslims that effectively symbolise notions of 'British Islam' today. From the initial need for post-war immigration, the attention turned towards assimilation, and when that appeared limited, integration, multiculturalism and anti-racism were all toyed with by successive Labour and Conservative governments. By the 1950s and 1960s immigration was regarded as undesirable, largely led by public opinion, so developments in anti-immigration policy and practice came alongside advances in anti-discrimination legislation. Visible minorities would be protected at home, while new migrant groups would find it harder to enter into Britain. Muslims who came to fill unwanted work in the declining manufacturing, engineering, heavy industrial and motor-vehicle sectors found their jobs disappearing at alarming rates. As a consequence of the immediate post-war racialisation of non-white migrant groups in the labour market and based on the dramatic decline of these traditional industrialised regions over the decades, Muslims found themselves to be socio-economically disadvantaged in particularly acute ways.

Thrust into vast urban metropolises, many rural-born Muslims, with distinct cultural affiliations to the sending regions, were initially unable to cope with the pressures and demands of urban, liberal, secular, Western-European life, as well as the limited opportunities for economic and social mobility. As a result of being unemployed, under-employed or simply discriminated against in the labour market, some turned to self-employment in historically and increasingly globally competitive economic sectors, such as retail and catering. Much of the Muslim entrepreneurial class, particularly outside of London, has remained geographically and economically isolated in the same deprived areas in which it first settled. Indeed, limited economic opportunities and the social injustices experienced by cultural, racial and religious minorities have, effectively, geographically concentrated groups in the least sought-after localities, with 'white flight' accelerating the process of residential clustering.[3]

By the end of the 1970s, Muslims, recognised largely as Pakistanis, Bangladeshis and also Indians, were experiencing severe instances of isolation, exclusion and disadvantage, and were mostly left to fend on their own. Found in clusters in parts of the south-east, the Midlands and the north, some of these groups were physically distinguishable, hence easily marked out for attention by right-wing fascists and violent nationalists known to make a sport of 'Paki-bashing'. Meanwhile, Muslim numbers grew relative to the majority population because of marriage, family reunification and high birth rates. This is in contrast to the fresh waves of Muslim immigration since the late 1970s; with for example the Arab elites from Saudi Arabia and the Gulf States or the Iranians fleeing the imminent arrival of the Ayatollah Khomeini and bringing with them considerable capital to some of most expensive parts of West London.

The 1980s revealed a particularly damaging economic recession brought on by neo-liberal economic policy and deregulation. The individual was champion, and the notion of society derided. The internationalisation of capital and labour, the forerunner of the globalisation of employment and education markets, affected a whole host of political, economic and social outcomes. Muslim communities, growing in numbers in the older parts of towns and cities, were particularly affected by the negative impact of the economic downturn, finding it difficult to live, work and organise as engaged communities. As the economic inequalities began to bite hard on Muslim groups, national cultural antipathy towards them began to increase. Since the publication of *The Satanic Verses* by Salman Rushdie in 1989, Muslim minorities in Britain have been portrayed and represented as individuals, groups and institutions that do not reflect the virtues of a liberal and apparently tolerant multicultural society, however ongoing a project as this might be in reality. Created by dominant Western media discourses, images beamed to the world of the 'Book Burnings in Bradford' illustrated the ostensible indifference that Muslims somehow exhibited towards majority society, as well as apparently demonstrating cultural, social and political traits regarded as antithetical to the needs and aspirations of the 'host society'. What these Muslim groups were broadly arguing was that they wanted sustainable employment, cultural acceptance, a voice and sincerity in their relations with majority communities. They desired to participate in society but lacked the trust, confidence and genuine physical support. Instead, the voices against the book were dismissed as reactionary zeal, with many political and media utterances regressing to the Orientalism of the

---

3 Peach, C. and G. Glebe (1995) 'Muslim Minorities in Western Europe', Ethnic and Racial Studies 18(1): 26–45.

'Muslim other'.[4] The idea of a multicultural Britain would remain problematised therein, with the year 1989 also witnessing the fall of the Berlin Wall and the emergence of a 'Clash of Civilisations' thesis that would persist throughout the 1990s and beyond.

During the 1990s, while the major Western powers enjoyed unprecedented global economic success, some Muslim nations were held back by famine, war, political instability and economic decline. After the first Gulf War of 1990–1, tensions in Bosnia, Sudan, Palestine, Kosovo, Chechnya and Afghanistan surfaced. These antagonisms fomented radical Islamisation on the part of politically motivated Muslims across the globe, and some disaffected individuals and groups began to find their way to Western Europe, with its already-significant presence of Muslims from once-colonised nations. These included the South Asians in Britain, Maghreb in France, Turks in Germany and the Albanians in Italy. With the arrival of Muslim 'refugees and asylum seekers' fleeing persecution and war, as well as the emergence of second and third generations frustrated with the lack of citizenship rights, many Muslims in Western Europe became angry about the condition of the *ummah,* their personal freedoms and the social progress generally experienced by majority 'others'. Negative external influence and the lack of internal cohesion made many young Muslim men particularly vulnerable to the political, ideological and theological forces of Islamism, and the call to violent jihad, with its everlasting promised rewards in Paradise.

In the late 1990s, a renegade Saudi of immense wealth, Osama bin Laden (1957–) was being influenced by Ayman Al-Zawahiri (1951–), who in the past was held captive and tortured in Egypt for his alleged association with a group thought to have assassinated President Anwar Sadat in 1981. The uncompromising ideologies of Al-Zawahiri gave Saudi-influenced Islamism a new prism. Osama bin Laden gained the status of mythical hero when he struggled against the Russians during their invasion of Afghanistan (1979–89), and he was present in Sudan for a short period before returning to Afghanistan to support the Taliban in the mid-1990s.[5] The latter are effectively the orphaned sons of the Mujahidin, victims of the 1980s Russian invasion, and subsequently 'rescued' by 'Islamist seminaries' expounding a literal reading of selected theology. The seeds of this radicalism were planted in the 1980s when the Mujahidin were initially bankrolled by Arab and by US-backed CIA funds channelled through Pakistan and its security services.[6] These seminaries acted as a starting point for many who would

4 Modood, T. (1990) 'British Asian Muslims and the Rushdie Affair', *Political Quarterly,* 61(2): 143–60.
5 Bergen, P. (2006) *The Osama bin Laden I Know: An Oral History of al Qaeda's Leader,* New York: Free Press.
6 Dreyfuss, R. (2005) *Devil's Game: How the United States Helped Unleash Fundamentalist Islam,* New York: Metropolitan.

later go on to training camps, learning the 'art of military jihad' without worry or attention from the outside world. This is not because of some intrinsic 'wahabification' of Islam, rather it was the limited educational spending by the Pakistani and Afghan states on education that meant parents were more content with schools remaining open and teachers at least turning up. In the mid-1990s, cementing its position as the single remaining superpower, seemingly crippling Iraq through sanctions with talk of its 'regime change' as early as 1998, the USA took its eye off the Islamist situation while paying greater attention to internal political scandal and division.

All this quickly changed with the dramatic fall of the Twin Towers in New York on 11 September 2001 (9/11). The USA was 'under attack', officially marking the beginning of the 'War on Terror'. The Western world was gripped with fear as the threat from violent Islamism was thought to be such that it could target any free Western individual or society at any time. The peril was presented as sophisticated, technologically advanced, well organised and ready to strike at any moment. No one was safe, and the only way to counter it was through 'smoking out' the threat 'dead or alive'. The USA and leading Western European nations were keen to react to this menace, and soon a 'coalition of the willing' went to war on Afghanistan, an already ruined country without effective social infrastructure or political stability, convinced that this was the only way to remove the 'head of the snake' that was thought to be Osama bin Laden. Part of an initiative of the 'New American Century' (as the only remaining superpower) was to remove all threats against it and the USA had the legitimacy it needed to make plans for military action, including for the invasion of Iraq in March 2003, defined as a process of bringing 'freedom and democracy' to ailing but 'dangerous' nations, later labelled as the 'Axis of Evil'.[7] In Britain, Prime Minister Tony Blair presented his messianic beliefs despite the nation being against him, 'dodgy dossiers' and the puzzling death of Dr David Kelly in July 2003 (the latter a top Ministry of Defence scientist who, arguably, knew most in Britain about the alleged weapons of mass destruction in Iraq). As anti-terror legislation began to erode civil liberties, the people of Britain, centre left think-tanks and political institutions, the intelligentsia, key columnists and political and social activists began to resist until Tony Blair was finally forced to leave office in July 2007.[8]

Since 2000, many Western nations have strengthened their anti-terror laws, giving policing and intelligence services unprecedented powers. Meanwhile, Islam and Muslims are often portrayed in negative-homogenised ways in media, political and cultural discourses. Excluded and disenfranchised,

---

7 Hiro, D. (2002) *Iraq: In the Eye of the Storm*, London: Nation.
8 Rawnsley, A. (2010) *The End of the Party: The Rise and Fall of New Labour*, London: Viking.

some Muslims in Britain and in other parts of Western Europe have further retreated into isolation as a defence against daily attacks on their presence in society. At home, they watch on their small screens the never-ending turmoil in Afghanistan, Iraq and Palestine. What is more, the 'fear psychosis' created by powerful states in the West during the most dramatic periods of war in Iraq and Afghanistan, in part, exacerbated the already loaded perceptions of vulnerable minds.[9] Some disaffected young Muslim men have viewed the 'War on Terror' as a war on Islam. The West is 'terrorised' by the 'other', which is defined in negative ways by the West itself. The most frustrated of the 'other' then react in the very terms set by the West.

In 2004, the Madrid train bombings and the murder of Theo van Gogh in Amsterdam caused great alarm in Britain. The essential question asked was: Could the same happen in Britain? On 7 July 2005, London experienced the first ever 'home grown' suicide-bombing in Western Europe (7/7), committed by second-generation young Caribbean, Kashmiri and Pakistani Muslim men from the north of England who attacked public targets in London. It was one of the most dramatic days in recent history for British Muslims, beyond doubt changing the course that 'British Islam' would take for ever. The subsequent conundrum is and still remains: How much are the events of 7/7, the failed terror attacks of 21/7 and the arrests and convictions of Muslim men, before and since, a problem of Islam or, indeed, the negative impact of limitations to domestic policy to effectively integrate Muslims at home with an apparently regressive foreign policy towards Muslim lands abroad?[10] It is arguably a position between grievance and ideology that defines the set of explanations here. While concerns remain in the context of the UK Muslim diaspora in relation to potentially twenty thwarted plots, a number of 'home-grown' plot attempts have also been foiled in other parts of the world, including Australia's Pendennis and The Toronto 18 Case, both in 2006.

As the questions become ever more complex, wider society has placed an emphasis upon the apparent unassimilability of Muslims, a policy focusing on 'community cohesion' as opposed to eliminating deep-seated structural inequalities, while there is a general widening of economic and social divisions in society as a whole. These attempts have placed the attention onto Muslims and not the workings of society. Policies seek to modify, improve or develop the behaviours of Muslims and the ways of Islam but not always the attitudes of majority society. Right-wing groups paint Muslims as the cause of all problems, i.e. whether it is to do with immigration or issues of perceived cultural relativism. At the same time, the relative economic, social

---

9 Furedi, F. (2007) *Invitation to Terror: The Expanding Empire of the Unknown*, London: Continuum.
10 Kundnani, A. (2007) *The End of Tolerance: Racism in 21st Century Britain*, London: Pluto Press.

and political positions of most Muslims have not improved since the days of the Rushdie Affair. Muslims in Britain are often weak and lack organisation and leadership, simply because 'the self' lacks confidence or capacity. The situation encourages the Government to talk of 'good Muslims are with us and bad Muslims are against us'.

A concentration on Muslim leadership reveals that it is often unrepresentative of most Muslims in society, while mosques and imams, in the main, are limited in their capacities. It is important to challenge and deal with these discrepancies as they were a concern well before 7/7 and have not merely emerged in the context of post-7/7 'prevent' policies. There is a worrying lack of knowledge of Islam, not just within majority society but also within Muslim communities, with protracted discussions in majority and minority politics focusing on values, identities and cultures on the one hand and individualised economics, sociology and politics on the other. The debate on the causes and solutions of radicalism sees the Left emphasise inequalities and the local impact of foreign policy, while the Right defends culture and nation. For Tariq Ali, the 'Clash of Civilisations' thesis has become 'a self-fulfilling prophecy', with projected power and influence resting with 'violent radical Islamists' on the one hand and 'neo-conservative Christian evangelicals' on the other – and, in the process, 'a clash of fundamentalisms' ensues.[11]

The potential for British Muslims to become involved in terrorism in Britain will remain if the status quo remains. To move forward, it needs to be recognised that the problems of violent extremism are not about the religion of Islam per se but global political ideology, a lack of national social cohesion and detrimental local area economic conditions. There is a genuine need to enhance and develop the appearance and application of Western European Islam, and one that is actively facilitated and encouraged by objective and rational-minded nation-states, improving the levels of trust, confidence, engagement and participation of existing and new Muslim minorities in Britain and in Western Europe.[12] If the global pressures in Muslim–West *and* Arab–Israeli relations are not alleviated, many more Muslim minorities in Western Europe will see the 'long war' as a 'war against Islam', the next global war, after the end of the Cold War.[13] While British Government policy struggles to deal with a whole host of security, policing, intelligence and community challenges, argumentation could be better connected. Reducing social and economic inequalities brings about

---

11 Ali, T. (2003) *The Clash of Fundamentalisms: Crusades, Jihads and Modernity*, London and New York: Verso.
12 Ramadan, T. (2005) *Western Muslims and the Future of Islam*, Oxford: Oxford University Press.
13 Rex, J. (2005) 'An Afterword on the Situation of British Muslims in a World Context', in T. Abbas (ed.) *Muslim Britain: Communities under Pressure*, London and New York, pp. 235–43.

social and community cohesion, helping to alleviate the potential for violent extremism. Whatever one can say about the nature and context of the events of 7/7, there is one thing that brings together all the many different young men found or thought to be involved in planning or executing acts of violent extremism or terrorism. They are all 'made in Britain'. For these young Muslims, radicalisation is as much about being British as it is about being Muslim.

Chapter 1 provides an historical account of the development of the religion of Islam and the character of early relations between the Muslim East and the Christian West, in particular, England. Chapter 2 explores the concept of 'Islamic political radicalism', based upon developments in Islam from the seventh to the twenty-first centuries, exploring different theological, political and cultural aspects of its growth. The immigration and settlement of British Muslims in the post-war era is dealt with in Chapter 3. It concentrates on the process of immigration, settlement and the sociological forces governing the lives of Muslim minorities in Britain. It also explores the current demographic position of British Muslims based on the 2001 Census, which posed the religion question for the first time since 1851. Chapter 4 examines the instances of education, employment and entrepreneurialism, as they are important structural concerns facing the British Muslim community, and how sociological research has attempted to rationalise the experience of underachievement and the 'Muslim penalty' in education and labour markets. Chapter 5 analyses the concepts of Orientalism and Islamophobia and how the negative images of Muslims and Islam are shaped by popular media and political discourses, and, in particular, in print news. Chapter 6 elaborates upon the concept of multiculturalism and how recent discussions in Britain have focused upon Muslims as somehow defining the problem of appropriately and adequately managing diverse societies, as well as introducing notions of how modernity is internalised by Muslims. Chapter 7 examines how violent Islamic political radicalism has emerged in the British case, exploring the nature of specific sociological, political and cultural processes in the context of challenges to individual and collective identities in an evolving local, national and global multicultural context. Chapter 8 is an analysis of the criminal-justice system and some of the specific prison, policing and anti-terror law concerns facing British Muslims in the post-9/11 and post-7/7 climate, including their impact on civil liberties. The final chapter concludes the debates in relation to the post-1945 experience of British Muslims and perspectives on political Islam through a sociological, economic, political science and social policy lens, and in an effort to determine the fundamental questions and potential solutions relating to issues of radicalisation and de-radicalisation in the current era.

1 From the historical to the contemporary …

How did Islam begin? What are its origins? How have Muslims arrived in Western Europe, and how are relations between Muslims and non-Muslims shaped? What are the origins of 'British Islam'? What are the implications for our present time? These are some of the many social, theological, cultural and political questions that need to be answered in any attempt to achieve an appreciation of the impact of Islam and Muslims on Western Europe and, specifically, on Britain in the current period. Without clear questions, it is not always possible to discern the nature of the contemporary experience. This opening discussion provides a broad introduction, not to explain the origins of the religion of Islam as merely a function of existing social, economic, political and cultural determinants but, rather, to elucidate its inception and to introduce current predicaments in the light of historical, theological, intellectual and political developments to the religion and its people since the seventh century. It also builds a foundation to better recognise the current issues of sectarianism, cultural relativism, the impact of colonialism and decolonisation, and the post-war immigration and settlement of a whole host of different Muslim ethnicities, nationalities and cultures across Britain. The current experience of violence, terror and radicalism is often presented as an association between Islam and Muslims, and this phenomenon is deconstructed through the lens of history, politics, economics and sociology.

The Arabian Peninsula is the birthplace of Islam. To the north lies Syria, and the land between the Tigris and the Euphrates rivers is modern Iraq, formerly the ancient land of Mesopotamia ('the cradle of civilisation') and the birthplace of both Judaism and Christianity.[1] To appreciate the nature of the lived experience that existed in Arabia before Islam, it is possible to take advantage of pre-Islamic history, as documented by Muslim and non-Muslim scholars, manuscripts from the Greeks and the Romans, and the discoveries of ancient relics and sites which have been

---

1 Armstrong, K. (2001) *Islam: A Short History*, London: Weidenfeld & Nicolson.

achieved through technologically advanced modern-day scientific excavations and observations.[2] In the centuries leading up to the inception of Islam in Arabia, the Near East was in political and economic turmoil. Once profiting from the Roman Empire through trade in incense in the south, the Arabian economy began to suffer because of the fewer numbers of pagans who were now converting to Christianity, as well as the general weakening of the Roman economy (Christianity became the religion of Roman Empire in 313 when Emperor Constantine (272–337) issued the 'Edict of Milan', legislating worship).[3] Because of ongoing conflicts strategic sea-trade routes were hard to find. Consequently, Arabian land routes became significant in the transport of vital goods and merchandise. They led to the development of the 'caravan trade' and, with it, contact and exchange with foreign cultures and beliefs. It created a settled, urbanised society with wealth, however, concentrated in the hands of the few. Social divisions, because of powerful tribalistic tendencies, led to particular forms of dissatisfaction in the region, raising questions about the underlying unequal social structures and the long-established religions and belief systems that seemingly justified them.

Before the arrival of Islam in Arabia, it was regarded by Muslims as in a state of *jahiliyah* (ignorance or barbarism). Arabian social life was based on a nomadic desert culture (bedouin), which relied on clan-kinship networks reinforced through patriarchy. It encouraged and facilitated values of tribal solidarity, and people generally believed in a primitive and fatalistic form of paganism. The region had a high level of cultural and social separation, but there was economic exchange and social contact with many civilisations, including Byzantium, Greece, Persia as well as Rome. Before the emergence of Islam in the seventh century, however, there was no political harmony in the Arabian Peninsula.[4] The nomadic tribes of the region pledged allegiance to a primordial religion where spirits were attributed to inanimate objects such as stones or trees. The pagan Arabs had no prescribed religious hierarchy, but, when wanting guidance, people conferred with soothsayers who would reply with oracular utterances. In Mecca, a central Arabian city at the heart of trade routes, tribes worshipped idols placed around and over the Ka'bah.[5] (According to Islamic tradition, Abraham and his eldest son, Ishmael, built the Ka'bah around 2000 BCE.) Many Islamic scholars have sought to explain the nature of this pre-Islamic period of idolatry and how it

2 Calder, N., J.A. Mojaddedi and A. Rippin (2003) (eds) *Classical Islam: A Sourcebook of Religious Literature*, London and New York: Routledge.
3 Crone, P. (1987) *Meccan Trade and the Rise of Islam*, Princeton, NJ: Princeton University Press.
4 Sardar, Z. (2006) *What Do Muslims Believe?* London: Granta
5 Rippon, A. (1990) *Muslims: Their Religious Beliefs and Practices, Vol. I: The Formative Period*, London: Routledge. The Ka'bah or Al-Bayt ul-Haram ('the honourable house') is a cubical building located at the centre of the mosque known as Al-Masjid Al-Haram in Mecca, Saudi Arabia. The mosque was built around the original Ka'bah.

impacted on the development of Islam. A renowned description is by Hisham ibn al-Kalbi (d. 819) in *The Book of Idols*, which makes reference to deities in pre-Islamic times that are also cited in the Qur'ān.[6]

Abraham is considered to be the patriarch of monotheism and the shared father of the Jews, Christians and Muslims. In Islam, the Israelite prophets were the progeny of Abraham's son Isaac, as well as profoundly important figures such as David, Jacob, Jesus, Joseph, Moses and Solomon.[7] The emergence of these celebrated prophets is seen as a blessing upon the people and nations of the Earth (through the lineage of Abraham). Such beliefs are unequivocally accepted by Muslims who state that faith in and respect of all the Abrahamic prophets are a critical aspect of belief. Knowledge of Abraham and views on the afterlife are comparable to Jewish and Christian values and beliefs. At the time of the origins of Islam in Mecca, religious persons were recognised as *kahins* (related to the Hebrew term, kohen, or priest), and the name of Allah equates with *Elohim* as God in the traditional Jewish perspective. The *Hanifs* (pre-Islamic monotheists) regarded Allah as *Al-Rahman* (the Merciful) in pre-Islamic times. *The Book of Idols* states that certain rituals associated with the Meccan pilgrimage are continuations of pre-Islamic rites and that these originally had pagan connotations.[8] Yet, Allah legitimises these traditions because they were found in Abraham and Ishmael, who had historically lived in Mecca, and that Abraham is the 'first Muslim'.[9]

Knowledge of pre-Islamic history is significant for historians and social scientists concerned with developing an understanding of the emergence of Islam, as well as for Muslims who accept the materialisation of Islam in relation to its wider socio-cultural past. Islam, as revealed and taught by Muhammad, who, of Arab origin would be the one to win over the Arabs to monotheism and the belief in the one true God, Allah.

In the year 570, Muhammad was born into the family of the Quraish clan, the ruling tribe of Mecca since the fifth century, and in the Hijaz region of north-west Arabia. The Ka'bah, located in the centre of Mecca, was originally a shrine of ancient origin, according to Muslims, to the time of Abraham himself. With the weakening of the southern Arabian economy, Mecca became a significant hub of sixth-century trade with the Byzantines, Ethiopians and Sassanians. The city of Mecca was regulated by formidable and prosperous trading families, with the Quraish clan unequalled. Muhammad's father, Abd Allah ibn Abd al-Muttalib (545–70), died before

6 Faris, N.A. (1952) *The Book of Idols, Being a Translation from the Arabic of the Kitab Al-Asnam by Hisham Ibn-Al-Kalbi*, Princeton, NJ: Princeton University Press.
7 Lowin, S.L. (2006) *The Making of a Forefather: Abraham in Islamic and Jewish Exegetical Narratives*, Leiden: Brill.
8 Bach, M. (1984) *Major Religions of the World*, London: DeVorss.
9 Rodinson, M. (2002) *Muhammad*, London: New Press.

the birth of his son. Muhammad's mother Amina bint Wahb (d. 577) passed away when he was six, and the orphan boy was put into the care of his grandfather, Abd al-Muttalib (497–578), leader of the Hashim clan. After the death of his grandfather within two years of his mother's, Muhammad was eventually raised by an uncle, Abu Talib (549–619). As was the case at the time, Muhammad as a young child lived away with a separate Bedouin family. This tradition was followed by the noble families of Mecca, Medina, Taif and in other towns of the Hijaz region. The experience had important implications for Muhammad. In addition to enduring the harshness of desert life, Muhammad developed an acute awareness of the rich language endeared by the Arabs, and whose oral traditions are a renowned cultural attribute.

In his early twenties, Muhammad built up a reputation as a successful trader of caravans, entering the employment of a wealthy widow named Khadijah al-Kubra (555–619 or 623). At some point soon after, Khadijah married Muhammad, with whom there were two sons (who did not survive) and four daughters. Muhammad did not take another wife until after her death. During this period in his life, Muhammad journeyed extensively. At the age of around 40, retiring to meditate in a cave on Mount Hira, which is just beyond the walls of Mecca, the first of the important events of Islam occurred. One day, sitting contemplating in the cave, a voice could be heard, which was later identified as that of the Angel Jibreel (Gabriel). It ordered Muhammad to, 'Read in the name of thy Lord who creates, creates man from a clot! Read, for your Lord is most Generous, (it is He) who teaches by the means of a pen, teaches man what he does not know.'[10] Three times Muhammad argued his incapacity to do so, but the same command was given on each occassion. Finally, Muhammad recited the words of what are now the first five verses of the ninety-sixth *sura* (or chapter) of the Qur'ān, words that proclaim Allah the Creator of humankind and the source of all knowledge. Instantly, Muhammad began sermonising the messages he received; Khadijah was the first convert, soon followed by his cousin and an eventual future successor, Ali ibn Abu Talib (599–661). As more revelations came to Muhammad asserting the oneness of Allah, his following expanded; first among the underprivileged and the enslaved and then later among the more powerful people of Mecca. The revelations received over the course of a twenty-three-year period are incorporated into the Qur'ān, the scripture of Islam or the 'Last Testament'.[11]

10 Qur'ān, 'The Embryo' (Al-'Alaq), 96: 1–5; Sardar, Z. (1978) *Muhammad: Aspects of his Biography*, Leicester: Islamic Foundation; Rogerson, B. (2004) *The Prophet Muhammad: A Biography*, London: Abacus.
11 Crone, P. and M. Hinds (2003) *God's Caliph: Religious Authority in the First Centuries of Islam*, Cambridge: Cambridge University Press.

Not everyone tolerated the words of Allah conveyed through Muhammad. In his own clan, there were those who vehemently rejected his words, with many powerful merchants actively opposing the message as it was a direct threat to their hegemony. The resistance, however, served only to strengthen the mission of Muhammad and his promulgation, understanding and appreciation of how Islam was distinct from paganism. The belief in the unity of Allah is supreme in Islam – from this all else ensues. Verses in the Qur'ān emphasise the uniqueness of Allah, cautioning those who refute it of the punishments in the afterlife that follows. The verses pronounce Allah's limitless compassion to those who submit to his will. For Muslims, they affirm the Last Judgement, when Allah, the Judge, will determine the balance of right and wrong and good and evil in the work of every man and woman, rewarding the faithful while chastising the disbelievers. Because the Qur'ān rejects polytheism and emphasises the moral responsibility of people, it presented a powerful but difficult challenge to the existing standing and authority of the worldly but pagan Meccans.

It is significant to note that Muslims believe that the transmissions from Jibreel to Muhammad came directly from Allah Muhammad was merely the messenger of Allah and Jibreel continued to convey messages from Allah to Muhammad until his passing away at the age of sixty-three, the last of which came nine days before Muhammad's end on Earth.[12] Islam states that this message is similar to that received by the early Hebrew prophets: that Allah is one; He is all-powerful; He is the Creator and Lord of the Universe; and that there will be a final judgement day when those who have obeyed the will of Allah shall benefit from Paradise in Heaven and those who have not will be condemned to Hell. The concepts of good and evil, right and wrong, and heaven and hell are also part of the Zoroastrian and Christian faiths which were well established in the region at the time.

By 615, Muhammad had acquired many followers. These early Muslims were, however, ill-treated in Mecca, predominantly by prosperous traders who dominated the city, fearing that the new faith would challenge their economic monopoly. That year, about 80 Muslims fled from Mecca to Abyssinia (present-day Ethiopia) to take refuge with welcoming Christians who were foes of the polytheistic Meccans. The Abyssinian Christians gave Muslims protection and support, which helped to shape a positive view of Christianity. Muhammad, throughout his time, regarded both Jews and Christians as *Ahl al-Kitab* (People of the Book), as both these faiths have a holy scripture. Muhammad considered Judaism and Christianity to be more advanced than the polytheistic and humanist religions of Arabia. Thus, Islam has several philosophies in common with these two older religions,

---

12 Rogerson, B. (2006) *The Heirs of the Prophet Muhammad and the Roots of the Sunni–Shia Schism*, London: Abacus.

and this is why it is deemed 'The Last Testament' and that Abraham is indeed the 'first Muslim'.

For Muslims, the Qur'ān is the final revelation from Allah. In Arabic, the Qur'ān is also presented as *Al-Kitab* (the Book), *Al-Furqan* (the Standard), *Al-Mashaf* (the Script), *Al-Dhikr* (the Invocation), as well as other designations. The Qur'ān is separate from the Hadith, which are the remarks of Muhammad himself, often compiled many hundreds of years after his death. It is recognised that Muhammad clearly distinguished between his own thoughts (the *Hadith*) and the words of Allah, which are ultimately the words found in the Qur'ān. Muslims and scholars of Islam believe that the Arabic Qur'ān contains the same Arabic that was conveyed to Muhammad (although there is evidence to support the view that the Qur'ān was codified soon after his lifetime).[13] Muslims believe that the words themselves are those revealed by Allah, and the act of reciting or reading the Qur'ān is believed to be a means of receiving *baraka* (blessing) from Allah. Thus, it is not unusual that Muslims study how to read the Arabic Qur'ān without necessarily always appreciating its meaning. Not always able to read the quranic letters, many Muslims believe that they can gain from hearing the poetry and inviolability of the original Arabic.[14] Muslims argue that the Qur'ān provides the complete set of codes for Muslims living an honest, chaste and satisfying life in obedience to the instructions of Allah, in this life and in the next. It is the teaching manual for every Muslim, and it is the 'constitution' of the Kingdom of Heaven on Earth. The Qur'ān is the eternal contemporary for all Muslims.[15]

While it is true that throughout history many have tried to challenge the Qur'ān, the historical and social contexts in which it became known relate to a dedicated field of knowledge. The fact that Western historians have given a great deal of attention to this text suggests much about modern attitudes towards its study but little about Muslim perceptions of the significance of the Qur'ān.[16] For Muslims, the divine word assumes a specific Arabic form, and this form is as essential as the meaning that the words communicate. Hence, only the Arabic Qur'ān is the Qur'ān, and translations are merely interpretations. Translations into local languages of the Islamic world, particularly Farsi and Persian, were carried out during the early period, arguably at the time of the revelations themselves. These were not separate works, but rather interlinear commentaries on the meaning

---

13 Whelan, E. (1998) 'Forgotten Witness: Evidence for the Early Codification of the Qur'an', *Journal of the American Oriental Society*, 118(1): 1–14; Crone, P. and M. Cook (1977) *Hagarism: The Making of the Islamic World*, Cambridge: Cambridge University Press.
14 Murata, S. and W.C. Chittick (1996) *The Vision of Islam*, London: I.B. Tauris.
15 Esposito, J.L. (1991) *Islam: The Straight Path*, Oxford: Oxford University Press.
16 Rippon, A. (2008) (ed.) *The Blackwell Companion to the Qur'an*, new edition, Oxford: Wiley-Blackwell.

of the text, and they acted to assist a deeper understanding rather than to change it.[17]

The Arabic form of the Qur'ān is in many instances more significant than the sense of the text. After all, Muslims have diverged over the reading of quranic verses as much as believers of other faiths have conflicted over their own scriptures. One of the foundations of Islamic intellectual history and its development is the diversity of explanations given for the same verses. Muslims often quote Muhammad who said that every verse of the Qur'ān has seven interpretations, commencing with the literal sense, and in relation to the seventh and highest meaning, 'Allah alone knows that'. The language of the Qur'ān is imaginistic, with each word having a vibrancy based upon the special nature of the Arabic language. Unsurprisingly, people comprehend diverse meanings from the same verse. The depth of quranic language and its openness towards different readings helps to explain how this single book gave rise to one of the greatest civilisations of the world. If people had understood exactly the same thought from the same text the religion would arguably never have spread as widely as it has done. The Qur'ān resonates its message to every man, woman and child as it does to the artist, the scholar or the poet.

The Qur'ān has been translated into English many times, but it is argued that each translation symbolises an individual appreciation of the text. Each is significantly different from the other and none is the Qur'ān itself. The quranic perspective is closely associated with the Arabic language, which, like Hebrew and Aramaic, is part of the Semitic family. Reasoning within the Semitic languages is distinct from that of Indo-European languages such as English, Latin, Persian and Sanskrit. Each word originates from a source made up of three letters, and from this root many different forms are built, and, typically, only a few of these are actually used. Without such a debate, it would be impracticable to articulate the richness of the linkage of meanings, the complexity of interpreting words into English and the inter-relationships among Arabic words that are clearer in the original.[18]

Thirty years after the death of Muhammad, the Caliphs ('successors to the prophet') spread Islam to the four corners of the world. The speed of this advance was remarkable. By the time of the fourth Caliph, Ali (599–661), half the known world was under Islamic rule.[19] This fact alone helps to explain the reason for tensions among the ruling elites of Mecca. After Ali was assassinated, Muawiyah (602–80), who was Governor of Syria for the previous twenty years, took over the caliphate. Muawiyah made succession

17 Robinson, N. (1997) 'Sectarian and Ideological Bias in Muslim Translations of the Qur'an', *Islam and Christian–Muslim Relations*, 8(3): 261–78.
18 Versteegh, K. (2001) *The Arabic Language*, Edinburgh: Edinburgh University Press.
19 Robinson, F. (1989) (ed.) *The Cambridge Illustrated History of the Islamic World*, Cambridge: Cambridge University Press.

hereditary, installing Umayyad dynastic rule in the process, and was eventually succeeded by his son Yazid (645–83). In response, the secessionists
gathered around Ali's youngest son, Hussain (by Fatima, daughter of
Muhammad), and they rose up against Yazid, who considered the caliphate
his birthright. Hussain, his entire family and a small group of loyal followers
were tragically slaughtered in Kerbala in 680 by Yazid. From this, the
Umayyad dynasty established power through conquest and industry.[20]
Moving the capital to Damascus, Umayyad Caliphs governed an extensive
empire that stretched from Europe to India. While Muhammad had lived in
modest accommodation inside the walls of the Medina mosque, less than
one hundred years later Caliphs were building vast palaces and fiefdoms.
They were economically wealthy and politically strong. The social revolution that Muhammad instigated, which led to the development of a pan-
Arab faith, based on eliminating inequality and delivering social justice,
arguably reverted to tribalist tendencies inherent in the Arabian culture in
pre-Islamic times. The accumulation of economic power combined with
military (and diplomatic) expansion led to political intrigue, and assassina-
tions were rampant throughout this period. The leading man in Mecca was
Abu Sufyan ibn Harb (560–650) when Muhammad preached his initial
message. His son, Muawiyah, founded the Umayyad dynasty. It was his son
and successor, Yazid, who was responsible for the cruel murder of Hussain,
grandson of Muhammad.

Under the authority of the Umayyads, political and social dominance
remained in the hands of a few merchant Arab families. The Muslims,
whose numbers had grown significantly as the empire expanded, became
increasingly disgruntled, especially as the Umayyads augmented their
income from raising land taxes. Resistance centred in Persia, where there
remained continued antagonism towards Syrian control, encouraging certain
groups to combine forces with the Abbasids – this dynasty takes its name
from its ancestor Abbas ibn Abd al-Muttalib (566–662), the youngest uncle
of Muhammad. These Abbasids overthrew the Umayyads in 750, executed
the Caliph Marwan II (688–750), acquiring the caliphate for themselves. All
the members of the Umayyad family were found and killed, except for Abd-
ar-Rahman I (731–88), who ran away to Cordoba in Spain in 756, briefly
ruling as an autonomous emir. In 762, the capital of the Islamic world was
moved to Baghdad and founded on the Tigris river by the second Abbasid
Caliph, Al-Mansur (754–75).[21] The Abbasids also ruled from Samara

20 The first four Caliphs were Abu Bakr Siddiq (close companion of the Prophet, died two
   years after); Umar al-Kattab from 634 to 644; Othman bin Affan, who was murdered
   twelve years later, in 656; and Ali, who was assassinated in 661.
21 Shaban, M.A. (1979a) *The Abbasid Revolution*, Cambridge: Cambridge University Press;
   Shaban, M.A. (1979b) *Islamic History: A New Interpretation: AD 600–750 (AH 132), Vol. I*,
   Cambridge: Cambridge University Press.

during the ninth century for a brief period. Ultimately, they gained control of the Islamic empire as it was then from the year 570 and remained in power until 1258 when Baghdad fell to the conquering Mongols, flattening the city and viciously slaying Al-Musta'sim Billah (1213–58), the last of the Abbasid Caliphs of Baghdad.

In the initial one hundred years of Islam, the Abbasids were omnipotent, both over Islam and over all the Muslims. Many Shi'a groups, however, spurned the authority of the Abbasids. Transformation came towards the end of the ninth century and it began with Sunni theologians taking over religious control and dismissing the Caliphs. This change in power was apparent after the *Mihna* ('inquisition') of the mid-ninth century. The *Mihna* was institutionalised in 833 by the Abbasid Caliph, Al-Ma'mun. He ordered the translation of Greek philosophy and science into Arabic. As a *Mu'tali-zite,* Al-Ma'mun believed the Qur'ān could be proven through reason. The *Mihna* involved questioning *Qadis* (judge) about their logical reasoning in relation to whether the Qur'ān was created or revealed. Those passing the 'test' were sent out to test others. Extensive actions were taken against those who failed the test, including removal from public office, imprisonment and even public flogging.

The Shi'a Buyids, originally from Persia, were the definitive commanders in chief from 945 until 1055.[22] These Buyids were strong enough to remove Caliphs at their own discretion. Eventually, the Caliphs lost their hold on power, and the unity of the Caliphate fell apart, leading to the formation of independent states. The authority of the Caliph was still recognised, but was only maintained in symbolic terms. In 1055, Turkish Seljuqs (1037–1157) took Baghdad. There was little to alter the status of the Caliphs. With Baghdad destroyed by the Mongols in 1258, a new strand of the Abbasid began in Cairo. Their authority, however, was restricted by locality, though this final subdivision of the Abbasids remained in power until 1517. Harun al-Rashid (763–809), the fifth and one of the most recognised of the Abbasid Caliphs, was infamously portrayed in *The Thousand and One Nights (Arabian Nights)*, compiled between 800 and 900, containing such renowned tales as *Aladdin, Ali Baba and the Forty Thieves* and *The Seven Voyages of Sinbad the Sailor.*[23]

This period in Islamic history was marked by significant scientific, cultural, technological and religious development. The Abbasid era (750–1258) is often considered the 'Golden Age' of Islamic history and civilisation. In the ninth and tenth centuries, classical European cultural and scientific

22 Busse, H. (1973) 'The Revival of Persian Kingship under the Buyids', in D.S. Richards (ed.), *Islamic Civilisation 950–1150*, Oxford: Bruno Cassirer, pp. 47–69.

23 Clot, A. and J. Howe (2005) *Harun Al-Rashid and the World of the Thousand and One Nights*, London: Saqi; Haddawy, H. (2008) *The Arabian Nights: Based on the Text Edited by Muhsin Mahdi*, London: W.W. Norton & Co.

achievement waned while the Muslim world flourished. Muslims mass-produced books after learning the art of paper-making from the Chinese. This fuelled the production of knowledge and the wide-ranging dissemination of ideas. Muslims translated all they could find into Arabic, including what were considered lost Grecian texts; the works of Aristotle and Plato became known to the Western world precisely because of the work of Al-Farabi (872–951). Through these translations, Islamic and Greek thinking came to be recognised in Western Europe, and Western schools of learning began to flourish as a result.[24] The oldest university in the world, still running to this day, is the Islamic University of Fez in Morocco, known as Al-Qarawiyin, founded in 859 by Fatima al-Fihri. (Al-Azhar University in Cairo, founded in 975, is slightly younger.) The Islamic system of education was imitated across Europe. The term 'chair' at a university reflects the idea of the *kursi* (Arabic for 'chair') upon which a teacher sits when instructing students in a *madrasa* (school of higher learning). Advances to astronomy, mathematics, chemistry, zoology, psychology, botany and veterinary science were made by the Muslims. Two hundred and fifty years before Galileo discovered the rotation of the Earth around its axis, Al-Biruni measured the circumference of the globe (between 950 and 1000). In 1121, Al-Khazini (d. 1130) published *The Book of the Balance of Wisdom*, which identified a universal force directed to the centre of the Earth, 566 years before Isaac Newton formulated the theory of universal gravitation. Muslims developed hospitals; there were sixty in Baghdad during the tenth century.[25] These were remarkably advanced for their time, and they laid the foundations for much of modern-day practice. They contained pharmacies, libraries, lecture theatres for medical students, separate wards for men and women, as well as out-patient facilities. Muslims excelled in surgery and medicine, and gained knowledge of the workings of the eye and in understanding the human blood system. They travelled extensively – indeed, to every part of the known world. Ibn Battutah (1304–68) is the Arab Marco Polo – Marco Polo is the Venetian Ibn Battutah.[26] Muslims developed charts and maps, even a full postal system. Town planning was developed with public spaces, organised streets and elaborate fountains, as well as through the conservation of natural and wildlife conservations. What remains of the architecture speaks for itself.[27]

24   Fakhry, M. (2004) *A History of Islamic Philosophy*, New York: Columbia University Press.
25   Surty, M.I.H. (1996) *Muslim Contribution to the Development of Hospitals*, Birmingham: Qur'anic Arabic Foundation.
26   Battutah, I. (2002) *The Travels of Ibn Battutah*, edited by Tim Mackintosh-Smith, London: Picador.
27   Sardar, Z. and Z. A. Malik (1999) *Introducing Muhammad*, Cambridge: Icon; Al-Hassani, S.T.S., E. Woodcock and R. Saoud (2007) (eds) *1001 Inventions: Muslim Heritage in Our World*, Manchester: 1001 Inventions; Wallace-Murhpy, T. (2007) *What Islam Did For Us: Understanding Islam's Contribution to Western Civilization*, London: Watkins.

As European civilisation entered the Middle Ages, there was barely a field of learning, art, literature or architecture that was not influenced by Islam. Islamic knowledge had become an essential part of Western civilisation. In the area of mathematics in particular, Muslims provided a range of important scientific developments. These made a significant contribution to the emergence of the Renaissance. Muslim scientists are acknowledged for having adopted an essential mathematical instrument from the Indian Hindus, the decimal system, and they are arguably most recognised for their advancement of algebra. It gave Muslim scientists a commanding tool: the capacity to handle variable quantities in mathematical equations and the means to generate solutions to questions of progressively escalating complexity. Muslims redefined Greek arithmetic operators, and devised concepts of their own. They expanded numerous practical rules in mathematics, enabling scientists to manage large numbers easily, significantly beyond the capacities of the techniques they supplanted. If it was not for the formalisation of the zero, the idea of abstract mathematical thinking would be inconceivable.[28] With these means at their disposal, Renaissance thinkers were able to carry out scientific study into many different areas of the pure sciences, specifically alchemy, astronomy, mathematics and physics.

In this 'Golden Age' of Islam, notable mathematicians and physicians emerged such as Al-Khwarizmi (c. 790–840), with geographers such as Al-Masudi (d. 956), scientists such as Al-Kindi (801–73), physicians such as Al-Razi (865–25), and talented scholars such as the eleventh-century Al-Biruni (973–1048), who, not content as celebrated mathematician and astronomer, wrote an important anthropological treatise on India while spending seven years studying and living there. This empiricism and robust scientific methodology arrived into Western Europe through Spain and remained to make a significant impact over the centuries. During the seventeenth century, texts in astronomy, chemistry, mathematics and medicine, written in the Arabic script, were indispensable to English higher education. The first chair of Arabic was created in Cambridge in 1633, with Oxford following in 1636. Muslim cerebral polymaths were identified by anglicised names: Alfarabi (Ibn Farabi, 872–951), Algazel (Al-Ghazali, 1058–1111), Avicenna (Ibn Sina, 980–1037) and Averroes (Ibn Rushd, 1126–98).

Within a century of the revelation of the Qur'ān, Islam came to interact with European civilisation and Christianity. Initially, Islam and Christian Europe learnt to cooperate with each other, helping to shape the history of the 'other'. One example of such interdependency was Offa of Mercia. An omnipotent eighth-century Anglo-Saxon monarch, he had coins inscribed with the Arabic declaration of Islam ('There is no god but Allah')

---

28 Al-Daffa, A.A. (1977) *Muslim Contribution to Mathematics*, London: Croom Helm; Berggren, L. (2004) *Episodes in the Mathematics of Medieval Islam*, New York: Springer-Verlag.

and used them to trade with the Muslims of Arabia. The Ballycottin Cross, which was located on the coast of southern Ireland, and which approximates to a period in the ninth century, also displays an inscription in Arabic *(Bismillah* – in the name of Allah). By the fifteenth century, more Europeans were living in North Africa than in the rapidly developing colonies of North America. British travellers to the East returned with extensive tales of their fellow countrymen thriving in service to the Ottomans. Queen Elizabeth I had strong commercial relations with the Ottomans, and was able to use the special relationship to strategically help protect against the threat from Catholic Europe.[29]

With the advent of the Renaissance, however, Western Europe not only moved away from its medieval past, but it also overlooked the influence of the Islamic world, one founded on intellectual admiration in spite of religious difference. The most significant episode in relation to this was the series of Crusades, the first of which was sanctioned by Pope Urban II (1042–99) and supported by a number of European monarchs.[30] The object, while political, was to bring the 'Holy Lands' back to Christianity, and in particular Jerusalem. Urban II evoked the religious passions of the knights by suggesting that Muslim Turks were stealing from and persecuting Christian pilgrims on their way to the 'Holy Lands'. The war gave the knights an opportunity for glory, wealth and martyrdom. Urban II urged that they waged war with Muslims as an alternative to fighting one another as they competed for wealth, status and plunder in an incohesive social and political world.

The first of the Crusades began on 27 November 1095. In the beginning, there were genuine military achievements, and local Western European rule was created in areas of Palestine and Syria, but Muslims regained dominance. In 1187, Salah ad-Din Yusuf Ibn Ayyub (Saladin, c. 1137–93), the celebrated Muslim leader, retook Jerusalem and overcame the Crusaders. The eighth and last of the crusades was in 1270, headed by Louis IX (1215–70), King of France, son of Louis VIII (1187–1226). There were no further attempts to recapture the 'Holy Lands' after 1291. The English contribution to the Crusades was nominal, with Richard I (the Lionheart, 1157–99), the only King of England to personally take part (Edward I took part as heir to the throne).[31] In the final analysis, the Crusaders were unable to retrieve the 'Holy Lands', but the conflicts had another outcome. Western Christian European men left their places of birth to fight long wars in faraway lands. In England, the narratives of the Crusaders returning with tales and accounts of the 'Muslim other' encouraged fellow countrymen to travel

29 Matar, N. (1998) *Islam in Britain, 1558–1685*, Cambridge: Cambridge University Press.
30 Riley-Smith, J. (2002b) *What Were the Crusades?* Basingstoke: Palgrave-Macmillan.
31 Riley-Smith, J. (2002a) *The Oxford History of the Crusades*, Oxford: Oxford University Press.

and see beyond their own towns and villages, effectively, for the first time in their history. The encounter brought to bear negative narratives of the 'Muslim other', as well as a desire for the material riches of the East, including jewels, silks and spices.[32]

At the same time, within the Islamic world there were divisions and feuds, and the corrupt and luxurious lifestyles of rulers made it difficult to sustain *asabiya* ('groupdom' or social cohesion); a concept conceived by the classical philosopher-historian Ibn Khaldun (1332–1406). The problems were initially compounded when Baghdad was sacked by the Mongols in 1258. Hulaga Khan (1217–65), grandson of Genghis Khan, conquered the then-centre of the Muslim caliphate, slaughtering its inhabitants and burning its great library, *The House of Wisdom*. Some Muslims regarded this military loss as an outcome of their overt recognition of ethnic and cultural diversity, and so the emphasis on *ijtihad* (logical spiritual struggle or individual reinterpretation of Islam in the light of 'modernity') was discarded with a newly transformed concentration on 'aggressive jihad'. Soon after, Ibn Taymiyyah (1262–1328), a Syrian mystic, established the fundamentals of a confrontational 'revivalism' that remains to this day the theological font for much of counter-ideological thinking among Muslims in the West (see Chapter 2). He was renowned for issuing *fatwas* (religious edicts) against the Mongols, who were viewed as 'unbelievers' regardless of their own claims. Matters were made more complex by the loss of Spain to Ferdinand and Isabella, with this period marking the end of the ascendancy of the Islamic world, as Abu Abdullah (c. 1460–1533), also known as Broadbil, the Caliph or Prince of Granada, knelt before Ferdinand on 2 January 1492, ending 800 years of Muslim dominance in Spain. These events fuelled a gradual decline, and by the end of the fifteenth century, the *ulema* (religious scholars) reduced the concept of *ilm* from 'all knowledge' to 'religious knowledge', and limited *ilma* from meaning the 'consensus of the community' to that of the *ulema* itself. The reading of the Qur'ān became frozen in time; it lost its dynamism, altering the Islamic lived experience from an open to a closed one. The printing presses were shut, depriving Islam and Muslims of the oxygen on which they once thrived.[33]

Contact between the Islamic and European worlds revealed the conceivable outcomes of a coming together of two of the pre-eminent civilisations in world history: hostility and partnership, conquest and capture and, conceivably, the greatest-ever exchange of ideas and knowledge. Islam arrived into Western Europe from the south of Spain which was then governed by Muslims for over eight centuries (711–1492). Sicily was governed by Muslims for over 200 years (831–1091). Gibraltar (Jabal Tariq, the rock

---

32 Lloyd, S. (1988) *English Society and the Crusade, 1216–1307*, Oxford: Clarendon Press.
33 Sardar, Z. and Z. A. Malik (2004) *Introducing Islam: A Graphic Guide*, second revised edition, Cambridge: Icon.

of Tariq) is named after the Muslim general, Tariq ibn-Ziyad (d. 720), whose ship landed there before capturing further territories on the Iberian Peninsula. Over many centuries, lesser independent Muslim settlements survived in France, Germany, Switzerland and southern Italy. When the Ottoman Muslim Turks came to power in the fifteenth century, they consolidated Islam in most of Eastern Europe, including the Balkans. Islam gave to these territories a dynamic civilisation, and the people welcomed the new religion, contributing to its enrichment and the maintenance of a global Islamic culture and civilisation. Christians, Jews and Muslims lived side by side in relative concord as followers of the principal Abrahamic faiths, and Western Europe achieved a genuinely successful period of remarkable affluence, cultural pluralism and scientific and technological development.

The era marking the creative expansion of both Islamic and Muslim culture came to a critical juncture with the capture of most of India in 1526 by Zahir ud-Din Muhammad, known as Babur (1483–1531), one of the Timurid princes. Established was a powerful Mughal Empire which produced such legendary rulers as Akbar (1542–1605), Jahangir (1569–1627), Shah Jahan (1592–1666) and Aurangzeb (1658–1707), with considerable developments in architecture, art, music, landscape gardening, cuisine and trading routes as well as the fusion of Persian and Sanskrit in the language and poetry of Urdu and Hindi.[34] After 1707, however, the Mughal Empire lost power to its various vassals – princes, maharajahs, sultans and other humble dependants – while the British colonial presence gradually took over.[35] With the weakening of Mughal central power, the period between 1707 and 1761 observed a growth in the provinces. The resurgence of regional identity accentuated both political and economic decentralisation as the Mughal military powers ebbed and the provinces became economically and politically autonomous. Assisted by intra- as well as interregional trade in local raw produce and local labour, these provinces became virtual kingdoms. Avadh, Bengal and Bihar in northern India were some of the new provinces where these advances were most evident, and rulers became independent warlords recognising the Mughal emperor in name only.[36]

The English East India Company (EIC), which began operations in 1600, aspired to take advantage of a financially lucrative spice trade. Rivalry with the Dutch drove the company to India. As a wealthy and mature civilisation, India was the focal point of a huge system of commerce. From a limited number of regional centres, the EIC built up a profitable model of

34 Mahmud, S.F. (1989) *A Concise History of Indo-Pakistan*, Karachi: Oxford University Press.
35 Shah, S.G.M. (1993) *The British in the Subcontinent*, Lahore: Ferozans.
36 James, L. (1997) *Raj: The Making and Unmaking of British India*, New York: St Martin's Press.

trade and this had a radical effect upon British economy and society. As the Mughal Empire declined, the Company gradually extended British rule over large parts of India, and this management of India through commerce and conquest gave rise to a steady migration of many different classes of Indians to Britain, including servants, sailors and students. The intermingling of Indian and British ideas, religions and ways of life led to a vibrant multiculturalism within the EIC; however, it did not linger long after the emergence of the Victorian Christian evangelicals and the arrival of the *memsahibs*.[37]

By the eighteenth century, the EIC had become even more powerful. It had its own army, made up of local Indians, which it used to conquer territories throughout the subcontinent. During this time, the EIC grew through the application of direct force and indirect economic control, finally removing the French from India after the battle of Plassey (1757), and subsequently commanding much of the South Asian subcontinent. British dominance in India was based on its militaristic power and as the Army seemed unconquerable; British power in India was guaranteed. However, this arrangement required the Indian Army to remain pliant and loyal, as it was made up of Indian soldiers who took their orders from British officers.[38]

British domination invariably took Westernised thinking and systems into India, but the proliferation of the Christian faith created immense unease for the Indians. The evangelistic Christian missions had limited comprehension or reverence for the traditional faiths of India, and their limited labours to win over the indigenous Indians gave rise to confrontations with localised religious communities. The missionaries were often English, and so the colonial regime arbitrated to defend them, which, unsurprisingly, presented a notion of authorised support for Christianity. Against this milieu of uneasiness, an '(up)rising' (or 'mutiny') occurred in 1857. The angry outburst was not because of ethno-religious confrontations, it was the 'first act of independence' sparked off by the knowledge that the grease applied in a new Enfield army rifle was lubricated with animal fat to help with loading of cartridge. Rumours circulated among the sepoys (Indian soldiers) that the grease was a combination of the fat of cows (sacred to Hindus) and pigs (abhorrent to Muslims). Therefore, biting the cartridge reduced the caste of the Hindu and contravened important Islamic faith principles. British Army officers finally grasped their oversight and modified the grease to beeswax and vegetable oils, but, in an environment of suspicion and mistrust, violent

37 Cavaliero, R. (2002) *Strangers in the Land: The Rise and Decline of the British Indian Empire*, London: I.B. Tauris; Dalrymple, W. (2003) *White Mughals: Love and Betrayal in Eighteenth-century India*, London: Harper-Perennial.
38 Ferguson, N. (2003) *Empire: The Rise and Demise of the British World Order and the Lessons for Global Power*, London: Basic.

conflict seemed unavoidable. By the mid-nineteenth century, social Darwinism was in full ascendancy, and the 'white British' had come to believe that they were a selected 'race', chosen to distribute the virtues of Western civilisation to apparent backward-looking regions of the globe.

Indigenous opposition in India frequently required military force against it, and few years would pass without the British Army being caught up in border encounters or punitive missions throughout the Empire. The British had been involved in European wars much more expensive in blood and glory than any overseas conquest, but this conflict did not seize the imagination of the British public in the same way as other colonial conflicts. When the 'mutiny' broke out in 1857, it swiftly became the most celebrated of all the colonial campaigns. British people at home followed with much excitement and anticipation various accounts of the 'mutiny' as it came from India. British soldiers were seen to be bravely fighting to serve a God-given sense of duty to defend their property, position and purpose – a manifestation of the confidence with which the British in the twentieth year of the reign of Queen Victoria viewed the world in general and the Empire in particular.[39] The 'mutiny' also showed the surprise and revulsion many in Britain had against the Indians, and pride quickly followed on the heels of a definitive triumph, one ostensibly accomplished against tremendous odds. The 'mutiny' continued for nearly two years. The British, in effect, fought and were ultimately triumphant through a series of assaults, sieges, atrocities and sheer savagery on the part of all.[40] Women and children were butchered by both sides. Vast cities were destroyed, and British forces, which sped across the north of India to alleviate overwhelmed comrades and to take revenge against their slain compatriots, were arguably the cruellest ever to have been put on the field by the government and people of Britain.[41]

The British perspective is to view the events of 1857 as a 'mutiny'. It is accurate in that there was an uprising by certain parts of the military, but it does not include vast numbers of civilians who were also involved in the conflicts. Most British writing and observation on the events is in agreement in describing it as a 'mutiny' because of the apparent limitations in the discipline and command of the army. However, the conventional Indian nationalist perspective on the events of 1857 is not as the British would view it (a number of sporadic and maladroit mutinies). Indeed, it was the first attempt by Indians to determine self-rule. After 1857, writings on the events

39 Said, E. (1993) *Culture and Imperialism*, New York: Vintage.
40 Mukherjee, R. (1990) ' "Satan Let Loose Upon Earth": The Kanpur Massacres in India in the Revolt of 1857', *Past and Present*, 128(1): 92–116.
41 Dalrymple, W. (2007) *The Last Mughal: The Fall of a Dynasty, Delhi, 1857*, London: Bloomsbury; Cohn, B. (1995) *Colonialism and Its Forms of Knowledge: The British in India*, Princeton, NJ: Princeton University Press.

were largely restricted to British commentators and intellectuals for nearly 50 years. European racial ideologies were in place at this time, with differences in attitudes concerning Hindus and Muslims codified through a range of differentiated behaviours towards them. Muslims were thought not to be open to Western education, for example, with measures put in place to ensure different educational paths.[42] Indian nationalist traditions define the post-1857 period as one of a return to Indian rule.

In a show trial, the British exiled *the last Mughal*, Bahadur Shah II (1775–1862), to Rangoon. Before his banishment, his sons, Mirza Mughal and Khizar Sultan, including his grandson, Abu Bakr, were viciously killed in front of him by Major W.S.R. Hodson. Their decapitated heads were then given to him on silver plates, while their bodies rotted for days, hanging on Delhi Gate. This event ensured that 331 years of Muslim rule came to a bloody end. India was the 'Jewel in the Crown' for the British Empire and the Raj managed to hold onto power with little effort. In the process, it brought to an end a remarkable civilisation.

As a result of commercial interests and growing racial pride, Edwardian and Victorian egotism permitted advances in Hellenophilia[43] and Philo-Semitism,[44] but not to 'Islamophilia'. It was not the case, however, that no English people were prepared to support Islam in the nineteenth century. Marmaduke Pickthall (1875–1936) had the purpose to support the Turks. Justice Syed Ameer Ali (1849–1928), who wrote *The Spirit of Islam* (1891) and *A Short History of the Saracens* (1927), dedicated his life to back the struggle to free the British of their Anglocentrism.[45] In 1897, however, a map of the British Empire included Egypt, India, Malaya and Nigeria, which were all large dominions with considerable Muslim populations. These Muslim lands supplied the human and material reserves that added significantly to the success of Edwardian and Victorian England. At the zenith of Western European expansion in the nineteenth century, most of the Islamic world was under colonial administration, with the exception of a few places such as Afghanistan, specific segments of Arabia and Yemen and the heart of Ottoman Empire and Persia. Even these regions were under foreign manipulation or, certainly in the instance of the Ottomans, under continuous risk.[46]

---

42 Perusek, D. (1992) 'Subaltern Consciousness and the Historiography of the Indian Rebellion of 1857', *Novel: A Forum on Fiction*, 25(3): 286–301.

43 The valuing of all things Hellenic and originating from ancient or contemporary Greece (or the Hellenic Republic).

44 Philo-Semitism is a specific interest in and the appreciation of Jewish people, their historical significance and the positive impact of Judaism.

45 Matar (1998), op. cit.

46 Saikul, A. (2003) *Islam and the West: Conflict or Cooperation?* Basingstoke: Palgrave-Macmillan.

After the end of the First World War and the dismantling of the Ottoman Empire, a number of Arab states, for example Iraq, took their independence. Others, such as Jordan for example, were fashioned as new nation-states, but Palestine, Syria and Lebanon were either mandated or became French colonies.[47] It was during this period that 'Saudi Arabia' was established. Egypt, which had been ruled by the descendants of Muhammad Ali (1769–1849) since the nineteenth century, became independent as a result of the demise of the Ottomans. Turkey was declared a secular republic by Mustafa Kemal Atatürk (1881–1938) in 1924, and the Pahlavi Dynasty began a new era in Persia when, in 1925, the country reverted to its traditional Eastern name of 'Iran'. This rule ended in 1979 with the Islamic Revolution of Iran.

From the fifteenth century onwards, the intellectual power that Muslims had in abundance eventually ebbed away, while Britain emerged as a focal point of industry, commerce and technological advancement, entering its own age of scientific discovery and development. It also began to change ideologically. The social Darwinian world-view did not always generate a positive view of the populations of the east or south, nor did it always give due regard to the cultural accomplishments of an ethnically diverse world. Simultaneously, Muslims closed the 'door of Ijtihad',[48] which has had consequences for how the faith has been practised ever since.

The colonial experience ultimately brought Muslims to Britain. During the nineteenth century, seamen ('lascars') created the original Muslim minority settlements in key English and Scottish ports.[49] At the start of the twentieth century, many hundreds of Muslim pedlars travelled to and finally settled in the more remote areas of Scotland. In 1889, there was the establishment of the first mosque in England (Shah Jahan in Woking, Surrey, and a co-located student residence). It developed under the benefaction of the Begum of Bhopal Sultan Shah Jahan (1838–1901) and demonstrated Muslims beginning to find a more determined presence in society. In 1937, Abdullah Yusuf Ali (1872–1953), recognised in the Islamic world for his translation into English and for his explication of the Qur'ān, eventually settled in Britain after years as a travelling educationalist. In the early part of the twentieth century, British Muslims came together to make a stand as a political group. One issue was the partition of Palestine. Muslims were opposed to the proposals for dividing the land as identified by the Peel

47 Smith, C.D. (2007) *Palestine and the Arab–Israeli Conflict: A History with Documents*, Basingstoke: Palgrave-Macmillan.
48 Rippon, A. (1993) *Muslims: Their Religious and Practices, Vol. II: The Contemporary Period*, London: Routledge, pp. 27–43.
49 Vishram, R. (1986) *Ayahs, Lascars and Princes: Indians in Britain 1700–1947*, London: Pluto; Halliday, F. (1992) *Arabs in Exile: Yemeni Migrants in Urban Britain*, London: I.B. Tauris.

Commission of 1936. Abdullah Yusuf Ali, with his direct understanding of the authorisations determined by the League of Nations, spoke widely on the injustices in Palestine at gatherings all over the UK.[50] At a war cabinet meeting on 24 October 1940, Prime Minister Winston Churchill authorised the funding for the building of the London mosque and King George VI visited what was then the Islamic Cultural Centre in Regents Park for its formal launch in 1944.[51]

Over a millennia, Islam and Muslims have emerged, evolved, expanded, strengthened, prospered and regressed. At the end of the nineteenth century, almost all of the Muslim lands were under colonial rule. After two world wars, post-war Muslim groups in Britain arrived as immigrants and settled as communities at a time of rapid globalisation, which has had implications for the economy, society and the development of the *ummah.*[52] After finalising the Qur'ān, the religion of Islam expanded into Central and Near Asia, Eastern Europe, North and Central Africa and South-East Asia. During that time, science, technology and civilisation advanced greatly, laying the foundations of modern Western European thought and civilisation – Renaissance, Reformation and Enlightenment. In this period, a sense of unity and diversity was central to how groups lived, worked and shared with each other to profit spiritually, intellectually and materially. With the advent of technology and industry in Western Europe, coupled with inner decay at the heart of the *ummah,* a significant change to the balance of world power ensued at the end of the fifteenth century. No longer were Muslim lands able to deal with external threats. They looked inwards, limiting both the culture and the ability to engage with the now powerful 'infidel' (the 'Muslim other'). The 'Jewel in the Crown' that was India under the British Raj provided considerable wealth creation for the English and the opportunity to develop the tastes and preferences of members of upper English and Indian society, but it also helped to drain a continent. And, as Britain eventually tried to break free from its inflated triumphalism, the region was in tatters, left to rebuild itself through a system of self-governance and administration, prematurely and divisively handed down in 1947. Once the 'cradles of civilisations', the regions of the Muslim world moved into the hands of Western European and US neo-colonial interests, dominated by foreign capital and exploited for the life-blood of the Western world: raw materials and natural resources. As a result of its suffocation, Islam and

50 Sherif, M.A. (2004) *Searching for Solace: Biography of Yusuf Ali, Interpreter of the Qur'an*, Kuala Lumpar: Islamic Book Trust.

51 Ansari, H. (2004) *The 'Infidel' Within: The History of Muslims in Britain, 1800 to the Present*, London: Hurst.

52 Ali, M. (2002) (ed.) *Islam Encountering Globalization*, London and New York: Routledge-Curzon.

Muslims developed reactively while external Western imperial interests busily played out the colonial game.

In the 1950s and 1960s, Britain experienced the largest growth of the Muslim population in its history, mainly due to the demand for labour in transport, textile and engineering industries. At present, based on the 2001 Census there are officially 1.6 million Muslims with around 1 million from Pakistan, Bangladesh and India, and they are predominantly Sunnis. At the time of writing, the figure of Muslims in Britain is nearer the 2.2 million mark, with Pakistanis alone nearing 1 million. As diasporic, transnational and multicultural communities, in some parts of the country they are successful and prosperous. In others they are poor and deprived. Yet, there are 1.5 million journeys between the UK and Pakistan ever year. South Asian Shi'a groups either have origins in the Punjab or the Gujarat (e.g. the Khojas) regions. Shi'a in Britain are also found to have origins in Lebanon and Iraq. The Al-Khoei Foundation, one of the most regarded Iraqi Shi'a families, is found in North London and has branches in a number of the major cities of the world. In relation to the Gujarati Ismaili Muslims, both the Dawoodi Bohras and the Nizaris are found in Britain. Pakistani Ahmadiya, who are regarded as heretics by most Muslims in the world, have moved their central headquarters to Tilford, Surrey. Presently, the congregation of the renowned Regent's Park Mosque in London hails largely from Arabs and Sunnis. Most Turkish Muslims are Sunnis, and many would argue that they are secularised.[53] At the same time, politically, Hizb ut-Tahrir (HT) is an Islamist political party originally founded in Palestine.[54] Currently, it has strong support among certain Muslim further and higher college and university students of various nationalities. However, it is also on the receiving end of significant criticism from various conservative and liberal Muslim and non-Muslim sections of society in Britain.

The vast majority of British Muslims originate from South Asia and therefore the religious practices of the Indian subcontinent dominate the profile of Islam in the UK. This experience is rich, diverse, complex and emerges out of colonialism and post-colonialism.[55] Nevertheless, the bulk of South Asian Muslims follow the Sunni Barelwi strand of Islamic thought, which amalgamates Sufism with exacting support of the Hanafi school. Deobandis are strongly represented among Muslims of Indian origin, and although sometimes puritanical, they nevertheless adhere to the Hanafi school. The Tabligh-i-Jamaat, which focuses on missionary work, is a

53 Küçükcan, T. (1999) *Politics of Ethnicity, Identity and Religion: Turkish Muslims in Britain*, Aldershot: Ashgate.
54 Taqi ud-Din al-Nabhani (1909–77), a Sufi Islamic scholar and appeals court judge (*qadi*), originally from Jerusalem, founded the organisation in 1953.
55 Lahiri, S. (2001) 'South Asians in Post-Imperial Britain: Decolonisation and Imperial Legacy', in S. Ward (ed.), *British Culture and the End of Empire*, Manchester: Manchester University Press, pp. 200–16.

significant sub-branch of the Deobandis. Their headquarters are found in Dewsbury. The Ahl-e-Hadith negates many of the influences of the different schools of law and Sufism, but they are firmly aligned with the 'Wahhabis' of Saudi Arabia. The vast majority of their followers in Britain come from Azad Kashmir ('Free' Kashmir) and the Punjab. Their headquarters, the Markazi Jamiat Ahl-e-Hadith UK, is in Small Heath, Birmingham. The UK Islamic Mission is a reflection of the Pakistani Islamist Jamaat-e-Islami (JI) party, which broadly espouses the political orientation of Maulana Sayyid Abul Ala Maududi (1903–79). These leanings are relatively popular among Muslim students, with the Islamic Society of Britain and Young Muslims demonstrating robust JI inclinations during the 1990s and until more recently.

The nature of relations between the Islamic world and Britain is one that is precarious at best, disingenuous at worst. When social Darwinism repelled the idea of a God, Muslims were largely subordinated people felt to be especially backward, thus legitimising existing plans for economic expansion and cultural domination. When the wider economic, social and political forces in Britain made it both important and necessary to woo workers to take up employment in declining industries in the post-war period, adequate reflection on the need to effectively integrate groups from relatively improvised sending regions, but who have defining religions and distinctive cultural practices of their own, was missing. Currently, these inequalities are as wide as ever, and, with the recent outpouring of literature that has attempted to dismiss the idea of God altogether,[56] and in the light of the events of 9/11, the subsequent 'War on Terror' and the events of 7/7, it is a time when the religion of Islam and Muslims as a body of people are persistently given negative attention. The positions of Islam and Muslims are being continuously re-examined in the light of further events and new challenges.[57]

56 Dawkins, R. (2006) *The God Delusion*, London: Banton; Hitchens, C. (2007) *God Is Not Great: The Case against Religion*, London: Twelve Books; Onfray, M. (2008) *Atheist Manifesto: The Case Against Christianity, Judaism and Islam*, London: Arcade; Amis, M. (2008) *The Second Plane: September 11, 2001–2007*, London: Jonathan Cape.

57 Ahmed, A.S. and B. Frost (2005) (eds) *After Terror*, Cambridge: Polity.

2   Islamic political radicalism
Origins and destinations

It is important to provide a deeper analysis of the radicalism of Muslims from its historical origins to more recent developments in the twentieth century, and how political Islam has permeated aspects of life in Muslim Britain today.[1] Apart from specific events that have taken place in Muslim lands throughout the 1990s and beyond, there has been British political activity within the Muslim world, for example in Egypt, Pakistan and Palestine, for many hundreds of years. The attempt here is to trace these developments and to discern the extent to which they have shaped the radicalisation of British Islam. There is a specific exploration of the lives and works of Sayyid Qutb and Maulana Sayyid Abul Ala Maududi, central figures who have been influential in shaping a radical Islam in the 1950s and 1960s. The roles of HT, the Taliban and Al-Qaeda are analysed to determine how a global Islamic political identity has emerged. In Britain, there have been important recent developments, for example the growth of Al-Muhajiroun in the mid-1990s. It was disbanded towards the end of 2004, but it did, however, spawn a number of offshoots, which have now also been prohibited: The Saviour (Saved) Sect, Al-Ghuraba ('the Strangers') and Islam4UK. After the Danish cartoons demonstrations of February 2006, these and other groups were officially proscribed by the British government only for them to be re-invented yet again. Given the negative media and political attention Muslims have received in the post-7/7 period, it is apparent that there will be many questions asked of existing and new Muslim organisations, especially in how they are regarded as potentially important (or not) in the radicalisation (and de-radicalisation) of young Muslims in Britain.

In exploring the ideas of the most important ideologues that have impacted on the Islamic revival movements over the past few hundred years,

1 Dreyfuss, R. (1980) *Hostage to Khomeini*, New York: New Benjamin Franklin House; Ali, T. (2006) 'Tortured Civilisations: Islam and the West', in C. Moores (ed.), *The New Imperialists: Ideologies of Empire*, Oxford: Oneworld, pp. 45–60; Milton-Edwards, B. (2004) *Islam and Politics in the Contemporary World*, Cambridge: Polity.

arguably the first person to provide a puritanical version of Islam as a response to the lived experience of Muslims was Ibn Taymiyyah (1263–1328). Since then, a whole host of other important figures in the Islamic revivalist movement have emerged, and their ideological perspectives are essential to analyse, particularly in the context of the anti-colonial and anti-imperial struggles of a range of oppressed Muslim states, lands and peoples. Of the many individuals and their thinking of interest in the current period, only one is of Shi'i origin, Ayatollah Ruhollah Khomeini (1902–89), while the others all emanate from orthodox Sunni schools. Khomeini largely concentrated on the Islamisation of the state of Iran, and the militant orthodoxy did not reach beyond the confines of the Middle East. Hezbollah was formed in Lebanon in 1982, after a civil war resulted in the arrival of French and US forces, and it was supported by the Iranian Revolutionary Guard. Today, in Iraq, there are Shi'a militia forces loyal to Muqtada al-Sadar (b. 1973),[2] and they arguably have some support from Iran. Rather, the focus here is on Sunni violent extremism, given that it is this which has caused greatest alarm in the West (Sunnis make up over 85 per cent of all the Muslims in the world). Many argue Sunni revivalist Islam is the greatest threat to Western neo-liberal socio-democratic hegemony and security, but it is also the case that Sunni lands have arguably suffered most at the hands colonial and post-colonial efforts of the past 500 years. The wider analysis here also focuses on the early Kharijite of the late seventh century, the 'Assassins' of the ninth to the eleventh centuries, Ibn Taymiyyah (1263–1328), Muhammad ibn Abd-al-Wahhab (1703–92), Jamal al-Din al-Afghani (1838–97), Ahmad Raza Khan (1856–1921) and the development of the Barelwi movement and, finally, the Darul Uloom (1866–), which is an expansion of the Deobandi movement. The latter three emerged under the colonial rule of the British in South Asia. In the twentieth century, Sayyid Qutb (1906–66), Taqi ud-Din al-Nabhani (1909–77), Maulana Sayyid Abul Ala Maududi, Osama bin Laden (b. 1957) and the formation of the Taliban in Afghanistan in 1994 have created the greatest interest among social thinkers studying British and Western European political Islam in the current period.[3]

In the late seventh century, soon after the death of Muhammad, there was much political conflict and disagreement. In the wake of turmoil and strife, it was the Kharijites who were effectively the first 'Muslim fundamentalists' in Islam. Khawarij philosophy underpins the ideological and political manifestations of the celebrated 'Muslim fundamentalist',

2 The fourth son of a renowned Iraqi Shi'a cleric, the late Grand Ayatollah Mohammad Sadeq al-Sadr (1943–99), one of the most influential religious and political figures in Iraq.
3 Lahoud, N. (2005) *Political Thought in Islam: A Study in Intellectual Boundaries*, London and New York: Routledge-Curzon.

Osama bin Laden. Indeed, the similarities could not be closer.[4] Over the years, this 'Salafi' (early Muslim) tendency later transformed into 'Wahhabism'. Here the term 'Salafi' refers to *al-Salaf al-Salih*, who were the original companions of Muhammad. The term 'Salaf' also refers to the first four generations of followers that came after Muhammad and also those who founded the four schools of Islamic jurisprudence. 'Salafis' argue that they are following the religious interpretation of Muhammad and his companions. 'Reformist' Salafis believe in individual and social change through spreading the message widely and its formal education, while some 'jihadi-Salafists' believe in the necessity of violence ('physical jihad') in achieving societal and religious goals.

Wahhabism has been exported to Muslim and non-Muslim nations all over the world by the Saudi Arabian government through the assistance of Saudi Arabian *ulema* (clerics). Modern-day Wahhabism or neo-Wahhabism represents the ideological merging of 1970s 'new Brotherhood' thinking and the revivalist strands of Wahhabism that emerged out of the Saudi state as a consequence of the oil-price boom. In the early 1970s, the Saudi state assumed the religious leadership of the Muslim world through the export of Wahhabism and its claim to be 'the one and true correct Islam'. In practical terms, this was facilitated by an alliance between exiled Egyptian Muslim Brotherhood members, which the Saudi state had given shelter to in the 1960s, the Saudi Arabian Wahhabi *ulema* and Saudi state funds. It resulted in the establishment of a number of organisations, which include the Islamic University in Medina, the Muslim World League, the Organisation of the Islamic Conference and the Islamic Development Bank. These organisations helped to spread Wahhabi ideology to other Muslim states.

During the 1980s, the Saudi Arabian government aligned with the USA and Britain to support the Mujahidin against the Soviet invasion of Afghanistan. Again, Saudi funds were used to support the anti-Soviet jihad, which included provision of weapons and supplies, as well as facilitating the movement and organisation of Islamist international fighters to Afghanistan. Some fighters travelled from Britain to join the anti-Soviet cause. In fact, it has been suggested that British foreign policy in the 1980s and early 1990s promoted and supported Afghan military resistance based on Islamic ideology, and that it favoured the training and financing of various groups. By the 1990s, however, the Saudi Arabian state had alienated a number of Islamist groups around the world and at home because of its alliance with the USA, and particularly in sanctioning the presence of US troops on Saudi soil during the 1991 Gulf War. The Islamist reaction to this development, together with their experiences as 'jihadi' fighters in Afghanistan, is thought to have succeeded in creating an international revolutionary

---

4 Oliver, H.J. (2002) *The 'Wahhabi' Myth: Dispelling Prevalent Fallacies and the Fictitious Link*, Oxford: Trafford.

Wahhabism opposed to the Saudi Arabian state. By the 1990s, Wahhabism fractured into different sects. 'Al-Qaeda' emerged out of this fracturing and it is strongly anti-Saudi Arabian. It remains to this day in the shape of the Taliban and the utterances of Muslim ideologues such as Osama bin Laden Ayman al-Zawahiri and their close followers.[5]

Historically, an internal ideological struggle between the *Mutazili* ('the leavers') and the *Ash'ari* (for whom the characteristics of God are superior to human intellectual capacity)[6] has underpinned the dispute between two powerful schools of thought. The Mutazilites are rationalists and regarded logic and reason, applying Greek philosophy, as essential in the appreciation and application of Islam in the present world, particularly in the separation of 'Mosque and State'. That is, state institutions could operate outside the immediate domain of Islamic thinking. The Khawarij and other similar factions did not recognise this difference between mosque and state, arguing that they are one and the same. They held close to relatively literalist and closed interpretations of Islam, and the Shariah that was derived from it. Al-Kindi was the first (Mutazilite) philosopher of the Arabs, and others such as Al-Farabi, Ibn Sina and Ibn Rushd are notable figures from this school of thought.[7]

To fully understand the processes of Islamic political radicalism in the Muslim world and in the West, it is important to start with first principles. To begin, it is necessary to make reference to the term 'jihad'. An Arabic word that essentially means 'to strive' or 'to struggle', Jihad is often considered an aggressive 'sixth pillar of Islam'. Orthodox Islam, however, distinguishes only five: the declaration of faith *(shahada)*, prayer *(salat)*, fasting (during the month of *Ramadan*), charity *(zakat)* and pilgrimage to Mecca once in a lifetime *(hajj)*. The notion of jihad as a sixth pillar originates from the Khawarij sect, a body of people that closely followed the teachings and practices of the Khawarijah, a sub-group that rebelled against existing Muslim leaders and, in the process, could be argued to have sowed the seeds of ongoing conflicts and persistent consternation across Muslim lands. The Khawarij position on *takfir* (excommunication) tends to be contradictory to the general Salafist interpretation. Salafism applies a limit on those who could be regarded as *kafir* (non-believer) and, as a result, excommunicated. Supporters of Khawariji thinking did not set a limit upon those who can be declared 'infidels', therefore justifying unhindered conflict or rampant violence against others. The vast majority of Muslims disqualify

5 Corbin, J. (2002) *The Base: In Search of Al-Qaeda*, London: Simon & Schuster; Gunaratna, R. (2002) *Inside the Al-Qaeda: Global Network of Terror*, London: Hurst; Bergen, P. (2006) *The Osama Bin Laden I Know: An Oral History of Al-Qaeda's Leader*, London: Simon & Schuster.

6 Founded by Abu al-Hasan al-Ashari (874–936), a tenth-century theologian of the Abbasid period (750–1258).

7 Sardar, Z. (2006) *What Do Muslims Believe?*, London: Granta, p. 91.

the obligation to spread Islam by compulsion, however, and regulate jihad to self-defence or, indeed, an inner struggle to master 'the self'.[8]

These Khawarij were essentially the earliest radical sectarian groups in Islam, but neither Sunni nor Shi'a. Initially supporting the leadership of Ali because of his supposed wisdom and piety, they turned against him when his dispute with Mauwiyah required arbitration. The event encouraged a small band of Ali's companions to accuse him of rejecting the Qur'ān. Ali fought against Mauwiyah (602–80) at the battle of Siffin (mid-July 657), but his authority was weakened. His followers alleged Ali had permitted a meeting when he was divinely chosen to represent the faith. In Mauwiyah calling a face-to-face confluence, all authority was lost in Ali (after Mauwiyah's fighters realised they were going to be defeated, they attached the Qur'ān to their weapons, compelling Ali to stop the fighting). The Kharijite regarded Mauwiyah as an upstart with a subordinate position to Ali. It was felt that judgement was in the hands of Allah alone. The Kharijite split from Ali, subsequently compelling him to engage in battle when they selected their own caliph from Kufa, named Abdullah ibn Wahb al-Rasibi. They created a military force to fight Ali but to no avail, losing 2,000 men at the battle of Nahrawan (late July 657). The downfall made the Kharijite strike surreptitiously, and, in 661, Abdur Rahman ibn Muljam assassinated Ali in Kufa while he prayed at a mosque.[9]

Presently, the remnants of the Khawarij are recognised by many different names. They came to be called the Khawarij because of their uprising (*khuruj*) against Ali. They have also been termed the Hukmiyya because of their rejection of the right of power of the two arbitrators (*Hakamain*), Abu-Musa al-Ashari (d. 662) and Amr ibn al-As (583–664), and because of their battle exclamations; 'the decision belongs to Allah alone; the two arbitrators have no power to decide!'[10] These Kharijite are an important aspect of the early history of Islam as it is a time when the Muslims had their first real schism *(fitna)*, and this division incorporated theological perspectives where the use of military power against other Muslims was regarded permissible. The Kharijite remained active throughout the Abbasid era by relocating to Basra. The term 'Kharijite' is a broad description, and today there are many sub-divisions of the group known in Iran as the *Azariqa* (followers of Nafi' ibn al-Azraq), in Arabia as the *Najdiya* (Najda ibn 'Amir al-Hanafi),

8 Hashmi, S.H. (2006) 'Interpreting the Islamic Ethics of War and Peace', in W. Evan (ed.), *War and Peace in an Age of Terrorism: A Reader*, Boston, MA: Allyn & Bacon, pp. 64–9.
9 Mahmud, S.F. (1989) *A Concise History of Indo-Pakistan*, Karachi: Oxford University Press, pp. 37–41; Esposito, J.L. (2003) (ed.) *The Oxford Dictionary of Islam*, Oxford: Oxford University Press.
10 Crone, P. (2004) *God's Rule: Government and Islam*, New York: Columbia University Press, p. 54.

in North Africa as the *Sufriyya*, and as the *Ibadiya* in Oman and throughout North Africa.[11]

From the murder of Ali, the Islamic world disintegrated into slaughter and rupture, with competing interests vying for rule over the *dar al-Islam* (the Abode of Peace). *Dar al-harb* is described as the 'Abode of War', and both these terms have starting points in the early days of Islam. They describe a metaphysical characteristic between the different worlds in which Muslims and non-Muslims exist. For some it is geographical, while for others it is without a physical divide. Effectively, these groups were applying the notion of *qital* ('fighting', but including murder and assassination), mitigating behaviour in the name of Muhammad, the Qur'ān and the Hadith.[12] After the assassination of Ali, two principal factions in Islam emerged and, to this day, still permeate the Muslim experience. There were sharp divisions inside the *ummah* as to how the caliph ought to be selected. Sunni groups believed that the caliph could only be selected through a consensus generated by the community of followers, where bloodline was not important if relevant at all. The Shi'a, however, argued that the successor to the caliphate should be someone from the same bloodline. Ja'far al-Sadiq (702–65), great-grandson of Hussain (murdered at Karbala), is the sixth Imam in the Shi'a tradition, and he had two sons, Ismail and Musa. When Ismail, the eldest, died, a number of Shi'a affirmed Musa, a younger brother, as the seventh Imam. A dramatic rift opened up that remains unresolved. Some Shi'a suggested that that as Ismail was the elder of the two, his son, Muhammad bin Ismail (746–809), should have accessioned.

Over the centuries, the family of Shi'as defined as Ismailis gave the world of Islam three significant figures: Qarmat, originator of the Qarmatians,[13] Ubayd Allah al-Mahdi Billah (903–34), founder of the Fatimid Dynasty in 909 (both these territories in North Africa),[14] and, most notably, Hasan ibn Sabah (1034–1124), originator of the 'Assassins', and better-known as Sheikh al-Jabal or 'Leader of the Mountain'.[15] As a powerful orator, Sabah was able to persuade his community of believers to follow only him and by doing so they would be guaranteed safe passage into Paradise. The expectation was that followers had to murder or terrorise those whom Sabah regarded as outside the domain of his influence. Alamut, the stronghold of

---

11 Ibid., p. 55.
12 Rahman, H.U. (1989) *A Chronology of Islamic History, 570–1000 CE*, London: Mansell, p. 13.
13 The Qarmatians ('Carmathians') were a radical Ismaili sect founded in Eastern Arabia, establishing a utopian community in 899. They are generally remembered for their rebellion against the Abbasid Caliphate, which caused major disorder and chaos, particularly when they seized the black stone from Mecca and desecrated the Zam-Zam spring with bodies of dead Muslims killed during the Hajj of 930.
14 Hitti, P.K. (2002) *History of the Arabs*, Basingstoke: Palgrave-Macmillan, pp. 617–19.
15 Mahmud (1989), op. cit., pp. 131–2.

the Assassins, was a mountain fortress located around 100 kilometres from modern-day Tehran. During their reign of terror, Abbasid Caliphs Al-Mustarshid (d. 1135) and his successor Ar-Rashid (d. 1136), were killed.[16] The stronghold of Alamut was prominent until it was sacked by Hulagu Khan who was on his way to destroy Baghdad soon after in 1258. The Assassins also attempted but ultimately failed to murder Salah al-Din Yusuf Ibn Ayyub (1138–93), better-known as Saladin. He was able to suppress the Assassin hunger for killing when he initiated a movement to fight against them. It was the efforts of Baibars al-Bunduqdari (1223–77), arguably the successor to Saladin, however, who ultimately eliminated the Assassins in 1265. According to Bernard Lewis, Sabah had used religious argument and symbolism to justify his actions.[17] There were no limits to the plans of the Assassins, and they even colluded with non-Muslims. Both Christian groups and the Assassins wanted notable Muslims killed, including Saladin.

Sabah promised his followers Paradise, and this reality on earth was depicted by Marco Polo as he came to visit one of the Assassin fortresses. Polo stated that Sabah had 'caused a certain valley [...] to be enclosed, and had turned it into a garden, the largest and most beautiful that ever was seen, filled with every variety of fruit'.[18] Rivers flowed freely, and there was wine, milk, honey and water in abundance. There were also stories of beautiful women who played musical instruments. All of this encouraged the followers of Sabah to believe that they were indeed in Paradise. The account of Heaven can be taken from an interpretation of aspects of the relevant sections of the Qur'ān, but it appears that the reason why people followed Sabah was because they believed they were entering Alamut as Heaven on Earth. Intoxicated by hashish, which was used to instil courage, fear and a determined concentration on the part of the Assassins, minds were easily swayed.

An important factor in why the Assassins managed to survive for so long is the Crusades. They lasted between 1095 until 1290, and, had they not happened, it is quite likely that the sultans who controlled minor principalities could have organised themselves more effectively against the threat from Western Europe. Ultimately, Sabah used the notion of *jihad al-qital* ('struggle through war') to justify a campaign of fighting and turmoil in relation to the existing order, whether in Baghdad, which was at the centre of the Abbasid caliphate, or Cairo, which was at the centre of the Fatimid caliphate. It is clear to see the ways in which the promise of infinite rewards in Paradise through martyrdom, including if it means the murder of other Muslims, has its political and ideological roots in this early period of Islamic history.

16 Lockhart, L. (1930) *Hasan-i-Sabah and the Assassins*, London: School of Oriental Studies.
17 Lewis, B. (1968) *The Assassins*, New York: Basic Books.
18 Polo, M. (1903) The Book of Sir Marco Polo the Venetian, Concerning the Kingdoms and Marvels of the East, trans. and ed. Henry Yule, third editior revised by Henri Cordier, Vol. I, Chapter 23, p. 702.

Whether the Kharijite are more important than the Assassins is contestable, but the Kharijite directly rebelled the order of the Caliphs and killed other Muslims without exemption. Assassins are an important group to consider, as they were Muslims who were prepared to kill non-Muslims *and* Muslims.

It is Ibn Taymiyyah (1263–1328), however, who is of greater significance because of his impact on later revivalist Muslims in relation to the concept of jihad. He is arguably the most important ideologue in the evolution of political Islam during the classic age. Born in Harran in modern-day Turkey, shortly after the end of the Abbasid caliphate, Ibn Taymiyyah was strongly opposed to the Mongols, who ultimately converted to Islam and governed over huge swathes of the Middle East. One of a small band of scholars to not only become well known at the time of the Mamluks,[19] Ibn Taymiyyah had already made quite an impression on Islamic thinking. In leaving Harran, initially because of the Mongols, Ibn Taymiyyah moved to Damascus and became a professor of Hanbali law (one of four main schools of law within Sunni Islam). Known as 'a great scholar, a fearless fighter, and outspoken in argument'[20] Ibn Taymiyyah was also recognised for promulgating a strict interpretation of the Qur'ān, which he viewed literally, emphasising that the purest form of Islam could only come from the early Muslims, or from the three generations after the death of Muhammad.[21]

Ibn Taymiyyah became notorious for his Islamic ideology and his involvement in combating the Mongols. When requested by the Sultan of Egypt to preach a jihad against the Mongols in 1299, which he did, Ibn Taymiyyah went further to physically wage war against them 'at Shakhab, near Damascus'.[22] Not only did Ibn Taymiyyah go into battle against the Mongols, there were also attacks against fellow Muslims, such as the Ismailis in 1305, and on the Armenians of Asia Minor, who had apparently conspired with the Crusaders.[23] Sent to the court of Cairo and interrogated, he was imprisoned in a dungeon, with his two brothers, for one and a half years for allegedly following anthropomorphic notions, which were seen as blasphemy. Already imprisoned in Cairo, he was sent to jail for an additional year and a half for making outrageous political aims. He was finally dispatched to Alexandria for eight further months to complete his term. In 1328, after further spells inside prison for issuing damaging fatwas, and

---

19 Mamluks were 'slave soldiers' who had converted to Islam and then worked for various Muslim Caliphs and the Ayyubid sultans. Over time, they became powerful military elites and on many occasions they gained authority on their own terms, e.g. when governing Egypt during the Mamluk Sultanate (1250–1517).
20 Mahmud (1989), op. cit., p. 173.
21 Peters, R. (1996) *Jihad in Classical and Modern Islam*, Princeton, NJ: Markus Wiener, p. 43.
22 Gibb H. A. and J. H. Kramers (1965) *Shorter Encyclopedia of Islam*, Ithaca, NY: Cornell University Press, p. 151.
23 Sivan, E. (1985) *Radical Islam*, New Haven, CT: Yale University Press, p. 100.

when his adversaries took away his books and papers, Ibn Taymiyyah finally gave up the fight and died in incarceration.

Ibn Taymiyyah believed fervently in adhering to the letter of the Qur'ān and the Hadith, but he also believed that Muslims needed to use *qiyas* (reason) to arrive at certain deductions on their own. Ibn Taymiyyah was an unswerving opposer of *bida* ('innovation'). Dismayed by Muslims looking for help from the saints, Ibn Taymiyyah argued that it was illegitimate to do so, a religious ruling given by many over the centuries, including Muhammad ibn Abd-al-Wahhab (1703–92). A believer of the Hanbali school, the latter would have a tremendous impact on political Islamism four centuries later. Countless tombs were smashed by Wahhab in the eighteenth century. Ibn Taymiyyah not only confronted the issue of tomb visitations, he argued with other Muslim Islamic thinkers, including Al-Ghazali (1058–1111), for purportedly repeating dubious Hadith. Ibn Taymiyyah wrote in opposition to Christianity and Judaism as belief systems that distorted their particular doctrine, arguing against the preservation of churches and synagogues.[24]

Ibn Taymiyyah developed his ideas through a literal interpretation of aspects of the Qur'ān and the Hadith. He argued that combat, economic penalties and also 'black' information were justifiable ways in which to bring back to Islam those who might be regarded as apostate. Furthermore, for Ibn Taymiyyah, although people adhered to the essential Islamic pillars, it did not automatically suggest they were Muslims. If someone is unable to respect or implement strict Shariah, they are no longer regarded as Muslim. Ibn Taymiyyah was arguably the first Sunni intellectual to suggest the use of force to remove someone from power. It is accepted Sunni thinking that a corrupt ruler should be supplanted by non-violent methods. For Ibn Taymiyyah, jihad was lawful against a leader who declined the implementation of rigid Shariah. One of the students of Ibn Taymiyyah, Ismail Ibn Kathir (1301–73), pointed out various verses in the Qur'ān as justification for insurrection against states that did not have Shariah as the foundation stone of their governance.

Through Taymiyyah, the notion of *qital fi-si-bi-Allah* ('combating in the way of Allah') was found in Central Asia, and both the Ottoman and Mughal empires utilised it to uphold their military action in Eastern Europe, the Indian subcontinent, the Middle East and North Africa. The Ottomans militarily controlled much of the Islamic world from the thirteenth to eighteenth centuries, and the Mughals dominated much of South Asia in the fourteenth to nineteenth centuries. Although these two huge empires had their conflicts, no significant theological figure in relation to jihad or *qital* emerges during this period. Even though many Islamic political individuals and groups today do not openly ascribe their behaviours to the writings and actions of the Kharijite, the Assassins or Ibn Taymiyyah, there are palpable lines of reasoning which connect all three. Like other revivalist Muslims

24 Gibb and Kramers (1965), op. cit., p. 152.

before them, twentieth-century ideologues justified their actions based on the Qur'ān and Sunnah. Breaking away from a society not practising Shariah and then returning to overcome it, which the Kharijites and Assassins carried out, or battling against other Muslims thought not to be holding true to Islam, can be seen from the actions of the Kharijite, the Assassins and Ibn Taymiyyah. These groups assembled a firm basis upon which many others who pursued it would later develop.

In the early eighteenth century, Muhammad ibn Abd-al-Wahhab (1703–92) founded a revivalist movement with the precise aim of determining a 'sociomoral reconstruction' of society. A Hanbali scholar, operating out of Arabia, Abd-al-Wahhab argued for the oneness of Allah (*tawhid*) as the essential doctrine of Islam, and his efforts began with the view that Arabian society was slipping into moral and political decline.[25] Believing in the return to a more purist reading and application of the Qur'ān and the Hadith, Abd-al-Wahhab also had a role to play in the destruction of Shi'a shrines in Najaf and Karbala in 1802. In 1747, forming close alliances with Muhammad ibn Saud (d. 1765), Abd-al-Wahhab eventually helped to formalise the rule of the House of Saud over Arabia. From the end of the eighteenth century, Ibn Saud and his followers spent a century and a half orchestrating a number of military offences to gain power over the whole of Arabia, ultimately gaining full supremacy in 1922. What emerged as a sociomoral and political movement culminated in the formation of a state. With the discovery of vast amounts of oil in the decades that followed, combined with control over the two most important geographical sites of Islam, Mecca and Medina, the House of Saud has had a particular vantage point in the proliferation of certain ideological, political, moral and theological paradigms, and particularly when related to 'Salafi' missionary zeal. People opposed to this movement describe them as 'Wahhabis', but they tend to call themselves 'Muwahhidun' or 'those upholding the doctrine of tawhid'.[26] Wahhab was directly influenced by Ibn Taymiyyah and his writings and sermons formulated four hundred years previously, although the impact his teachings have had in relation to the policy and practice of Osama bin Laden has been acknowledged by some but disputed by others.[27]

The role of colonialism is important in the formation of anti-Western discourses and practices on the part of Muslims, and nowhere is this better exposed in relation to the British than in South Asia. An important figure in the development of a literalist interpretation of Islam is found in South Asia, from the time of the British Raj and the Muslim responses that began to define an anti-colonial struggle in the face of oppression, subjugation and

25 'Ibn Abd al-Wahhab', in Laoust, H. (1979) *The Encyclopedia of Islam*, Leiden: Brill, pp. 677–8.
26 Esposito (2003), op. cit., p. 333.
27 DeLong Bas, N. (2004) *Wahhabi Islam: From Revival and Reform to Global Jihad*, New York: Oxford University Press, pp. 278–9.

vilification. Jamal al-Din al-Afghani (1838–97), philosopher and politician, born in Iran but claiming Afghan descent, encouraged the idea of harmony among all Muslims in opposition to British rule in particular and against global Western interests in general. His plea for Muslim cohesion impacted on many other parts of the world, including Egypt, Turkey and Iran. In 1855, in travelling to India, British colonialism was introduced to him. Recognising how Muslims were being discriminated against in relation to appointments in government as well as opportunities in institutions of higher learning. He absorbed the Indian Muslim psyche, which suggested that the British were against Islam. The writings and sermons of Al-Afghani caught the imagination of the populations in Muslim India and in Iran, Turkey and Egypt. He worked tirelessly to create a pan-Islamic front to fight off the yoke of imperialism and colonialism. His actions became a catalyst for other individuals and groups in South Asia, who were beginning to formalise their response to the British, particularly since the 'mutiny' of 1857 or 'the first war of independence'.[28] Al-Afghani remains of interest to the Muslim world today because of his wide-ranging emphasis upon pan-Muslim solidarity against the Christian and Western worlds, but less so for his forward-looking, pragmatic approach to the reinterpretation of Islam.[29]

Ahmad Raza Khan (1856–1921), Muslim scholar and a Sufi from Bareilly, a city in northern India, was a follower of the Hanafi school that dominates much of South Asia to this day. Regarded as having inspired the formation of the Barelwi movement, which is named after his place of birth, his defining principles were based on utter devotion to Muhammad, paying particular attention to his birthday. The Barelwi tradition is concentrated in particular areas in rural Azad Kashmir and the Campbellpuri districts of north-eastern Punjab. Barelwi Islam is a folk religion specific to particular localities, and it places significant emphasis upon the worship of Pirs (saints as intermediaries) and their tombs as shrines of worship. It is influenced by the Sufi tradition within Islam. Barelwi imams in Britain are largely recruited from their district of origin in Pakistan. These imams played an important role for the first-generation Muslim community in Britain in acting to help legitimise and reinforce various traditions from the sending regions and villages. In Britain, Islamic reform movements, especially the Ahl-e-Hadith and Deobandis, strongly criticise Barelwis for some of their practices and customs, which they argue as being un-Islamic. The Barelwis counter these criticisms by accusing the various reform groups of being Wahhabis and therefore falling outside the fold of mainstream Islam. They argue that it is acceptable within Islam to follow both local custom and the universally prescribed laws of Shariah as long as there is no compromise of the central

28 Keddie, N.R. (1972) *Sayyid Jamal al-Din al-Afghani: A Political Biography*, Berkeley: University of California Press.
29 Esposito (2003), op. cit., p. 7.

tenets of Islam. The counter-attack by the Barelwis in opposition to these reformist tendencies gave rise to bitter conflicts for power inside mosques in the 1970s and 1980s. The Barelwi form of Islam involves a huge spectrum of written and oral traditions brought together and formalised in a particular geographical locality through the focus around a Sufi shrine. The community is more likely to be fragmented as loyalty is directed to individual Pirs, and there are significant variations among groups because of the language spoken, the place of origin, and the nature of practice and participation, or not as the case may be, within a range of different Sufi orders.

It has been suggested that it is challenging for Muslim communities to organise themselves on a national basis in Britain precisely because of these sub-differences. In recent years, attempts have been made to formally organise the community on a national level, but with only moderate success.[30] Many of the South Asian Muslims in Britain today are of the Barelwi school of thought. It needs to be emphasised that Barelwis are pious and peaceful Muslims whose devotion to a spiritual and moral framework transcends their worldly constraints. The Deobandi movement, on the other hand, was formed as a direct response to the 1857 'uprising' and, it could be argued, is stricter because of its more distinctive counter-ideological manifestations. The group derives its name from the Indian town of Deoband, which is located 150 kilometres north-east of Delhi. It was where the first Deobandi school, Darul Uloom ('House of Knowledge'), was formed in 1866 by Maulana Muhammad Qasim Nanotwi (1832–79). After the British ended Mughal power over India in 1858, it established direct rule. In an effort to prevent further 'uprisings', all Muslim schools were immediately closed down. After the Al-Azhar University in Cairo, the Darul Uloom is the second largest focal point of Islamic research and teaching. Upon graduation, Muslims in Saudi Arabia, Malaysia and China open up many hundreds and thousands of *madrasahs* (religious schools) throughout South Asia, specifically in parts of Afghanistan and Pakistan.[31]

Since the mid-1990s, the Darul Uloom has been an unremitting supporter of the Taliban. When the Taliban destroyed the 1,500-year-old Buddhas of Bamyan in March 2001, Darul Uloom supported the action. Darul Uloom, unlike the Muwahhidun (or Wahhabis) who are hostile in their proselytisation, pouring many millions into the construction of mosques and schools all over the Islamic world, does not fund *madrasahs* in other countries. Darul Uloom does not encourage its students to forcefully uphold Islam. Indian Deobandis project a milder character, regarding the practices of the Taliban as a particular fierceness based on Pashtun culture – the ethnic and

30 Geaves, R. (1996) *Sectarian Influences within Islam in Britain with Reference to the Concepts of 'Ummah' and 'Community'*, Leeds: University of Leeds.

31 Johns, A.H. and N. Lahoud (2005) 'The World of Islam and the Challenge of Islamism', in N. Lahoud and A.H. Johns (eds), *Islam in World Politics*, New York: Routledge, p. 12.

tribal groupings from which most of the Taliban materialises. All the same, the combination of Deobandi and Wahhabi persuasions on Pakistan have all but shattered the mystical Sufi presence there, making a distinct impact on the governance and religious institutionalisation of the country. Historically, in an effort to protect Islam from the forces of British colonialism, it was felt that the solution should be to develop religious schools devoted to preventing the dilution of Islam. That is, it was thought that in order to bring back ascendancy, Islam needed to be purer in form and practice. What began as a Sunni Islamic revivalist pressure group, which began in India, now finds itself in countries such as Afghanistan, South Africa and Britain. Followers of the Deobandi school, like the Muwahhidun, are puritanical in nature: there is a desire to remove Islam from any Western or modernist sway, and institutions that establish the Qur'ān and Hadith as primary guiding forces are bitterly defended. As practised in India, Deobandi schools have sought to 'purify' Islam of fashionable practices suggested to have been derived from Hinduism, including the idea of visitation to shrines and graves of saints (the Muwahhidun have sought to do the same in Saudi Arabia). Given the various challenges from Hindu fundamentalism over the years, the Deobandi movement in India continues to exist apolitically while recognising a certain allegiance to the Indian state.[32]

The Deobandi emphasis upon custom and Shariah is translated into a conservative form of Islam. It is shown in the emphasis upon correct religious practice, and also the approach to *ijtihad*; they argue that *ijtihad* must not be used to establish new views in support of developments occurring in present-day society. Deobandis stress correct dress, length and style of beards and proper Islamic manners as derived from the Sunnah. It has been argued that this emphasis upon the outward manifestations of the religion has its origins in the nineteenth-century colonial situation in India. In order to protect the community from outside influence and domination, Muslims set out to construct a fence of correct ritual practice that defined the parameters of Muslim life. It has been noted that the obsession to copy the details of the lifestyle and appearance of Muhammad is not a dominant issue in Muslim majority countries. The fascination is thought to be a defence mechanism against the forces of other cultures and influences – one that has been introduced and reinforced by South Asian Deobandis in the context of a minority Muslim community living in Britain.

Thus, it can be seen that the Deobandi movement developed its strategies for reformation and protection of Islam in the context of nineteenth-century colonial India. These approaches institutionalised the specific Deobandi practices and ideologies it reproduced, utilising the strategy of withdrawal, initially used in British India, in the context of seemingly having to protect

---

32 Zaman, M.Q. (1999) 'Religious Education and the Rhetoric of Reform: The Madrasa in British India and Pakistan', *Comparative Studies in Society and History*, 41(2): 294–323.

Islam from the threat of secularisation in modern Britain. Deobandis define the world of religion as a private domain that is separate from the public arena of politics and government. For Deobandis, it is politically acceptable to live as a minority in a non-Muslim environment if that nation can be defined as *dar al-amn* (a place of tolerance where Muslims are guaranteed the freedom to practise their faith).

The founders of the first mosques in Britain were more often than not non-Barelwi Pakistanis, mostly better educated and originating from the cities. The Deobandi–Barelwi division is along urban–rural lines as well as by various class and ethnic groups originating from the South Asian subcontinent. In particular, it is thought that the movement has a pre-dominance of Muslims that originate from India, either via East African immigration or as North Indian migrants (Muhajir) to Pakistan during the time of partition. The style of worship in the first mosques established in Britain needed to accommodate the needs of all Muslim groups. In order to achieve this, practical aspects of worship were stripped down to the basics of Islam in order to avoid potential conflict. With the growth of immigrant and ethnic-minority communities, and particularly with family reunification, mosque committees organised matters such that qualified *ulema* would be sent from the subcontinent. These early imams reflected the belief systems and world-views of the mosque committees and they were often graduates of Deobandi schools. Problems soon started to emerge when some imams would preach against the customs of the majority Barelwi congregation. Once the Barelwis managed to organise themselves behind their own leaders, several bitter hostilities broke out for the control of mosques.

By the end of the 1960s, there were only nine mosques in Britain. By 1974 this had risen to 81 registered mosques. In 1983, it was estimated that there were 450 registered mosques in Britain, a figure that had doubled to around 900 in 1993.[33] At present, it is considered that there are anything between 1,500 and 2,000 mosques and Islamic centres in Britain.[34] The rapid expansion of the number of mosques led to an increase in the numbers of imams being recruited from the subcontinent. In the past, there had been little or no central organisation to coordinate imam recruitment as each mosque committee traditionally made its own arrangements with organisations in the subcontinent. Most of the mosques are Barelwi, but the Deobandis have also founded schools in Britain, with the Bury and Dewsbury seminaries being the most influential. After completing their studies, the more pliable students go on to further study at the Al Azhar in Cairo or at the Medina University in Saudi Arabia.

Among South Asian ideologues with an intimate relationship to the Deobandis was Maulana Sayyid Abul Ala Maududi. Born in Hyderabad,

33 Geaves (1996), op. cit.
34 Masood, E. (2006) *British Muslims: Media Guide*, London: British Council.

India, Maududi was educated at home, obtaining religious education upon instruction from his learned father and a range of other specially employed teachers, later studying at the Darul Uloom in Hyderabad itself. His early career was in journalism, but it was in 1941 when he formed the Jamaat-e-Islami (JI), a religious political movement aimed at enhancing the application of Islamic values and principles.[35] After the partition of Pakistan and India in 1947, the JI party gave its support to the Islamic state of Pakistan, and to this day it remains the oldest religious political party in the country. Originally opposing Indian nationalism in favour of pan-Islamism, JI subsequently dropped this approach.[36] Maududi was president of the party until 1972, when ill health caused him to move aside. In writing many books and articles and having made many speeches and public utterances, his most memorable work is his Urdu translation of the Qur'ān, becoming widely read across the region and translated into many different languages.

Maududi believed that an Islamic society could not be complete without Shariah and the necessary development of an Islamic state – a 'theodemocracy'.[37] The system would incorporate all aspects of the lived experience, including social and economic matters, a judicial system and the full rights and responsibilities of all its citizens. He argued that this system needed to be exported to the wider world replacing un-Islamic states with those that are purely Islamic and where non-Muslims would have to accept Muslim rule, through the payment of a *jizya* (a tax). Notwithstanding, considerable criticism has been levelled against Maududi. Regarded as an ideologue who narrowly defined the concept of *hukm* (to act and judge wisely), his definition of an Islamic state would be one where freedoms would be limited, genders would be segregated and non-Muslims would be discriminated against. Branches of JI in Pakistan and Bangladesh have endorsed harsh discrimination of the Ahmadiya. However, the ideas of 'Islamic theodemocracy' and the 'Islamic economy' have not materialised, although it remains an aspiration among its current leadership.

Their limitations in Pakistan are contrary to their relative accomplishments in backing Islamists abroad. Faith in violence (physical jihad) provided an observable popularity amongst the Mujahidin in Afghanistan and Kashmir. They have also had associations with a number of global revolutionary movements, for example the Hizb-i-Islami (founded in 1977 by Gulbuddin Hekmatyar) at the time of the Soviet invasion of Afghanistan.[38]

35 Davidson, L. (2003) *Islamic Fundamentalism: An Introduction*, Westport: Greenwood Press.
36 Ahmad, A. (1967) *Islamic Modernism in India and Pakistan 1857–1964*, Oxford: Oxford University Press, pp. 216–19.
37 Maudidi, S.A.A. (1955) *Islamic Law and Its Introduction*, Lahore: Islamic Publications, pp. 13–14; Choueiri, Y.M. (1997) *Islamic Fundamentalism*, London: Cassell.
38 Edwards, D.B. (2002) *Before Taliban: Genealogies of the Afghan Jihad*, California: University of California Press.

It has been argued that JI is buttressed by the Pakistani state in its activities in Kashmir, as it is the only separatist movement in Kashmir dedicated to unification with Pakistan. It has also been claimed that JI supports training camps in Kashmir, both Kashmiri and foreign, principally for 'Jihad against India'.[39] Jamaat-e-Islami-influenced organisations are thought to include Dawatul Islam, the East London Mosque, the Islamic Foundation, the Islamic Society of Britain, the Markfield Institute of Higher Education, the Muslim Council of Britain, the Muslim Education Trust, the UK Islamic Mission, the Young Muslim Organisation UK and Young Muslims UK. The Islamic Foundation and the Islamic Mission arguably gave guidance and a degree of leadership to the Muslim community at the time of the Rushdie affair of 1989. In addition, they helped to formalise the establishment of the UK Action Committee for Islamic Affairs. This organisation was able to bring together a number of Muslim groupings to help generate a united platform from which to campaign in opposition to the publication of *The Satanic Verses*. The process gave status to JI-influenced groups within the community during this period.

The writings of Maududi influenced Sayyid Qutb, and there are close 'brotherly' associations with Islamist groups operating in different countries, chiefly those affiliated with the Muslim Brotherhood (*Akhwanal-Muslimeen*). Qutb, an Egyptian national, was a member of the Muslim Brotherhood (founded in 1928 by Hassan al-Banna in Egypt – Muslim Brotherhood chapters have since been founded in other countries, including Syria and Jordan). A significant Islamist revivalist, his ideas were highly influenced by the revolutionary radicalism of Maududi. Qutb's contributions to Islamic political thinking started in 1954 when incarcerated and tortured in the infamous Egyptian prisons under Gamal Abdel Nasser (1918–70). Following an assassination attempt in 1954, Nasser gathered up many in the Muslim Brothers, including Qutb, placing an authoritative prohibition on the organisation. In 1964, Qutb, undergoing torture and with ten years behind bars, published his most recognised work, *Milestones* (*Ma'alim fi'lTariq*; or 'Signposts'), a book seemingly encouraging zealous manifestations of Islamic revivalist political projects, such as Islamic Jihad[40] and Takfir wa-l Hijra.[41] A primary hypothesis of the book, the idea of *jahiliyah,* was fashioned largely because of a period spent in the USA (1948–50). Employed by the Egyptian Ministry of Education at the time, Qutb was sent to study US educational establishments. Profoundly displeased by the racism

39 Grare, F. (2001) *Anatomy of Islamism: Political Islam in the Indian Subcontinent*, New Delhi: Jamaat-e-Islami Manohar Publishers.

40 The Organisation for Jihad claimed it had assassinated Egyptian President Anwar al-Sadat on 6 October 1981.

41 In 1977, the Islamist group *Takfir wa'l-Hijra* (condemnation and migration), also recognised as the Society of Muslims, struck out at nightclubs in Egypt.

he saw (as well as experienced himself) he became incensed by the apparent sexual and cultural freedoms in the USA. Following his return to Egypt, accumulated feelings of frustration and anxiety led Qutb to join the Muslim Brotherhood in 1952.

Based on a powerful call for the militancy of Islam, Qutb urged the development of a front line of believers who would lead the battle against *jahiliyah*. These ideas had an important basic role in developing the notion of a *sahwa* (an 'awakening'); a combination of Qutbist thought and extremist Wahhabist expression, which developed from the endeavours of the Muslim Brothers who had been banished from Egypt in the early 1960s but had gained some notoriety in Saudi Arabia by the 1980s. As such, Qutb is regarded as the pioneering twentieth-century Islamist, and there is much anecdotal evidence to suggest that Sayyid Qutb and Taqi ud-Din al-Nabhani, founder of Hizb-ut-Tahrir in 1953–4, both influenced each other. A central aspect for most modern Islamists is their belief that all types of authority over Muslims are unacceptable, except in the Islamic caliphate. For Qutb, the 'unity of God and His sovereignty' results in the human condition being subservient to Allah alone, and not governments, which are examples of 'illegitimate human rule'.[42] On 29 August 1966, Qutb was hanged. Muhammad Qutb, his younger brother, went to Saudi Arabia, eventually becoming professor of Islamic studies. One of his keenest students and an ardent follower was Ayman Al-Zawahiri, later becoming the ideological mentor to Osama bin Laden, apparently remaining his 'right-hand man' to this day.

Arguably, Maududi and Qutb are regarded as the 'founding fathers' of the worldwide Islamic revival movement, sometimes simply referred to as 'Islamism'. Both Maududi and Hassan al-Banna recognised the importance of science and technology, and they concurred that technology could only usefully be developed by Islamic, not Western approaches, as they believed the Qur'ān and Sunnah provide the guidance to all aspects of life, including governance.[43] The presuppositions and methods of the work of Maududi were characteristically Salafist, and accepting contemporary knowledge of Islam was fraudulent because of the loss of understanding of classical Arabic over the centuries. Developing that presupposition, Maududi re-examined the Qur'ān, the Hadith and the text of past scholars in painstaking detail, reinterpreting the original meanings. Determining a revised perspective, known as 'new jahiliyah',[44] it influenced latter-day Islamists. It proposed that the essence of Islam had lost its original aims, and, therefore,

42 Benjamin, D. and S. Simon (2002) *The Age of Sacred Terror: Radical Islam's War Against America*, New York: Random House, p. 62.
43 Esposito, J.L. (2002) *Unholy War: Terror in the Name of Islam*, New York: Oxford University Press, pp. 52–3.
44 Sivan (1985), op. cit.

its leaders were apostates for having appropriated divine power, developing laws for their own gain.[45] Chastising states in Muslim lands that did not enact rigorous Shariah laws against apostasy, the 'true believers' were encouraged to wage jihad against such people and groups.[46] What follows is that a revolutionary group of true believers must act as a vanguard, remaining outside the workings of the so-called *jahili* states until all of society has been Islamised.[47]

Hizb ut-Tahrir (Party of Liberation, HT) is an independent Islamist political party. Established in 1953–4 by Taqi ul-Din al-Nabhani, previously a member of the Muslim Brotherhood and a religious *qadi* (judge) of Jerusalem, the party claims to be dedicated to the re-establishment of the caliphate and the eradication of what it regards as imperialistic non-Islamic control of Muslim lands seized by the *kuffar* (non-believers). For HT, this includes what was once Muslim Spain as well as the current external influences on Muslim lands. While concentrating on the local problem of the Palestinians, the establishment of HT was also based upon disappointment in relation to the Brotherhood – that is, of Palestinians and Arabs who apparently failed to overthrow the colonial powers and prevent the establishment of the state of Israel – believing this failure gave rise to the lack of unity and a well-expressed ideology among Arab Muslims. To transform these ideals into reality, this movement was established to unify all Muslims under the banner of the caliphate. It initially focused on Palestine and the Middle East but it presently operates in forty countries around the world. In seeking to expand its basis, HT actively distributes a range of paraphernalia, including books, leaflets, DVDs and audio CDs. Even though it promotes a rigorous reading of Islam, contemporary technological advancements are not forsaken, including fully utilising the Internet. In Western Europe, HT is banned in certain countries such as Denmark and Germany, but operates relatively freely in Britain.[48]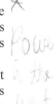

While the Brotherhood supports the motto 'Islam as solution' without giving any details of the form of the state to be established, HT proposes detailed policies and constitutions such as domestic and foreign affairs in relation to the future Islamic state. HT calls for the revitalisation of Islamic life and order (*ist'inaf al-hayah al-islamiyah*) in Muslim countries through the establishment of an Islamic caliphate that collapsed at the end of the

45 Euben, R.L. (1999) *Enemy in the Mirror: Islamic Fundamentalism and the Limits of Modern Rationalism, a Work of Comparative Political Theory*, Princeton, NJ: Princeton University Press.
46 Sagiv, D. (1995) *Fundamentalism and Intellectuals in Egypt, 1973–1993*, London: Frank Cass.
47 Davidson (2003), op. cit.
48 Karagiannis, E. and C. McCauley (2006) 'Hizb ut-Tahrir al-Islami: Evaluating the Threat Posed by a Radical Islamic Group That Remains Nonviolent', *Terrorism and Political Violence, 1556–1836*, 18(2): 315–34.

Ottoman Empire.[49] HT has been in Britain since the early 1980s, and its first leader was Omar Bakri Mohammed who went on to establish al-Muhajiroun as, arguably, a front for HT to help recruit members from universities. In 1996, al-Muhajiroun split from HT. According to Bakri, they did so because HT was 'too soft'.[50] It is argued that to have a desired impact, the recruitment process is a critical phase for the movement to establish an identity among its members. The recruitment process of HT mainly works through student networks. They disseminate their propaganda through campuses, and it is largely done secretively. By the mid-1990s, HT was banned by most student unions and college authorities in Britain.[51] In the current period, to avoid detection, HT often uses different names, for example, the 'Millennium Society', the 'Pakistan Society' and the '1924 Committee'.[52]

The concept of the *ummah* has become the designation of a collective identity since it can unite Muslims from many different backgrounds. Manuel Castells and Roger Scruton consider this collective identity as a form of defensive identity that functions as resistance and cohesion to protect against hostile globalisation.[53] Kevin McDonald, on the other hand, sees the concept of *ummah* as more of an alternative identity towards globalisation rather than being inherently defensive.[54] The framing of the identity-building process is important for the rise of HT. Framing is also important as it intercedes between political opportunity and the mobilisation of resources. It is also crucial in the construction of a collective identity for a movement that, in turn, could lead to collective action. It is essential to regard HT more as a 'local' movement rather than global as it is impotent without its interconnections within a local context. It encourages Muslims to go back to a purely Islamic way of life under the authority of the caliphate and it wishes to organise the Muslim communities so that they live exclusively through Islam, developing and maintaining a strong and purposeful Muslim identity. It recognises Islam as a complete way of life, with no separation between religion and politics. It completely disputes political engagement and argues that partaking in a Western-style

49 Al-Nabhani, T.A. (1953) *Mafahim Hizb al-Tahrir*, n.p.: The Liberation Party; Taji-Farouki, S. (1996) *A Fundamental Quest: Hizb ut-Tahrir and the Search for the Islamic Caliphate*, London: Grey Seal, p. 116.

50 Siddiqui, M. (2004) 'The Doctrines of Hizb ut-Tahrir', in Z. Baran (ed.), *The Challenge of Hizb ut-Tahrir: Deciphering and Combating Radical Islamist Ideology*, Washington, DC: The Nixon Centre, p. 20.

51 Siddiqui (2004), op. cit.

52 Koyaleski, S.F. (2006) 'For Britain's Young Muslims, Forks in the Road', *International Herald Tribune*, 30 August.

53 Castells, M. (1997) *The Power of Identity: The Information Age – Economy, Society and Culture*, Oxford: Blackwell; Scruton, R. (2003) *The West and the Rest: Globalization and the Terrorist Threat*, London: Continuum.

54 McDonald, K. (2006) *Global Movements: Action and Culture*, Oxford: Blackwell.

democracy is often in conflict with the objective of determining an Islamic state. Hizb ut-Tahrir is adamant that it does not support violence and that it is not a path towards terrorism, although these perspectives are found in many other radical Islamist organisations, many of which argue that violent action is a solution. Three British HT members (Maajid Nawaz, Ian Nisbet and Reza Pankhurst) were jailed in Egypt in 2004, where the organisation is proscribed. They were thought to be plotting against the Egyptian state. All three were released and returned to Britain in 2006, with Maajid Nawaz taking a lead role with Ed Husain, author of *The Islamist*, in the establishment of the UK-government funded 'world's first counter-extremism' think-tank, *The Quilliam Foundation*, after he publicly rejected HT, after having served a time as a leading figure within its UK ranks.

Since the dawn of Islam in the seventh century the religion has expanded vigorously across the world and with tremendous inroads made into various Eastern, Asian and North African regions. Part of Southern Europe was also under Islamic influence for many hundreds of years. It is also true that this was carried out through a programme of jihad, the struggle for Islam, sometimes displaying characteristics of violence, despotism and disregard for implicit humanism, as argued by some.[55] It is apparent that today two twentieth-century Islamist ideologues, Maulana Sayyid Abul Ala Maududi and Sayyid Qutb, are arguably the most influential on the young, angry and disenfranchised Muslims, both in the East and the West.

Unofficially, there are approximately 17 million members of Muslim minorities in Western Europe and 6 million in the USA. There are over 1.2 billion Muslims in the world as a whole, with Arabs forming around 16 per cent of this population. From the attacks on the Paris Métro (1996), a Moscow theatre (2002), trains in Madrid (2004) to the assassination of Theo van Gogh (2004), the first-ever suicide-bombings by home-grown terrorists in Western Europe in 2005 in London and the Glasgow Airport attacks (2007), and even the 'underpants bomber' plot of Christmas Day (2009), there are discernible connections between Muslim violence in Western Europe and geopolitics in relation to the Muslim world.[56] The events of 7/7 were not the first time British-born Islamic political radicals have came to the fore. The 'Seven in Yemen' (1999) included five British-born Muslims. After 9/11, there were the two failed 'shoe-bombers', Richard Reid (2001) and Saajid Badat (2005); and the 2003 'Mike's Place' bombers in Tel Aviv were Omar Khan Sharif and Asif Mohammed Hanif. Terrorism on the part

55 Boston, A.G. (2007) (ed.) *The Legacy of Jihad: Islamic Holy War and the Fate of Non-Muslims*, New York: Prometheus.
56 Reuter, C. (2002) *My Life as a Weapon: A Modern History of Suicide Bombing*, Princeton, NJ: Princeton University Press; Abbas, T. (2007), op. cit.

of these violent 'Islamists' is largely justified in reaction to violence inflicted on Muslims by external dominant forces.[57] Their motivations for their actions are based on their experiences of 'Being British' as much as about 'Being Muslim'.

In modern urban centres there is an increasingly cosmopolitan environment evident, through the diversities of people, politics and places. It is the increase in these differences between individuals in society, perceived or actual, that leads to an increasing need for recognition and status.[58] The rise in diversification has redefined what conformity there essentially is by expanding the boundaries of identity, recognising it as multiple and no longer singular, fixed or uncontested. As the world becomes increasingly globalised, individuals align themselves with parochialisms of different kinds, including certain radicalisms. In more global terms, the deterioration of Islamic institutions in Muslim countries has been cited for the rise in Islamic political radicalism at home and overseas, with leaders of Muslim countries acting in a self-fulfilling manner, rather than actively protecting Muslims. On the other hand, militant groups gain popularity by highlighting this progressive deterioration (usually associating it with 'Westoxification') and then portray themselves not as revolutionaries but as saviours trying to rescue the old society from self-destruction. In many cases, these groups give the impression not of radicalism but of conservatism which has as its main ideology two powerful concepts: the concept of the *ummah* together with Muslim suffering. It is attractive to a broad section of the community that identifies itself as Islamic and Muslim. On the surface, it encourages an Islamic identity that transcends ethnicity and stimulates emotions that could be thought of as positive, including ideas of charity and empathy.

Where most of the Muslim world is still facing up to the challenges of modernity and democracy, Muslim minorities in the West face a whole host of issues in relation to ethno-national identity, the adaptation of religio-cultural norms and values and issues in everyday matters of social and legal citizenship.[59] In Britain today, and more widely in Western Europe, there is the phenomenon of the indigenous-born, native-language-speaking, Muslim youth politicised by a Islamicised political radicalism. The analysis of what drives these young people needs to explore a combination of complex

---

57 Pape, R.A. (2006) *Dying to Win: Why Suicide Terrorists Do It*, London and New York: Random House; Sutton, P. and S. Vertigans (2005) *Resurgent Islam: A Sociological Approach*, London: Polity.

58 Michaels, W.B. (2006) *The Trouble with Diversity: How We Learned to Love Identity and Ignore Inequality*, New York: Metropolitan Books.

59 Cesari, J. and S. McLoughlin (2005) (eds) *European Muslims and the Secular State*, Aldershot: Ashgate; Modood, T., R. Zapata-Barrero and A. Triandafyllidou (2005) (eds) *Multiculturalism, Muslims and Citizenship: A European Approach*, London: Routledge.

factors in relation to cultural, economic, social and political dislocation, compounded by national and international neo-Orientalist, Islamophobic, political and media discourses,[60] and given the processes of post-war immigration, settlement and community development. It is important to analyse these issues further.

60 Said, E. (1997) *Covering Islam: How the Media and the Experts Determine How We See the Rest of the World*, London: Vintage; Abbas, T. (2001) 'Media Capital and the Representation of South Asian Muslims in the British Press: An Ideological Analysis', *Journal of Muslim Minority Affairs*, 21(2): 245–57; Poole, E. (2002) *Reporting Islam: Media Representations and British Muslims*, London: I.B. Tauris; Macdonald, M. (2003) *Exploring Media Discourse*, London: Hodder Arnold.

3 Post-war immigration and settlement
Ethnicity, identity and spatiality

There has been a relatively significant Muslim presence in Britain since the beginning of the nineteenth century when Muslim seamen and traders from the Middle East began settling around the major British ports.[1] Many Muslims from the British Raj came to England to study or engage in commerce, however the major growth of the Muslim population dates from the post-war immigration of Pakistanis, Bangladeshis and Indians to fill specific labour demands in certain declining industrial cities in the south-east, the Midlands and the north of England.[2] The British Muslim population has significantly increased in size since then, with many political, economic and social concerns influencing the patterns of migration and the resulting areas of settlement. Factors such as British labour-market needs, dispersion from the country of origin and family reunification have been the main propellants for much of the Muslim migration to Britain and, similarly, in other Western European countries.[3] As a result of the limited employment positions Muslims attained at the outset, the majority of Muslim immigrants and subsequent generations became concentrated in a few large cities and manufacturing towns, where certain types of work were originally available but later disappeared, revealing a whole host of deep-seated socio-economic predicaments, which still have not been properly addressed to this day. While there are acute challenges to the lived experience, South Asians nevertheless make an important contribution to

1 Halliday, F. (1992) *Arabs in Exile: Yemeni Migrants in Urban Britain*, London: I.B. Tauris.
2 Anwar, M. (1979) *The 'Myth of Return': Pakistanis in Britain*, London: Heinemann; Werbner, P. (2002) *The Migration Process: Capital, Gifts and Offerings among British Pakistanis*, Oxford: Berg.
3 Vertovec, S. and C. Peach (1997) 'Introduction: Islam in Europe and the Politics of Religion and Community', in S. Vertovec and C. Peach (eds), *Islam in Europe: The Politics of Religion and Community*, Basingstoke: Macmillan, pp. 3–47; Cesari, J. (2003) 'Muslim Minorities in Europe: The Silent Revolution', in J.L. Esposito and F. Burgat (eds) *Modernizing Islam: Religion in the Public Sphere in the Middle East and in Europe*, New Brunswick, NJ: Rutgers University Press, pp. 251–69.

society through the arts, cuisine, politics and the cultural life of Britain in the post-colonial era.[4]

From the early nineteenth century onwards, there were population flows from a range of Muslim countries, mainly determined by material and resource needs. The growing imperial and colonial domination of many territories containing Muslim populations, such as India, Africa and the Middle East, resulted in a firmly established connection between these places and Britain. As Britain exercised political and economic power over its colonies, many Muslims migrated from their materially deprived circumstances to meet the demands for cheap labour in Britain. It was accelerated by the needs of the First World War, when migration to many British ports increased significantly, largely to meet the needs of the shipping industry; in particular significant numbers of stokers working in coal-fired steamships, jobs that Europeans avoided at all costs.[5] Migration decreased in the inter-war period as there was less economic necessity; however, the relationship between economic pull in Britain and migration push from Muslim territories became generally well established and would continue for many years.[6] The associations between the politics of 'race', ethnicity and immigration policy were also formalised, and they are fundamentally important to appreciate in relation to this period in recent history.[7]

At the end of the Second World War, Britain was no longer able to hold on to many of its colonies. As a parting gesture, the Raj gave Pakistan the independence it wanted in 1947. However, the region experienced turmoil with the displacement of 10 million people and the death of up to 1 million – the largest forced exodus in the twentieth century. There was now a Pakistan (East and West), with India in between. It was widely held that Kashmir ought to have arrived into the hands of newly formed Pakistan, as understood by Muhammad Ali Jinnah (1876–1948), the first Prime Minister of Pakistan. For many Pakistani historians, the associations between Pandit Jawaharlal Nehru (1889–1964) and Lord Mountbatten (1900–79) led to Kashmir being disputed by both Pakistan and India (the countries have gone to war three times over this territory).[8] Consequently, Jinnah's vision

4 Ali, N., V.S. Kalra and S. Sayyid (2005) (eds) *A Postcolonial People: South Asians in Britain*, London: Hurst.

5 Ballard, R. (1990) 'Migration and Kinship: The Differential Effect of Marriage Rules on the Processes of Punjabi Migration to Britain', in C. Clarke, C. Peach and S. Vertovek (eds) *South Asians Overseas: Contexts and Communities*, Cambridge: Cambridge University Press, pp. 219–49.

6 Ansari, H. (2004) *The 'Infidel' Within: The History of Muslims in Britain, 1800 to the Present*, London: Hurst.

7 Small, S. and J. Solomos (2006) 'Race, Immigration and Politics in Britain Changing Policy Agendas and Conceptual Paradigms: 1940s–2000s', *International Journal of Comparative Sociology*, 47(3–4): 235–57; Wolton, S. (2006) 'Immigration Policy and the "Crisis of British Values"', *Citizenship Studies*, 10(4): 453–67.

8 Choudhury, G.W. (1968) *Pakistan's Relations with India 1947–1966*, London: Pall Mall.

for the new Pakistan has never been fully realised. Although the end of the Second World War left Britain short of domestic labour to meet growing indigenous demand, this workforce scarcity was also common to a number of other Western European economies at the time, including France and Germany. British policy, however, differed from other Western European nation-states because it failed to capitalise upon initiatives to 'exploit' immigrant labour for the specific purposes of domestic economic expansion. Realising that newly recognised British citizens from the Caribbean and South Asia would make Britain their home, the restriction of net immigration in response to public opinion effectively hindered domestic economic growth. The Labour Government of the time, in essence, reduced the inflow of migrant labour to meet domestic political concerns, regarded by Robert Miles as a 'paradox'.[9] Labour demonstrated a profound preference for 'aliens' from Eastern Europe rather than, effectively, British citizens. These attitudes towards visible ethnic-minority migrant labour remained largely hidden from the public.[10]

In Britain, labour was needed to work in certain industrial sectors which were in decline and in which the 'host' population no longer wished to be employed. It was a racist perception that only ethnic minorities would work in these menial, dirty jobs, unable to perform other advanced functions. The economic recession of the late 1950s, however, eliminated the need for both domestic and migrant labour in these industries. By then, local communities and national institutions had already developed outward hostilities towards ethnic minorities.[11] It was increasingly becoming the case that ethnic minorities were concentrated in the inner areas of older industrial towns and cities. They lived in close proximity to working-class white British indigenous communities unable to escape economic decline. The somewhat limited acceptance on the part of the indigenous working classes was based on the belief that ethnic-minority and Muslim workers would eventually return to the sending regions once their employment terminated. Rarely was it imagined, or for that matter desired, that ethnic minorities would remain, forming and establishing communities over time. In many senses, migrant labour to Britain, as was the case in many other advanced Western European economies, originating invariably from once-colonised lands, filled the gap at the lower echelons of society. These British South Asian Muslim migrants were, in effect, placed at the bottom of the labour market, disdained by the host society and ethnicised and racialised in the sphere of capital accumulation. Workers were recruited into those industrial sectors most in decline, and, as such, their positions in society were located below the white British

---

9 Miles, R. (1989) *Racism*, London: Routledge.
10 ibid.
11 Layton-Henry, Z. (1984) *The Politics of Race in Britain*, London: Harper-Collins.

working classes, with the latter arguably having greater opportunity to attain social mobility.[12]

At the beginning of the 1960s, the number of immigrants entering Britain from South Asia reached its zenith. Towards the end of the 1960s, however, immigration from South Asia had all but ended. Both the peak in 1961–2 and the decline to 1968 were the result of the Commonwealth Immigrants Act 1962 and the Commonwealth Immigration Act 1968. Labour demands continued the unrestricted migration trends up until the 1962 Act. The new legislation had the effect of significantly increasing the rate of immigration in the eighteen months prior to its enactment. The rise in immigration was not only due to the introduction of the Act but also to the construction in 1960 of the Mangla Dam in Pakistan. In the Mirpur district of Azad Kashmir, large numbers of people were displaced due to the flooding of approximately 250 villages in this region, and many of these South Asian Muslims came to Britain through a process of chain migration.[13] The state of Azad Jammu and Kashmir, usually shortened to Azad Kashmir ('Free' Kashmir), is part of a Pakistani-administered section of the Kashmir region, along with the Northern Areas. Although defined as Pakistanis, the Pakistanis in Britain predominantly originate from the Mirpur district of Azad Kashmir. The term 'Mirpuri' is also interchangeable with Pakistani or Azad Kashmiri. It is difficult to estimate the proportion of Pakistanis in the UK who are actually from the Azad Kashmir district, but it is suggested that it could be as high as two out of three Pakistanis in Britain, with the 'Mirpuris' making up a significant component of this figure. Many of the Pakistanis in the West Midlands and in the north of England are Azad Kashmiris, although the category itself is not recognised in official statistics. The term 'Azad Kashmiri' has not quite become accepted parlance in academic or practitioner discourse. It is also important to state that some people would not consider Azad Kashmir to be part of Pakistan at all, nor would they wish to be identified as Pakistanis for political or cultural reasons. In effect, the 1962 Act changed the pattern of South Asian immigration: rather than 'pioneer' men, it was their wives, fiancées and children who arrived, with many South Asians from India and Pakistan seemingly rushing in an attempt 'to beat the ban' created by the Act.[14]

The unintended rise in immigration continued beyond the implementation of the Act in 1962 when those who had already settled in Britain were joined by their dependants.[15] The Act was initially intended to halt

---

12 Castles, S. and G. Kosack (1973) *Immigrant Workers in Western Europe and Class Structure*, London: Oxford University Press.

13 Anwar, M. (1979), op. cit.

14 Deakin, N. (1970) *Colour Citizenship and British Society*, London: Panther.

15 Anwar, M. (1998) *Between Cultures: Continuity and Change in the Lives of Young Asians*, London: Routledge.

immigration due to growing public and political concern over the desirability of large-scale immigration of 'coloureds'. Almost 130,000 Pakistanis arrived in Britain in the eighteen months preceding the 1962 Act.[16] A voucher system was introduced that encouraged patterns of chain migration. Those who were already in Britain could help their friends and relatives to migrate. Subsequent amendments to the original 1962 Act in 1968 led to wider restriction of immigration from New Commonwealth countries. On each occasion, the move reflected the politicisation of ethnic minorities in Britain. As a consequence of changes to the legislation, the South Asian settlement became more permanent and family-orientated.[17] At the beginning of the 1970s, Britain had a large number of distinct South Asian Muslim communities living and working in distinguishable parts of the country.

Historically, Muslims have arrived and settled in Britain for over a thousand years, entering the economy and society as traders, bankers, spice merchants, medical students, sailors and servants.[18] In the late nineteenth century, during the British Raj, Indians from upper-class backgrounds came for the specific purposes of education and enterprise. It could be argued that the current South Asian Muslim population possesses similar educational and entrepreneurial ambitions, but, it is, however, drawn from the more impoverished areas in the sending regions of Azad Kashmir in north-west Pakistan, the Sylhet region of north-west Bangladesh and the Punjab region of India. Invariably, the principal aims of South Asian Muslims at the beginning of the 1960s were to create as much wealth as possible before returning to their countries of origin, supported by a 'myth of return'. It did not happen – whether by chance (opportunity) or by design (legislation).

East African Asian Muslims arrived in the 1960s and the early 1970s essentially because of the 'Africanisation' of former colonised lands by the British. Their economic characteristics were middle class and professional in the sending societies and they sought to achieve those very ends in Britain. In 1973, Ugandan Asians were forced out of their country and those accepted by Britain were encouraged to settle away from already densely populated South Asian pockets known as 'red areas'.[19] Bangladeshis arrived when civil war, severe economic hardship and the desire for family reunification forced many to seek refuge in Britain during the late 1970s and early 1980s. In the 1990s, there was an intake of Eastern European and Middle Eastern Muslim refugees, emanating from such places as Bosnia, Kosovo,

16 Nielsen (2005), op. cit.
17 Modood, T. (1990) 'British Asian Muslims and the Rushdie Affair', *Political Quarterly*, 61(2): 143–60.
18 Commission for Racial Equality (1996) *Roots of the Future: Ethnic Diversity in the Making of Britain*, London: CRE.
19 Rex, J. and S. Tomlinson (1979) *Colonial Immigrants in a British City: A Class Analysis*, London: Routledge.

Afghanistan, Somalia and Iraq.[20] Indeed, for most Muslims, the most recent phase of immigration is largely because of political dislocation. Many Muslims had to emigrate from their home countries due to political troubles, decolonisation or displacement after various wars, conflicts or various forms of political persecution.[21] The 'Africanisation' processes in such countries as Kenya and Uganda, the political unrest in Cyprus, the civil wars in the former Yugoslavia and Lebanon, and the Islamic Revolution in Iran in 1979 are among the many number of reasons that have led to an increased flow of Muslims since the late 1970s. Many Muslims caught up in these upheavals took flight from their homelands to claim political or refugee status in various Western European countries, including Britain. A recent example of forced migration is given by Akbar S. Ahmed in his analysis of how the 'ethnic cleansing' in Bosnia, Serbia and Croatia in the mid-1990s compelled white European Muslims to seek refuge in Western Europe and elsewhere.[22]

The 1971 Census showed second-generation ethnic minorities, in particular South Asian Muslims, remaining within the same geographical locations as their parents. Two decades later, the 1991 Census showed second-and third-generation South Asian Muslims choosing to do the same.[23] The trend is argued to be a function of the younger generations maintaining the religious and cultural traditions of the generation before them as well because of negative experiences found in the labour market (see Chapter 4).[24] Many of the South Asian Muslims, specifically those from the rural areas of Azad Kashmir in Pakistan and Sylhet in north-west Bangladesh, are found working in the declining or highly competitive manufacturing, textile and catering sectors. They are living in inner-city housing built at the turn of the twentieth century, which is often in need of substantial repair and maintenance, and as joint and extended families in relatively restricted ethnically and culturally homogeneous communities. They remain close to kith and kin, extending religious and cultural manifestations of life, helping to directly shape their presence in Britain. It is also a period in which subsequent generations have begun to question their religious and cultural values, as well as the emergence of the increasing link between local and

20 Al-Ali, N., R. Black and K. Koser (2001) 'The Limits to "Transnationalism": Bosnian and Eritrean Refugees in Europe as Emerging Transnational Communities', *Ethnic and Racial Studies*, 24(4): 578–600.
21 Vertovec and Peach (1997), op. cit., p. 15.
22 Ahmed, A.S. (1995) ' "Ethnic Cleansing": A Metaphor for Our Time', *Ethnic and Racial Studies*, 18(1): 1–25.
23 Phillips, D. (1998) 'Black Minority Ethnic Concentration, Segregation and Dispersal in Britain', *Urban Studies*, 35(10): 1681–702.
24 Robinson, V. (1996) 'Inter-generational Differences in Ethnic Settlement Patterns in Britain', in P. Ratcliffe (ed.), *Ethnicity in the 1991 Census, Vol. III: Social Geography and Ethnicity in Britain: Geographical Spread, Spatial Concentration and Internal Migration*, London: HMSO, pp. 175–99.

global capitalism (see Chapter 7). As with other groups in society, de-industrialisation, technological innovation and the internationalisation of capital and labour have helped to ensure that British South Asian Muslims remain close to the bottom of the pile.[25] These were the patterns early on in the immigration and settlement of South Asian Muslims, but these social divisions remain today largely as a function of structural and cultural racism, as well as the fact of increasingly competitive education and labour markets.[26]

Pakistanis in the Midlands and the north of England almost exclusively originate from the Mirpur district of Azad Kashmir. A number of British Pakistanis also come from the Punjab region of Pakistan, but these groups have largely settled in the de-industrialised inner cities to the north or southeast. Before immigration, many of the Pakistanis in the Midlands and the north lived and worked in rural areas. Families were usually extended, with up to three generations living in one household. The men worked on small land holdings or in specialist craftwork, while women maintained domestic order and looked after livestock.[27] Families lived in close proximity to each other and were knowledgeable of what each member was doing. A recent socio-anthropological study of a Pakistani community in Oxford shows how strong the village–kin network is in the sending regions. Among rural-origin immigrants from northern Punjab, it has remained relatively intact as part of adaptation to Britain.[28] In the 1950s and 1960s, only men were prevalent, and they initially regarded their stay as temporary. Eventually, younger men from the sending regions replaced older Pakistanis, and a cyclical pattern emerged. Early Pakistani immigration was dependent upon this form of chain migration and, in particular, the regular remittances of capital sent back to the sending regions.[29] It is how the Pakistani immigration process differed from that of the Punjabi Sikhs and the African Caribbeans. These 'pioneer' Pakistanis worked hard to ensure their existence, as did other South Asians. Many had to fully adapt to the host society to persevere and, for some, it resulted in forsaking distinct cultural and religious traditions and habits for more 'Westernised' ones, such as the consumption of alcohol.[30]

25 Massey, D. and R. Meegan (1982) *The Anatomy of Job Loss*, London: Routledge.
26 Babb, P., H. Butcher, J. Church and L. Zealey (2006) (eds) *Social Trends, no. 36*, London: Office for National Statistics.
27 Dayha, B. (1974) 'The Nature of Pakistani Ethnicity', in A. Cohen (ed.), *Urban Ethnicity*, London: Tavistock, pp. 97–125.
28 Shaw, A. (1988) *A Pakistani Community in Britain*, Oxford: Basil Blackwell.
29 Saifullah-Khan, V. (1976) 'Pakistanis in Britain: Perceptions of a Population', *New Community*, 5(3): 222–9.
30 Dayha, B. (1988) 'South Asians as Economic Migrants in Britain', *Ethnic and Racial Studies*, 11(4): 439–56.

The Indian Muslims in the main are more affluent than their Bangladeshi and Pakistani peers and are not generally restricted to the same inner-city areas. These Indians tend to be occupationally more mobile and are more likely to be engaged in entrepreneurial activity.[31] Indian Muslims in London, Leicester and Birmingham have originated from the Punjab and the Gujarat areas of India or via East Africa, and are from a combination of urban and rural settings. The East African Muslims arrived via Kenya, Tanzania and Uganda, bringing with them the acumen for business.[32] As a result of this distinction at the point of entry into English society, many Indian Muslims are successful across a number of economic and occupational spheres. The Indian economic success story is also related to struggles experienced in the labour market, leading to self-employment as a way in which to realise upward social mobility, positively utilising the human (intellectual, social, cultural and economic) capital they regard as having been potentially mis-recognised by majority society. Unlike their white British peers, certain Indian small-business owners are a well-established section of the petty bourgeoisie.[33] Bangladeshis in Britain are a group almost exclusively originating from the Sylhet region, and the largest British concentration is found in the deprived neighbourhoods of the East End of London.[34] The second largest Bangladeshi community in Britain is found in parts of inner-city Birmingham. As with Pakistanis, Bangladeshis live in close-knit communities in ethnically distinctive localised settings. Increasingly, they too are establishing an entrepreneurial presence as well as becoming more organised at the level of the community. British Bangladeshis, however, remain an impoverished group, with large families being the norm and with men working predominantly in the catering industries or otherwise unemployed.

In relation to religion, there is presently a desire for the 'Islamisation' of second- and third-generation British Muslims. Present-day British-born South Asian Muslims, which include all Bangladeshis and Pakistanis and approximately 15 per cent of all Indians, are increasingly distinguishing their ethnic from their religious identities. The nature of Islam among these groups is questioned and re-examined in the light of inter-generational change. Young Bangladeshis experience a similar reality to young Pakistanis as the re-evaluation of their individual, political, cultural, ethnic and religious identities has involved a return to a more literal Islam.

31 Desai, R. (1963) *Indian Immigrants in Britain*, London: Oxford University Press for the Institute of Race Relations.
32 Mattausch, J. (1998) 'From Subjects to Citizens: British "East African Asians"', *Journal of Ethnic and Migration Studies*, 24(1): 121–41.
33 Ram, M. and T. Jones (1998) *Ethnic Minorities in Business*, Open University, Milton Keynes: Small Business Research Trust.
34 Eade, J. (1989) *The Politics of Community: The Bangladeshi Community in East London*, Aldershot: Avebury.

In contemporary Islam, there are two main sects, Shi'a and Sunni. In addition, the Barelwis and Deobandis are all variants of Sunni Islam (see Chapter 2).[35] In many of the concentrated urban centres where Muslims are found, by far the majority of all Muslims are Sunni, and the high number of mosques is evidence of a commitment to remain in Britain and teach younger Muslims the values and ways of Islam. In certain localities, there are specialist goods and services outlets, such as *halal* butchers, travel agents, clothing stores, fruit and vegetable retail outlets, restaurants, jewellers and bookshops – all owned and managed by Muslims and all helping to form and establish distinct ethnic enclave economies. Such entrepreneurial activity reinforces a sense of community as local businesses gear their activities towards the needs of the local people and, in the case of South Asians, whether they are Muslim, Sikh or Hindu. It further helps the creation of communities that hold close various manifestations of religious and cultural life (see Chapter 4).[36]

The size of the Muslim population in Britain was the topic of considerable discussion in the 1980s and 1990s. The rise in the political importance of Islam, internationally and domestically, in particular after the Iranian Revolution of 1979, led to various estimates being made. The number was thought to be as low as 900,000[37] or as high as 1.5 million in the 1990s.[38] Today, because of the 2001 Census, it is possible to show how the official 1.6 million population of Muslims in Britain is residentially clustered into a small number of large urban areas: in particular, London (607,000), the West Midlands Metropolitan County (predominantly Birmingham – 192,000), Greater Manchester (125,219) and the West Yorkshire Metropolitan County (the Bradford–Leeds urban area – 150,000).[39] London boroughs make up ten of the twenty local authorities with the greatest number and highest proportions of Muslims in England, including Tower Hamlets. In 2001, Tower Hamlets had the highest percentage of Muslims of all the local authorities in Britain (36 per cent) as well as being third biggest in number. It remains the focal point of the Bangladeshi community in Britain as it holds approximately one-quarter of all Bangladeshis in the country. Although increasing in size by 66 per cent between 1991 and 2001,

35 Robinson, F. (1988) *Varieties of South Asian Islam*, University of Warwick: Centre for Research in Ethnic Relations.
36 Lewis, P. (2002) *Islamic Britain: Religion, Politics and Identity Among British Muslims*, London: I.B. Tauris.
37 Peach, C. (1997) 'Estimates of the 1991 Muslim Population of Great Britain', *Oxford Plural Societies and Multicultural Cities Research Group Working Paper 1*, Oxford University: School of Geography.
38 Anwar, M. (1993) *Muslims in Britain: 1991 Census and Other Statistical Sources*, University of Birmingham: Centre for the Study of Islam and Christian-Muslim Relations.
39 Peach, C. (2006a) 'Muslims in the 2001 Census of England and Wales: Gender and Economic Disadvantage', *Ethnic and Racial Studies*, 8(4): 629–55.

the proportion of Bangladeshis residing in Tower Hamlets has stayed the same.[40]

In the urban industrialised zones in which they have formed communities, Pakistanis and particularly Bangladeshis show high rates of residential clustering (or 'segregation'). This is a highly contentious subject as it tends to be politically and culturally charged as well as being a genuinely difficult concept for statisticians and geographers to fully determine. Using the 2001 Census, on a scale from 0 (no segregation) to 100 (complete segregation), Pakistani segregation from white Britons averaged 54, while the Bangladeshis averaged 65. Bangladeshis showed the highest degree of segregation of any ethnic minority population in Britain in the 1991 Census.[41] They showed a relatively high level of segregation from the Pakistanis (46), while Pakistani segregation levels compared with Indians was lower than it was with Bangladeshis (39 versus 46). Therefore, although Pakistanis and Bangladeshis adhere to the same religion and historically once held the same nationality, ethnicity appears to be a stronger bond than religion among these groups of South Asian Muslims.[42]

The 2001 Census demonstrated that 72 per cent of the population of the UK considered themselves Christian (around 42 million people). Muslims were the second largest religion with 2.7 per cent (around 1.6 million). Hindus accounted for 1 per cent, Sikhs for 0.6 per cent, Jews for 0.5 per cent and other religions for 0.3 per cent; just under one-quarter of the population had 'no religion' or did not state one. The 2001 Census also revealed that 68 per cent of British Muslims were South Asian. Pakistanis on their own accounted for 43 per cent of all Muslims, and remained the single dominant group. The number of white Muslims in England and Wales (179,000) was higher than expected, with one-third defined as 'white British' (around 61,000 people). The remaining two-thirds are described as 'other white'. These include Turks,[43] Bosnians, Kosovans and Albanians, but also those originating from North Africa and the Middle East. The religion-by-birthplace data suggest 60,000 Muslims were Eastern European-born. These groups are assumed to be largely Bosnian and Kosovan refugees. Moreover, '36,000 Muslims were born in North Africa, and 93,000 Muslims were born in the Middle East'.[44] It is thought that many of these would have been

40 Peach, C. (2006b) 'Islam, Ethnicity and South Asian Religions in the London 2001 Census', *Transactions of the Institute of British Geographers*, 31(3): 353–70.
41 Peach, C. (1996) (ed.) *The Ethnic Minority Populations of Great Britain, Vol. II: Ethnicity in the 1991 Census*, London: ONS and HMSO.
42 Peach, C. (2006a), ibid.
43 Küçükcan, T. (2004) 'The Making of Turkish-Muslim Diaspora in Britain: Religious Collective Identity in a Multicultural Public Sphere', *Journal of Muslim Minority Affairs*, 24 (2): 243–58.
44 Peach (2006a), op. cit., p. 634.

counted among the 'white' population and therefore for much of the 116,000 'other white' Muslims.

'There were also found to be 96,000 Black African Muslims in England and Wales, but there were 7,500 Nigerian-born Muslims and a further 11,000 from "Other Central and [West] African countries". It is [suggested] that a substantial part of the Black African Muslim population is of Somali origin'.[45]

While Pakistanis accounted for 43 per cent of British Muslims, only 13 per cent of the Indians in Britain are Muslim. It confirms that 'around half of the South Asian population, taken as a whole, is Muslim'.[46] With the Muslim population estimate at around 2.2 million in 2010, and given that two out of three of all South Asian Muslims are Pakistanis (1 million), with approximately two out of four Pakistanis of Azad Kashmiri origin (approximately 667,000), it can be estimated that more than one in four of all British Muslims are quite probably Azad Kashmiri in origin.[47]

The ethnic diversity of the Muslim population, as revealed by the 2001 Census, permits a calculation of its estimated growth. This is achieved by applying the 2001 percentages of the different ethnic groups to the estimated ethnic minority populations in the Census years 1951 to 1991. It is an inexact approach as ethnic diversity in relation to the Muslims of Britain has grown in the past two decades due to the emergence of refugees and asylum-seekers from Afghanistan, Iran, Iraq, Somalia and former Yugoslavia. Nevertheless, the proportions from non-Asian or African sending regions do not vary too significantly because of the relatively small ethnic minority populations between 1951 and 1981. Based on this analysis, the 'Muslim population of the UK rose from about 21,000 in 1951 to 55,000 [in] 1961, a quarter of a million in 1971, nearly 600,000 in 1981, 1 million in 1991 and 1.6 million in 2001'.[48] Population growth rates are high while British Muslims remain, on average, relatively young.

It is true that British Muslim communities have remained concentrated in the inner-city areas of older towns and cities in Britain. It is an indicator of how they have not benefited from the levels of social mobility enjoyed by other immigrant and ethnic minority communities, past and present, but also of their inability to move out of areas facing high levels of social tension and economic deprivation, as well as direct discrimination, racial

---

45   Ibid., p. 635.
46   Ibid.
47   Abbas, T. (2009) 'United Kingdom and Northern Ireland', in J.S. Nielsen, S. Akgönül, A. Alibašić, B. Maréchal and C. Moe (eds) *Yearbook of Muslims in Europe 2009*, Leiden: Brill, pp. 363–73.
48   Peach, C. (2005) 'Muslims in the UK', T. Abbas (ed.), *Muslim Britain: Communities under Pressure*, London and New York: Zed, p. 23.

hostility and cultural exclusion. The Islamic Human Rights Commission has extensively mapped the physical, racial and cultural discrimination and violence experienced by Muslims in Britain in all spheres of social life, including in relation to health, education and policing services, as well in how Muslims have been attacked by random members of the majority society.[49] Birmingham, located at the centre of the West Midlands region, is a post-industrial city in which many of the challenges faced by Muslims across the country are typified. The experience of Birmingham Muslims brings into sharp focus the fact that economic opportunities have tended to bypass these communities, even when others have prospered. Where other cities with large Muslim populations, such as Bradford, are trapped in economic decline, the economic performance of Birmingham has been rather favourable. Despite the decline of its manufacturing and engineering sectors, the city is undergoing regeneration with considerable expansion in service (retail) and commercial sectors. These opportunities, however, have largely evaded most Muslims, and they may have even entrenched some of the barriers faced by this group. While most of the white British indigenous population has moved out of the inner cities through 'white flight', many Muslim groups have failed to move beyond the inner-city areas to which they originally migrated. These areas have become further disadvantaged, with new employment created elsewhere and in other economic sectors.[50]

In the city of Birmingham, presently home to 1 million people, Muslims accounted for 14.3 per cent of the population, with Pakistanis numbering just over 104,000 (74 per cent of all Muslims in the city) in 2001.[51] This total number of Muslims is twice as large as the highest concentration outside London.[52] In April 2001, 9 per cent of the 1.6 million Muslims in Britain and 16 per cent of the entire population of 658,000 Pakistanis in Britain were found to be in the city of Birmingham, arguably home to the largest expatriate Azad Kashmiri community in the world. Nevertheless, it is important to reflect on the fact that 'Pakistanis' do not comprise a single homogeneous religio-ethnic group: ethnically, Punjabis, Kashmiris, Pathans, Sindhis and Blauchis can all be Pakistani. Religiously, these Pakistanis are Barelwi or Deobandi, subscribing to the Hanifi school and, politically, aligned with various groups and organisations. Most of the Azad Kashmiris are Barelwi Hanifis. The independence of former East Pakistan (now Bangladesh)

49 Ameli, S.R., M. Elahi and A. Merali (2004) *British Muslims' Expectations of the Government Social Discrimination: Across the Muslim Divide*, London: IHRC.
50 Owen, D. and M. Johnson (1996) 'Ethnic Minorities in the Midlands', in P. Ratcliffe (ed.), *Ethnicity in the 1991 Census, Vol. III: Social Geography and Ethnicity in Britain: Geographical Spread, Spatial Concentration and Internal Migration*, London: HMSO, pp. 227–70.
51 Birmingham City Council (2003) *Population Census in Birmingham: Religious Group Profiles*, Birmingham: BCC.
52 Office for National Statistics (2008) *Census 2001: Ethnicity and Religion in England and Wales*.

in the early 1970s and the fact that the vast majority of Pakistanis in Britain are from the Azad Kashmir region masks certain ethnic characteristics of people ordinarily identified as 'Pakistanis'. Moreover, there is a considerable body of people who have originated from the north-west frontier. In the movement of populations from Afghanistan to Pakistan, largely a result of the Russian–Afghan war and more recent events since 9/11, ethnic identities such as Pushtun or Pathan are subsumed under that of Pakistani.[53] As much as there is a great deal of heterogeneity among Muslims in Britain, there is also considerable homogeneity, particularly in Birmingham with its large Pakistani or, more specifically, Azad Kashmiri community, where South Asian Muslims in Birmingham predominantly originate from the Mirpur district of Azad Kashmir and the surrounding areas, including Attock, Jhelum and Rawalpindi.

Post-war South Asian Muslim migrants and now ethnic-minority communities have largely entered and settled in Britain as a workforce for the unwanted jobs indigenous Britons did not want to carry out, then and now. At present, Pakistani and Azad Kashmiri groups continue to live near or at the bottom of local area economic and social realities, largely in the postindustrial cities to the north, the Midlands and the south, all of which are at various stages of regeneration after the collapse of the traditional economic sectors. The fact that one in six of working Pakistani men in Britain is a taxi driver is indicative of the labour experiences faced.[54] Birmingham Pakistanis have some of the highest rates of unemployment: up to three times as much as others across the city.[55] These Birmingham inner cities reveal that it is the Muslims (largely Pakistanis and Bangladeshis but also African and Arabs) who occupy the areas in highest numbers and that it is they who are at greatest disadvantage. In Birmingham, Muslims appear to have been neglected by the local state and various 'third way' public services.[56] In the early 1990s, while the local authority and community groups helped to dismantle the ailing race relations equality structures, the replacement was an experimental partnership network without adequate political and financial ownership or investment.[57]

53 Mahmood, J. (2009) personal communication, 22 August.
54 Office for National Statistics (2006) *Employment Patterns: Pakistanis Most Likely to Be Self-Employed*, London: ONS.
55 Anwar, M. (1996) *British Pakistanis: Demographic, Social and Economic Position*, University of Warwick: Centre for Research in Ethnic Relations.
56 Shukra, K., L. Back, M. Keith and J. Solomos (2004) 'Black Politics and the Web of Joined-up Governance: Compromise, Ethnic Minority Mobilisation and the Transitional Public Sphere', *Social Movement Studies*, 3(1): 31–50; Smith, G. and S. Stephenson (2005) 'The Theory and Practice of Group Representation: Reflections on the Politics of Race Equality in Birmingham', *Public Administration*, 83(2): 323–43.
57 Abbas, T. and M. Anwar (2005) 'An Analysis of Race Equality Policy and Practice in the City of Birmingham, UK', *Local Government Studies*, 31(1): 53–68.

The most significant influence on the city has been the need to shift from an industrial city renowned throughout the world for its engineering and manufacturing to a post-industrial global city of corporate consumerism. The early phases of the recent developments have focused on re-establishing the economic strengths of the city in relation to the region, and the most expedient way to do it has been to concentrate on the global-corporate commercial retail service sector. Over the years, there are plans to develop the arts, media and cultural sectors but how this process will include or exclude ethnic and religious minorities is still to be tested. Until recently, any developments to local economic areas have concentrated on service-sector investment. The city's Muslims are often excluded from this experience of change and development because of structural subordination and existing conditions of exclusion, racism, poverty, disadvantage and limited political impact, which is perennially constrained by internal divisions and external challenges.[58]

It could be reasoned that clustering reflects limited population movements outside the original areas of settlement, therefore raising the issue of social mobility.[59] An important debate here centres on the issue of whether residential clustering among ethnic-minority groups is better defined as 'segregation' or 'concentration'. The question of segregation has been of particular interest in recent times, not least during the disturbances in the north in 2001 when the former Chair of the Commission for Racial Equality (CRE), Herman Ousley, talked of the 'parallel lives' of Pakistanis in Bradford and, more recently, in the wake of the events of 7/7, when the very last CRE Chair, Trevor Phillips, spoke of 'sleep-walking into segregation'.[60] Research and statistics are extensive in their availability and detail but they do not clarify the matter at hand. Rather, what tends to speak loudest is the political rhetoric that this subject has become. It does not stop at 'segregation' either. Commentators use it to evoke the 'problems of multiculturalism', which is often more about the 'problems of multiculturalism in relation to Muslims' (see Chapters 6 and 7).

Arguably, Pakistanis and Bangladeshis, between them, number more than half of all Muslims in Britain. Apart from London, where there are approximately 1 million Muslims of every national and ethnic origin, the Muslims in the Midlands and in the north are relatively homogeneous. It is here that it is possible to recognise the greatest issues in relation to 'segregation', and they are invariably a function of limited economic and social opportunities

58 Back, L. and J. Solomos, J. (1992) 'Black Politics and Social Change in Birmingham, UK: An Analysis of Recent Trends', *Ethnic and Racial Studies*, 15(2): 327–51.
59 Open Society Institute (2004) *Muslims in the UK: Policies for Engaged Citizens*, New York: OSI.
60 Phillips, T. (2005) 'After 7/7: Sleepwalking to Segregation', speech delivered to the Manchester Council for Community Relations, 22 September.

compounded by direct and indirect racism and discrimination that keeps communities 'locked in' and majority society 'locked out'. It is these Muslim communities that faced the brunt of the focus when the policies of 'community cohesion' were first propounded at the end of 2001. Emerging as the New Labour response to the northern disturbances, the idea of 'community cohesion' adopts a socio-pathological blame-the-victim approach, placing the onus of responsibility firmly onto the marginalised communities themselves, taking it away from local and national government.[61]

The continued local ethnic, racial and religious profiling of the 'Muslim' perpetuates a negative focus, creating wider majority hostility and encouraging Muslim communities already in isolated localities to become even more fearful of their limited opportunity structures. The continued national focus on domestic Islamic political radicalism and the apparent threat of Muslim local residents who are regarded as potential policing and security risks develops fear and confusion in the minds of many, Muslims and non-Muslims (see Chapter 8). The international 'War on Terror' has maintained a siege mentality in relation to Muslims; perpetually characterised in blanket, homogenised and caricatured terms such as 'radicals', 'fundamentalists' or 'terrorists'. At the same time, Azad Kashmiri and Sylheti Muslims in the Midlands and the north are continuing to marry within a certain clan-based system of networks and family associations, some of whom are also 'marriage migrants' joining British-born spouses in the UK.[62] If ethnic and cultural integration is a 'two-way street', many Muslims are clearly in a cul-de-sac, as is argued by some right-of-centre commentators. It applies to the majority of Muslims who live in the Midlands and the former mill towns, but hardly at all to those who live in the south-east of the country. There are specific differences by region that are important to take into consideration when attempting to discuss the nature and significance of segregation. However, in reality, the question as to whether this is about the nature of communities or discrimination and racism will not change unless there is a transformation of the political landscape on the subject matter.

It could be argued, therefore, that rather than Muslim groups segregating themselves from wider society it is the inequalities based upon 'race' and ethnicity that have contributed to this segregation. It can be primarily seen in the example of the housing market, where discriminatory practices

61 Kundnani, A. (2001) 'From Oldham to Bradford: The Violence of the Violated', in *The Three Faces of British Racism: Race and Class*, 43(3): 41–60; Amin, A. (2003) 'Unruly Strangers? The 2001 Urban Riots in Britain', *International Journal of Urban and Regional Research*, 27(2): 460–3.
62 Charsley, K. (2005) 'Unhappy Husbands: Masculinity and Migration in Transnational Pakistani Marriage', *Journal of the Royal Anthropological Institute*, 11(1): 85–105; Shaw, A. (2001) 'Kinship, Cultural Preference and Immigration: Consanguineous Marriage Among British Pakistanis', *Journal of the Royal Anthropological Institute*, 7(2): 315–34.

are found to exist. Not all are necessarily intended because some result from the unwitting outcomes of routinised institutional processes.[63] Such discriminatory practices result in 'excluded neighbourhoods' and lead to 'separateness'. Segregation here emerges as a result of discrimination and certain opportunities unavailable to ethnic-minority groups. Half of the white British population lives in neighbourhoods containing no ethnic-minority residents.[64] An important indicator of segregation is the fact that Muslims live in areas that are part of an older housing stock. They are in towns and cities where urban obsolescence is greatest, and are clustered in localities where the services of education and health are in limited supply, but where the need is significant and continues to grow, and particularly in relation to the older members of minority groups.[65]

It is clear that the economic marginality of these Muslim groups constrains the choices they can make in relation to the locations in which they live. If given the alternative, most Muslim minorities would not elect to live in the poorest and most deprived areas; rather, their choices are inhibited due to the limited opportunities available to them, and, as such, groups become 'segregated' (or residentially clustered) through a lack of choice. It is doubtful that residents make an active choice to live in such areas as they are likely to experience social stigma and economic marginalisation as a result of association with a particular spatiality. The problems are especially acute for Pakistani and Bangladeshi groups who are heavily concentrated in the poorest sections of the housing market; for example, most Muslim minorities in Bradford experience high rates of housing stress. The problem can indeed be linked to the lower position of such groups in the labour market and their higher levels of unemployment.[66]

Susan Smith points to the persistence of residential segregation among ethnic and religious minorities in Britain, and that the segregation can indeed be seen as a product of British racism. The process perpetuates the marginal economic opportunities of ethnic minority groups, outweighing the notion that certain ethnic minorities tend to segregate themselves and thus raising the issue of 'self-segregation'. Segregation can indeed be linked to racialised notions of space, where minority mono-ethnic communities are

63 Rex, J. and R. Moore (1967) *Race, Community and Conflict: A Study of Sparkbrook*, London: Institute of Race Relations and Oxford University Press.
64 Phillips, D. (2006) 'Parallel Lives? Challenging Discourses of British Muslim Self-Segregation', *Environment and Planning D: Society and Space*, 24(1): 25–40.
65 Hussain, S. (2008) *Muslims on the Map: A National Survey of Social Trends in Britain*, London: I.B. Tauris; Ahmad, W.I.U. and R. Walker (1997) Asian Older People: Housing, Health and Access to Services, *Ageing and Society* 17(2): 141–65.
66 Ratcliffe, P. (1999) 'Housing Inequality and "Race": Some Critical Reflections on the Concept of "Social Exclusion"', *Ethnic and Racial Studies*, 22(1): 1–22; Sellick, P. (2004) *Muslim Housing Experiences*, London: Housing Corporation and Oxford Centre for Islamic Studies.

perceived to be a threat to social cohesion.[67] Concerns arise about the 'black inner city' and the 'transformation of whole areas into alien territory'.[68] The argument in relation to segregation and the issues of 'self-segregation' can be seen as legitimising 'the discriminatory practices underpinning […] the racialisation of culture'.[69] It is reflected in the rise of cultural racism, where the emphasis has shifted from differentiating on the basis of 'race' to religion, language and nationalistic loyalties; 'it is in our [white British] biology to defend our way of life, traditions and customs against outsiders not because they are inferior but because they are parts of different cultures'.[70] It captures the essence of cultural racism, an adaptation of racism to the modern world.[71] The primary message that re-emerges, as echoed by former Prime Minister Margaret Thatcher in a television interview for Granada's *World in Action* (27 January 1978), is that 'this country might be swamped by a people with a different culture'.[72]

The debate as to whether ethnic residential clustering is best defined as concentration or segregation is a highly complex one. It also raises the issue of whether Muslims, for example, are 'Islamising' the city, a notion that has been taken forward by certain right-wing commentators in recent periods.[73] It reflects an ideology that supports the notion that Muslim minorities are segregated through choice. As stated, this is highly questionable since the residential areas they choose to live in are effectively determined by class position. It can be legitimately argued that economic marginality and restricted opportunities have played a large part in the formation of residential clusters. If segregation can be deemed to exist, it is not a choice of the individual but rather a constraining factor. As Ludi Simpson argues, the growth of the South Asian Muslim population certainly creates areas of concentration, 'which official reports have most recently acknowledged in an unhelpful, victimising and accusatory manner with the false label of self-segregation'.[74]

Thus far, the different Muslim groups who arrived and settled in Britain and how they were initially incorporated into the workings of post-industrial British society have been introduced. The essential elements of this

67 Smith, S.J. (1993) 'Residential Segregation and the Politics of Racialisation', in M. Cross and M. Keith (eds), *Racism, the City and the State*, London: Routledge, pp. 128–43.
68 Barker, M. (1984) 'Het nieuwe racisme [The New Racism]', in A. Bleich and P. Schumacher (eds) *Nederlands Racisme* [Dutch Racism], Amsterdam: Van Gennep, pp. 62–85.
69 Ibid., p. 78
70 Ibid.
71 Mac an Ghaill, M., M.J. Hickman and A. Brah (1999) (eds) *Thinking Identities: Ethnicity, Racism and Culture*, Basingstoke: Palgrave-Macmillan.
72 Smith, S.J. (1993), op. cit.
73 Caldwell, C. (2009) *Reflections on the Revolution in Europe: Immigration, Islam, and the West*, London: Allen Lane.
74 Simpson, L. (2004) 'Statistics of Racial Segregation: Measures, Evidence and Policy', *Urban Studies*, 41(3): 661–81.

discussion explore the processes of decolonisation and the post-war immigration of Muslims to Britain, the impact of legislation on immigration and settlement patterns, in particular the 'push' and 'pull' factors impacting on specific population movements. Analysis has been provided of the different sending and settling regions involved. Official statistics in relation to the British Muslim population, and in exploring geographical distribution and socio-economic status suggest that as well as being a heterogeneous community it is also one that experiences severe structural inequalities. The topic of segregation has been looked into in the light of the continuing arguments it raises in the popular imagination, in political discourses and whether indeed there are issues that imply Muslim communities are 'sleep-walking into segregation', as has been suggested by some.

It is understood that there are theoretical intersections but British racial discourse on minorities has transformed from 'colour' in the 1950s and 1960s, to 'race' in the 1960s, 1970s and 1980s, 'ethnicity' in the 1990s and 'religion' in the present climate, with Islam having the most exposure.[75] There has been a movement away from regarding minorities as homogeneous entities to discerning differences within and between 'Blacks' and Asians, and then within South Asians, to differences between Indians, Pakistanis and Bangladeshis, and, currently, between Muslims, Hindus and Sikhs. It appears that religion has surfaced as the primary social descriptive category. In Britain, this burgeoning interest in religion has come from both awareness of Islam within the Muslim population and from its heightened national and international profile.[76] The particular social, cultural and religious needs of different Muslim ethnic, religious and cultural groups have become important issues on the British political landscape, especially after the events of 9/11 and 7/7.

The experience of British South Asian Muslims is a complex mesh of ethnicity, migration, identity, culture and religion, as well as the maintenance of strong transnational links to the sending regions.[77] There are also various political and material factors involved in the different phases of immigration and the patterns of settlement resulting from this. There has been a continuing increase in the Muslim population of Britain in the post-war period, and different factors have influenced the demographic profile of this group. The ethnic characteristics of British Muslims are predominantly those of Pakistani (in particular Azad Kashmiri), Bangladeshi and Indian

---

75 Peach, C. (2005) 'Muslims in the UK', in T. Abbas (ed.), *Muslim Britain: Communities under Pressure*, London and New York: Zed, p. 18.

76 Ibid.

77 Ballard, R. (1994) (ed.) *Desh Pardesh: The South Asian Presence in Britain*, London: Hurst; Grillo, R. (2004) 'Islam and Transnationalism', *Journal of Ethnic and Migration Studies*, 30(5): 861–78; Werbner, P. (2004a) 'Theorising Complex Diasporas: Purity and Hybridity in the South Asian Public Sphere in Britain', *Journal of Ethnic and Migration Studies*, 30(5): 895–911.

Muslims living and working in older parts of established towns and cities in Britain, and this population is largely young. It is also, on average, relatively poor, badly housed, poorly educated, experiencing relatively low rates of male employment and also has a distinctively limited female participation rate in the labour market. Survey accounts show it is also a 'religious population' that holds strong family values,[78] and marriage is a within-ethnic-group phenomenon: in 1991; '99 per cent of married Bangladeshi women in 1991 were married to Bangladeshi men, 95 per cent of Pakistani women to Pakistani men'.[79]

It is true that South Asian Muslims reflect Islam in Britain but there is a risk of homogenising the religion by suggesting that South Asian traits are wholly typical of Islam itself. Pakistanis and Bangladeshis are nearly always Muslim, but there are British Muslims of 'Arab, Albanian, Bosnian, Iranian, Nigerian, Somali, Turkish'[80] and many other origins whose cultural, social, economic and theological profiles directly contrast the South Asian Muslim experience. There are also within-group variations to consider; for example, there are huge differences between Sunni Barelwi Pakistanis and East African Ismailis, but they are both South Asians by definition. The experiences of Pakistanis and Bangladeshis are not at all reflective of individuals and communities from other ethnic Muslim backgrounds in Britain, but as a combined group they continue to retain a dominant demographic and cultural profile.

Since immigration to Britain from the subcontinent began on a large scale during the 1950s and 1960s, the Muslim population has often clustered together, residing in close proximity to one another, and around certain ethnicities. Many South Asian Muslims in Britain have worked to actively shape and re-establish a range of social and cultural practices found in the Indian subcontinent, a number of which have a basis in Islam. It has led to large communities of Muslim origin living in specific areas, the largest of which is London. Most of these groups live in the less affluent areas of London including the poorest borough, Newham, in which 40 per cent of all London-based Muslims are found. It has a significant impact on the Muslim population as a whole as the areas in which most young Muslims live are in run-down and deprived localities, and it will be difficult for subsequent generations of Muslims to break free from the socio-economic and cultural (internal and external) constraints that they face. Other areas that exhibit large pockets of Muslims include the West Midlands (10 per cent of the Muslim population) and the north-west (13 per cent of the Muslim population). These areas were part of the traditional manufacturing and textile

78 Modood, T., R. Berthoud, J. Lakey, J. Nazroo, P. Smith, S. Virdee and S. Beishon (1997) *Ethnic Minorities in Britain: Diversity and Disadvantage*, London: Policy Studies Institute.
79 Peach (2006a), op. cit., pp. 638–9.
80 Ibid.

industries that many came to work in after the Second World War. Their demise left widespread unemployment in these areas. Growth in the communities of Muslims and other ethnic and religious populations in Britain results in the increased importance of issues such as multiculturalism, integration and identity. The changing demographic profile of British Muslims has been a major factor in determining the extent to which multiculturalism has become significant in both the political and public arena. Before exploring these issues further, it is important to look more closely at the nature of socio-economic mobility and its impact on cultural relations between Muslims and non-Muslims in wider society.

4 The formation of Muslim capital
Education, employment and entrepreneurialism

In recent periods, there has been much discussion about identities, achievements, faith schools, the national curriculum and citizenship. The current focus on 'citizenship education' is the latest acceptance of the role education can play in engendering a 'civic morality' amongst young people.[1] It is apparent that state education systems have historically tended to reinforce the status quo, and the needs and aspirations of Muslims have only in recent periods been met by local and national policy initiatives, namely through state-funded Muslim schools since 1997.[2] The latter development has created consternation in some quarters who regard their existence as a potential for 'fundamentalism' while tentatively acknowledging that they ought to be granted funding because of the precedents set by Jewish, Church of England and Roman Catholic schools.[3] At the time of writing, there are seven state-funded Islamic schools in England (compared with forty in the Netherlands).[4] This figure can be 'compared with more than 4,700 Church of England schools, 2,100 Catholic schools, 37 Jewish and 28 Methodist [state-funded] schools'.[5]

The education of British Muslims has remained a topic of concern since groups first came to the country in large numbers in the post-war period.

1 Crick, B. (2000) *Essays on Citizenship*, London: Continuum.
2 Halstead, M.J. (2004) 'Education', in Open Society Institute (ed.), *Muslims in the UK: Policies for Engaged Citizens*, London and Budapest: OSI, pp. 101–92.
3 Walford, G. (2004) 'English Education and Immigration Policies and Muslim Schools', in H. Daun and G. Walford (eds), *Educational Strategies among Muslims in the Context of Globalization: Some National Case Studies*, Leiden: Brill, pp. 209–28.
4 Bartels, E. (2000) '"Dutch Islam": Young People, Learning and Integration', *Current Sociology*, 48(4): 59–73; Walford, G. (2003) 'Separate Schools for Religious Minorities in England and the Netherlands: Using a Framework for the Comparison and Evaluation of Policy', *Research Papers in Education*, 18(3): 281–99.
5 Meer, N. (2007) 'Muslim Schools in Britain: Challenging Mobilisations or Logical Developments?', *Asia-Pacific Journal of Education*, 27(1): 55–71, p. 57.

Early problems involved language, integration and teacher expectation issues,[6] and all of these factors were thought to affect educational outcomes, directly and indirectly.[7] It appears that many of these issues remain important today, with South Asian Muslims, in particular young men, often performing the least well of all ethnic-minority and majority groups in education.[8] It is important to consider the range of forces impacting on the education of Muslims. These concern not only the home and school (as studies continue to show) but also the wider social world. Furthermore, the ways in which identity and religiosity impact upon individual and group experiences, how they are manifested in educational settings, and the ways in which they influence achievement are also important to discern.

In the inner-city areas where there is high 'ethnic residential clustering', in a number of comprehensive schools Muslims are the overwhelming majority, particularly in the East End of London, parts of the West Midlands and in the north. Most teachers ensure that what they do embraces the diversity and multi-faith nature of the children who enter their institutions, but questions of institutional impact, as well as identity and religio-cultural maintenance on the part of both teachers and pupils, however, remain unanswered. Many of these issues are thought to impact on the persistent educational underachievement of young Muslim men. Many Muslim communities have created independent Islamic schools to supplement mainstream education through religious and linguistic teaching. The impact this has for Muslim groups needs to be explored in detail, including the view that this somehow demonstrates an unwillingness to integrate *or* adapt to majority society. There is a need to recognise the issues of professional capacity and how concepts of citizenship are embedded in the religion of Islam itself (and which are not always appreciated). Poor performance in schools can lead to unemployment or reduced earning capacity, and a lack of positive opportunities to develop. Combined with limited facilities for recreation and leisure, this can thrust some younger Muslims towards crime or a potential sensibility towards extremist behaviour of other kinds.[9]

Numbering 2.2 million in the current period, Muslims form a significant group whose educational needs are of particular interest to Government.

6 Rose, E.J.B. in association with N. Deakin, M. Abrams, V. Jackson, A.H. Vanags, B. Cohen, J. Gaitskill and P. Ward (1969) *Colour and Citizenship: A Report on British Race Relations*, London: Institute of Race Relations and Oxford University Press.

7 Tomlinson, S. (2005) *Education in a Post-welfare Society*, Milton Keynes: Open University Press and McGraw-Hill.

8 Abbas, T. (2004b) *The Education of British South Asians: Ethnicity, Capital and Class Structure*, Basingstoke: Palgrave-Macmillan.

9 Macey, M. (1999) 'Class, Gender and Religious Influences on Changing Patterns of Pakistani Muslim Male Violence in Bradford', *Ethnic and Racial Studies*, 22(5): 847–9.

The Muslim population in Britain is indeed young, with one in three British Muslims under the age of fifteen.[10] This adds considerable importance to debates surrounding the educational achievement of Muslim groups who constitute a large segment of the future workforce population. The Open Society Institute (OSI) asserts: 'with Muslims set to comprise almost a quarter of the growth in the working age population in Britain between 1999 and 2009, integrating British Muslims into the mainstream labour market must now be a priority for the government'.[11] Statistics for educational performance reveal that young Bangladeshi and Pakistani men have some of the lowest average levels of attainment at General Certificate for Secondary Education (GCSE) level, marginally ahead of Caribbean groups. Official statistics in 2003–4 showed that 31 per cent of Muslims of working age in Britain had no qualifications, exceeding all other religious groups. Similarly, Muslims are the least likely of all groups to have higher education degrees.[12] Compared with other South Asian religious groups, such as the Sikhs and Hindus, on average, they consistently underperform in education (particularly outside of London). The most rudimentary reasons seem to be social class and the educational levels of parents (as is the case with all groups in society), how majority society views and acts in relation to Muslim minorities, and the negative general outcomes that emanate from various social and institutional encounters and modes of cultural and political exchange.

The educational experiences of British Muslims are closely linked to the history of their immigration in the UK, with the late 1960s witnessing Muslim family reunification because of government immigration legislation that effectively shut the door on primary migration. Wives and dependants were 'rushed over'. It was during this time that immigrant Muslim children, predominantly of Pakistani ('East and West') origin, first had an impact on the British education system. The 1960s was a time of assimilationist government policy in education, with 'different' cultures assumed to be 'deprived' cultures needing to be internalised into the dominant English culture.[13] Some regarded this as an illegitimate surrender to racism and an attempt to dissolve the rights and identities of minorities into an imagined unitary whole.[14] Changes in government approach followed in the 1970s with programmes of integration and multiculturalism, promoting the

10 Peach, C. (2005) 'Muslims in the UK', in T. Abbas (ed.), *Muslim Britain: Communities under Pressure*, London and New York: Zed, pp. 25–6.
11 Open Society Institute (2004b) *Aspirations and Reality: British Muslims and the Labour Market*, New York: OSI, p. 8.
12 Office for National Statistics (2004) *Education: One in Three Muslims Has No Qualifications*, London: National Statistics.
13 Walford (2004), op. cit.
14 Troyna, B. and J. Williams (1986) *Racism, Education and the State: The Racialization of Educational Policy*, Beckenham: Croom Helm.

positive recognition of other cultures.[15] These were criticised as instruments of social control by the left for concentrating upon individuals rather than inequalities in the institutions and structures of wider society.[16] A shift towards anti-racist policies was called for in the 1980s, where schools would be urged to deliver anti-racist education, but these were only partially implemented.[17] The various approaches here were accused of being over-simplistic, generalising not only the plight of all ethnic minorities but also the apparent culpability of all white groups in relation to racism. Ultimately, the study of Muslims in relation to their potential to engage and participate successfully in everyday life has the effect of focusing on individual and group differences rather than structures and opportunities, as suggested by Ash Amin in responding to the 'community cohesion' reports and Tariq Modood in his analysis of the various 'capitals' (cultural, social and economic) that impact upon the experiences of ethnic minorities entering higher-education institutions in Britain.[18]

A potentially useful way in which to explore educational outcomes is to utilise the concept of social capital. Recent socio-anthropological research shows the extent to which certain social and cultural norms and behaviours exist within Muslims as specific ethno-religious characteristics that could be defined as social capital, some of which could be seen to impact on education.[19] There are strong associations between family, ethnicity and social capital, as argued in the general discussions of the intersection between ethnicity, religion and culture.[20] However, more conceptually, relatively homogeneous ethno-religious communities may be characterised by strong trust and cooperative norms within the community but low levels of trust and cooperation with the rest of society. Strong bonding ties provide Muslims with a sense of identity and common purpose, but without 'bridging' ties that transcend various social divides (e.g. religion, ethnicity and social class), 'bondedness' can potentially act as the foundation for pursuing

15 Walford, G. (1998) *Doing Research about Education*, London: Routledge.
16 Abbas (2004b), op. cit.
17 Walford (1998), op. cit., pp. 214–15.
18 Amin, A. (2002) 'Ethnicity and the Multicultural City: Living with Diversity', *Environment and Planning A*, 34(6): 959–80; Modood, T. (2004) 'Capitals, Ethnic Identity and Educational Qualifications', *Cultural Trends*, 13(2): 87–105; Modood, T. (2006) 'Ethnicity, Muslims and higher education entry in Britain, *Teaching in Higher Education*, 11(2): 247–50.
19 Anwar, M. (1979) *The 'Myth' of Return: Pakistanis in Britain*, London: Heinemann; Ballard, R. (1994) (ed.) *Desh Pardesh: The South Asian Presence in Britain*, London: Hurst; Shaw, A. (2000) *Kinship and Continuity: Pakistani Families in Britain*, London: Routledge.
20 Campbell, C. and C. McLean (2003) 'Social Capital, Local Community Participation and the Construction of Pakistani Identities in England: Implications for Health Inequalities Policies', *Journal of Health Psychology*, 8(2): 247–62; Goulbourne, H. and J. Solomos (2003) 'Families, Ethnicity and Social Capital', *Social Policy and Society*, 2(4): 329–38.

narrow interests that can potentially exclude outsiders.[21] While ethnic networks may serve as a source of 'adaptive change' when immigrants first arrive, it is bridging capital that enables greater participation in the 'host society'. That is, bridging capital is crucial for immigrant groups to expand upon networks beyond existing ethnic and religious communities and to eventually acculturate into society. Importantly, the accumulation of bridging capital requires not only the willingness of ethnic-minority groups to integrate into society at large but also, more importantly, the willingness of the receiving society to accept ethnic groups, and in cases where these other ethnic groups are also religious groups, i.e. Muslims. As such, some ethnic Muslim minorities are potentially excluded *or* included in majority *and* minority society because of 'race', ethnicity *and/or* religion.

'Bonding' and 'bridging' between Muslims is strengthened by the religio-cultural characteristics of the group as well as by the impact of economic and social exclusion. For Muslims, the religion of Islam binds people by certain specific norms, values and practices. These can transcend accepted boundaries of nation and state, even language and culture, and existed long before the modern social era. Yet, the Muslim world is not as it once was, and it is currently held siege by its own internal divisions as well as by its place in the current epoch of globalisation. Relations with non-Muslim ethnic majorities are restrained by 'segregation' (both occupational and residential) and alienation. There are instances of rising Islamophobia ('the fear or dread of Islam', see Chapter 5) as well as general hostility towards Muslims in the post-9/11 and post-7/7 climate. 'Linking' involves precisely the notion of developing improved relations with those who hold power in government, media, civil society and the academy. They require bearing influence and obtaining resources. The ability of Muslims to link positively is, however, hampered by their existing positions. As they remain susceptible, polarities continue to widen, exacerbating the existential experiences of Muslims. Bonding is desirable as part of the building of social capital, but too much bonding with same-ethnicity groups can serve to reinforce social and cultural modes of behaviour which can prevent the community's effective integration into majority society. In general, at the onset of adaptation, immigrant groups bond with same-ethnicity groups but eventually move towards integration by broadening community networks to develop relations with majority communities and society to become integrated and effective ethnic minorities. When these immigrant communities as an ethnic minority community do not move forward as would be expected, it is said there is a preponderance of 'bonding' social capital.

Social-capital theory can usefully engage with some of the micro-dynamic concerns impacting on groups, but it has no role for the historical, political

---

21 Portes, A. and P. Landolt (1996) 'The Downside of Social Capital', *The American Prospect*, 26 (May–June): 18–23.

or psychological. In relation to educational outcomes, there is some mileage in the application of social-capital theory to help limit the ethno-centricity of social-class analyses and the potential denial of individual agency when faced with such issues as 'institutional racism'; however, it also risks the possibility of victim-blaming and the potentially negative emphasis upon 'difference' that can emerge with any concentration on a range of cultural and social characteristics of specific groups. Important here also are anthropological discussions of the 'starting points'[22] of immigrant groups, sociological debates about identity, ethnicity and mobility, and the policy framework behind the post-'third way' political agenda.

A direct relationship between social capital and various patterns of inequality can be determined by a focus on the concepts of 'bonding', 'bridging' and 'linking'.[23] 'Bonding social capital operates as a resource for poorer ethnically homogeneous communities[,] protecting them from market inequalities, while providing' richer and more 'exclusive communities the means to consolidate' their advantage.[24] 'Bridging' social capital can offer ways of building trust across different groups, potentially 'reducing inequalities between communities and facilitating social mobility. The contribution of social capital to reducing inequality and building the capacity of poorer communities also' depends upon the relationship between 'community networks [and] political power, which can be seen as "linking" social capital'.[25]

It is often argued that social class rather than ethnicity or social capital is the best indicator for determining the process of academic performance. As has been discussed, the majority of Pakistani and Bangladeshi Muslims in Britain are children of immigrants from rural origins, and they are often poor and badly housed. Bangladeshis in particular represent one of the poorest ethnic-minority groups in Britain. The marginalised occupational positions which first-generation groups found upon arrival have been reproduced for their children in the inner city areas in which they continue to live. If social status is the main influencing factor on educational performance, then these characteristics could certainly explain the educational underachievement of British Muslims. Language barriers are also seen to undermine the education of British Muslims. An OSI study found that many bilingual pupils, for whom English is an additional language, require support to improve language skills in order to achieve their full academic

22 C. Clarke, C. Peach and S. Vertovec (eds), *South Asian Overseas: Migration and Ethnicity*, Cambridge: Cambridge University Press.
23 Bruegal, I. and S. Warren (2003) 'Family Resources and Community Social Capital as Routes to Valued Employment in the UK?', *Social Policy and Society*, 2(4): 319–28.
24 Edwards, R., J. Franklin and J. Holland (2003) *Families and Social Capital: Exploring the Issues*, South Bank University: Families and Social Capital ESRC Research Group, p. 19.
25 Ibid.

potential, but it tends to be insufficiently provided.[26] Islamophobia, discrimination, low teacher expectations, a lack of Muslim role models in schools and wider societal experiences of a sense of lack of belonging are all possible influences. There is a palpable sense of alienation, disadvantage and discrimination felt by many young Muslims in inner-city secondary schools in particular.[27]

British Muslim children of school age make up approximately 6 per cent (500,000) of the school population from around 3 per cent of the national population.[28] The educational underachievement of British Muslims in secular comprehensive schools is a matter of much current concern, but the establishment of Muslim faith schools has been suggested as a solution to the limitations facing Muslims schoolchildren in the British educational system. The question raised is whether such schools should be supported by the state in order to reap the benefits of a well educated Muslim population who have largely underperformed in mainstream schools. A combination of cultural needs and structural obstacles has led to an increase in the demand for Islamic schools among Muslims, regarded by some as remedies for the issues of persistent underachievement in state schools. With increasing numbers of Muslims opting for a faith-based education, and with the relative success of the few current Muslim state-funded schools, the Government has been encouraged to take further steps. These developments could potentially not only improve the education of British Muslims but could also put the Government in a better position to help build social cohesion.

It is acknowledged, however, that there are structural factors to be addressed. Islam attaches great importance to notions of education 'from the cradle to the grave'.[29] The first revelation to Muhammad was a commandment to 'Read in the name of the Lord ... [who has] ... taught man what he did not know'.[30] Such a proclamation sets in stone the idea that knowledge should be at the forefront of Muslim life. Muhammad is reported to have said 'whoever treads a path seeking knowledge, Allah will make easy for him the path to Paradise'.[31] These teachings urge Muslims to seek knowledge and that this education is a duty for all Muslims, irrespective of gender. The idea of attaining knowledge is intended to encourage practising Muslims to become more diligent in their educational endeavours. That the Islamic moral code of a Muslim could be transmitted in the

26 Open Society Institute (2004), op. cit., p. 180.
27 Abbas, T. (2004) 'Structural and Cultural Racism in the Educational Underachievement of British South Asian Muslims', in K. Jacobson and P. Kumar (eds), *South Asians in Diaspora: Histories and Religious Traditions*, Leiden: Brill, pp. 269–93.
28 Halstead (2004), op. cit., pp. 101–92.
29 ibid.
30 'Qur'a-n, 'The Embryo' (Ai-'Alaq), 96: 1–5.
31 Hadith (found in Imam al Bukhari and Imam Muslim.)

environment of a Muslim school (this may be regarded as the case for all faith-based schools) is worthy of attention. Specifically, Islam teaches that good morals are the epitome of human development. These principles include truthfulness, patience, tolerance, kindness, cooperative treatment of non-Muslims and the unwillingness to live on the charity of others, all of which, if achieved in an individual, would make these groups of real value to any society. Such a work ethic and an appeal to morality would be present in Muslim faith schools based upon these Islamic as well as wider principles of respect and tolerance for others, and civic engagement and social responsibility in relation to society in general.

The propagation of education to students as a religious duty could bring about relative improvements in performance. Evidence does suggest that Islamic schools which have received state funding have been academically successful.[32] Feversham College, a secondary school for girls in Bradford, was top of the 2004 national league tables in the value-added category. Head teacher Jane Tiller related this achievement to a 'shared Islamic vision to work hard and succeed'. The school remains heavily oversubscribed.[33] In reality, many independent Islamic schools are often situated near the bottom of the academic ladder, often with humble funds generating limited results. Therefore, state funding of religious schools has a number of important effects. Under voluntary-aided status, grants can be allocated for the purchase, upkeep and running of school buildings, with staff salaries paid by local authorities. Extending the remit of the Education Act 1944, criteria for acceptance include local-education-authority support for the proposal, the suitability of premises and the ability of the school to deliver the national curriculum. Such state control of funded Islamic schools may be necessary for efficiency. Many independent Muslim schools struggle as they await funding decisions, with some schools forced into closure in the early years of their inception, largely because of the lack of sustained funding.[34]

The question raised is whether the establishment of proficient Muslim schools could remedy the problems surrounding the education of British Muslims. Since 9/11, however, faith schools in general have been accused of certain detrimental influences upon education and society. They are said to limit the personal autonomy and religious judgement of pupils, and to impose a restricted view of religion promoted by external sponsors. Another concern is the apparent erosion of social cohesion through the suggested separation of young people of different religious and non-religious

32 Parker-Jenkins, M. (2002) 'Equal Access to State Funding: The Case of Muslim Schools in Britain', *Race Ethnicity and Education*, 5(3): 273–89.

33 Blair, A. (2005) 'Muslim School Offers Best Added Value', *The Times*, 13 January.

34 Parker-Jenkins, M. and K.F. Haw (1998) 'Educational Needs of Muslim Children in Britain: Accommodation or Neglect?', in S. Vertovec and A. Rogers (eds), *Muslim European Youth: Reproducing Ethnicity, Religion, Culture*, Aldershot: Ashgate, pp. 193–215.

backgrounds, who, it is argued, should be learning to live together despite their differences.[35] In addition, there are fears raised in relation to Muslim schools in particular. Some of these are concerned with the nature of independent Muslim schools, which, as stated, often lack basic facilities due to limited funds. David Bell, the Chief Inspector of Schools in 2005, warned that independent Muslim schools give pupils 'little appreciation of their wider responsibilities and obligations to British society', potentially widening the gap between cultures.[36] There have been claims that it was polarised schooling that contributed to community divisions in relation to the 2001 disturbances in Oldham, Bradford and Burnley, as expounded by former CRE chair Herman Ousley.[37] Similarly, Women Against Fundamentalism pose their objection to state-funded faith schools, suggesting that Islamic schools 'bring up girls to be dutiful wives and mothers', without offering adequate facilities for academic achievement.[38] In the media today, Islamic schools have been associated with ideas of 'Muslim fundamentalism', an expression holding connotations of violent extremism in the current period.[39] The fears that Muslims could harbour or even nurture extremist sentiments in students are regularly maintained in the popular imagination, perpetuated by negative media and political discourses.

Proponents of faith schools, however, claim that they in fact provide a positive response to racism and promote justice and fairness for all children, parents and religious communities. They can also promote 'social cohesion and the integration of minority communities into the democratic life of the state'.[40] Historically, government subsidies for separate Catholic schools facilitated the integration of Irish Catholics into British society. Here, Islamic schools could foster the religious and cultural needs and the basic obligations of Muslim life given their positions in a non-Muslim land. These include prayer duties, religious instruction in assemblies, celebration of festivals, dress codes and dietary regulations.[41] Critics raise concerns regarding the nature of the curriculum expressed in relation to issues of sex

35 Jackson, R. (2003) 'Should the State Fund Faith Based Schools? A Review of the Arguments', *British Journal of Religious Education*, 25(2): 89–102.
36 Guardian Unlimited (2005) 'The Full Text of a Speech Made by David Bell, the Schools Inspector, to the Hansard Society in London Today', *The Guardian*, 17 January.
37 Bradford Vision (2001) *Community Pride, Not Prejudice: Making Diversity Work in Bradford*, Bradford: Bradford City Council.
38 Yuval-Davis, N. (1992) 'Fundamentalism, Multiculturalism and Women in Britain', in J. Donald and A. Rattansi (eds), *Race, Culture and Difference*, London and New York: Sage.
39 Osler, A. and Z. Hussain (2005) 'Educating Muslim Girls: Do Mothers Have Faith in the State System?', in T. Abbas (ed.), *Muslims in Britain: Communities Under Pressure*, London and New York: Zed, pp. 127–43.
40 Jackson (2003), op. cit.
41 Parker-Jenkins and Haw (1998), op. cit.

education, music and choice of modern language study, in addition to the 'Islamisation' of subjects such as history and geography. Language gaps could be bridged by Muslim schools, as pupils arriving with a weak grasp of English would be accommodated by teachers with bilingual and inter-cultural skills and gradually socialised into the system.[42] Islamic schools could also deal with predicaments facing Muslim parents in relation to the educational environment of their children, such as how to effectively negotiate issues of morality in a secular society, and the structure of educa-tion and society as a whole, which may well have driven Muslims to search for other educational options in the first instance.[43] The autonomy of children need not be circumscribed by religious views any more than it is by encounters with teachers in secular institutions.[44]

Perceptions of racism within existing state-funded schools have incenti-vised the setting up of institutions where the community feels safe and secure.[45] Islamic schools allow students to avoid discrimination, which can often take place in the mainstream education system. One study suggested that 50 per cent of head teachers in state schools identify racism awareness as a concern, whereas this was of no concern to head teachers in Muslim schools.[46] It would be expected that problems of Islamophobia and a lack of Muslim role models could be eradicated in well organised Islamic schools, as well as the issue of having to attend evening religious education classes as an additional educational need. It would suggest that state support for Muslim schools may be the best way to counter discriminatory forces in the education system, with previous multiculturalist and anti-racist initiatives failing to achieve the desired effects. Evidence suggests that demand for Muslim schooling has increased for these reasons. The number of indepen-dent Islamic schools is said to be growing as well as the increase in parental demand. The importance of this type of education for British Muslims was illustrated in the fourth Policy Studies Institute (PSI) survey of 1994, which showed that 48 per cent of Muslims supported state-funded faith schools in Britain compared with just over half of the white-British respondents (26 per cent).[47] It is apparent that this interest in state-funded schools has grown since then.

It is clear that the socio-economic status of British Muslims has a huge effect upon standards of education. Bangladeshis and Pakistanis continue to achieve low levels compared to national averages; 'differences in exam results attributable to ethnic group are very much smaller than

42 Sarwar, G. (1991) *British Muslims and Schools*, London: Muslim Educational Trust.
43 Parker-Jenkins and Haw (1998), op. cit., p. 194.
44 Jackson (2003), op. cit.
45 Walford (1998), op. cit., pp. 214–15.
46 Parker-Jenkins and Haw (1998), op. cit., p. 208.
47 Modood, T., Berthoud R., Lakey J., Nazroo J., Smith P., Virdee S., Beishon S (1997) Ethnic Minorities in Britain: *Diversity and Disadvantage*, London: Policy Studies Institute.

those attributable to the school [...] some schools are much better than others'.[48] If the quality of institution is a major factor, school funding holds considerable significance, and by merely funding more of the schools which British Muslims choose to go to, the Government can potentially improve educational standards for all. There are a only a handful of Islamic schools that have students who leave with relatively strong grades; but questions in relation to the reinforcement and promotion of Islamic identity remain significant. Additional state funding would put these schools in a better position to educate Muslim children through adequate facilities and a better appreciation of their needs.

From an analysis of achievement in education and the questions of faith-based state-funded schooling, it is possible to explore the transformation of human capital into certain labour market and human resource outcomes. Here, it is necessary to explore the experiences of British Muslims in the labour market with particular reference to changing notions of the 'ethnic penalty' and the idea of a 'Muslim penalty' in the light of secondary statistical analyses of the fourth PSI survey. A focus on Muslim minorities has added to researcher and policy-maker interest on the experiences of disadvantage and discrimination in the labour market. Based on official statistics (Labour Force Survey, Social Trends), it is possible to discern how Muslim employment patterns are negatively differentiated. In analysing the degrees of ethnic inequality in relation to employment and entrepreneurialism, the extent to which British Muslims are socially and economically excluded can be better explicated. It is argued that much can be characterised by the patterns of Islamophobia, structural disadvantage and institutionalised racism.

Analysis of first-generation economic immigrants and their labour market experiences found that, generally, all ethnic minorities experienced an 'ethnic penalty', including East African Asians, who were better qualified compared with other ethnic minorities. It is African-Caribbeans, Pakistanis and the Irish, however, who suffered greatest. Indians, Pakistanis and African-Caribbeans all underwent substantial 'ethnic penalties', even after controlling for their age and education.[49] A 'racial division of labour' ensured African-Caribbean and South Asian workers, including Muslims, were kept apart and therefore prevented from organising together as part of a wider collective struggle. The process deskilled workers, kept wages down and segregated ethnic minorities in the low paid jobs that majority society workers did not want.[50] Analysis of 1991 Census data reveals that the

48   Smith, D. and S. Tomlinson (1989) *The School Effect: A Study of Multi-racial Comprehensives*, London: Policy Studies Institute.
49   Cheng, Y. and A. Heath (1993) 'Ethnic Origins and Class Destinations', *Oxford Review of Education*, 19(2): 151–66.
50   Sivanandan, A. (1982) *A Different Hunger: Writings on Black Resistance*, London: Pluto.

'ethnic penalty' or 'ethnic disadvantage' experienced by first generations was largely transmitted to second generations. Some elimination of the 'ethnic penalty', as second generations are British-born and have received their education in Britain, was expected. Both direct discrimination and cultural differences, therefore, must play a part as the range and magnitude suggest complex explanations, as Anthony Heath et al. have argued.[51] The extent to which different ethnic minorities experience racism and discrimination in the labour market in the current period is largely a function of the different historical periods of post-war immigration and settlement.

National Labour Force Survey (LFS) estimates made at the end of 2002 indicated the variability of economic activity between ethnic minorities. 'Black Caribbean' women (72 per cent) had almost as high an economic activity rate as white women (74 per cent). Bangladeshis had the lowest economic activity rates among men (69 per cent) and women (22 per cent). Pakistani women had economic activity rates of 28 per cent.[52] Low rates of education for Bangladeshi and Pakistani women reflect their limited education levels before immigration, combined with its negative consequences for subsequent generations.[53] Among women with children in paid employment, however, ethnic minorities are more likely than white women to be in full-time employment, irrespective of their occupational group.[54] Current analysis of labour-market participation suggests that many young South Asian Muslim women demonstrate high aspirations as well as levels of participation in contrast to the educational and occupational levels of their parents.[55] National statistics have shown a recent increase in the numbers of young Pakistani and Bangladeshi women in full-time undergraduate courses.[56]

It remains questionable whether religion is an important dimension in the ethnic inequality experienced in the labour market. An analysis of the PSI survey confirms that there is a multifaceted picture in relation to

51 Heath, A.F., D. McMahon and J. Roberts (2000) 'Ethnic Differences in the Labour Market: A Comparison of the SARs and LFS', *Journal of the Royal Statistical Society A*, 163(3): 341–61; Heath, A.F., C. Rothon and E. Kilpi (2008) 'The Second Generation in Western Europe: Education, Unemployment, and Occupational Attainment, *Annual Review of Sociology*, 34: 211–35.

52 White, A. (2002) (ed.) *Social Focus in Brief: Ethnicity 2002*, London: Office for National Statistics.

53 Brah, A. and S. Shaw (1992) *Working Choices: South Asian Young Muslim Women and the Labour Market*, London: Department of Employment Research Paper No. 91.

54 Dale, A. and C. Holdsworth (1997) 'Issues in the Analysis of Ethnicity in the 1991 British Census', *Ethnic and Racial Studies*, 20(1): 160–80.

55 Basit, T.N. (1997) *Eastern Values; Western Milieu: Identities and Aspirations of Adolescent British Muslim Girls*, Aldershot: Ashgate.

56 Dale, A., N. Shaheen, E. Fieldhouse and V. Kalra (2002) 'Routes into Education and Employment for Young Pakistani and Bangladeshi Women in the UK', *Ethnic and Racial Studies*, 25(6): 942–68.

employment patterns found within the Muslim–non-Muslim dichotomy. It would appear that Bangladeshi and Pakistani Muslims suffer a detrimental experience in the labour market compared with their Indian Muslim counterparts. Even though over half failed to report their earnings in the survey, Muslims were found to be over-represented in the lowest income band. Almost one-quarter earned less than £115 per week compared with one in ten Sikhs and Hindus, and less than one in twenty for those with no or 'other religion'.[57] Seventeen per cent of Pakistani men were in the lowest income bracket, whereas 40 per cent of Bangladeshi men earned less than £115, compared with only 4 per cent of 'others' and people who had stated 'no religion'. In comparison with other South Asians, Muslims from Pakistan and Bangladesh, in particular, are found to be underperforming in the labour market.

At the other end of the spectrum, 12 per cent of Muslims were found to be in the top income bracket of over £442 a week compared with the 'other religion' average of 29 per cent. In comparison to Hindus, who had 27 per cent of their population earning in the top bracket, Muslims do not fare well in relation to these higher levels of income. Given these results, some caution needs to be exercised because the levels of income cannot be verified since they are based upon individuals reporting on an optional question in the survey. What is inferred is that in this sample group, Hindus and, to a lesser extent, Sikhs generally receive a higher weekly wage than Muslims. The results point to under-representation of Muslims in the labour market, and, where employment is successful, a 'penalty' seems to have been imposed in the form of lower earnings. It tends to be true for both men and women but the percentage of Muslim women in the bottom wage differential category is equal to other South Asians. Only a small percentage is represented in the highest wage category, with Hindu women performing best overall. Clearly, there are large differences within the Muslim population when it comes to the performance of women in the labour market. As well as cultural issues, it is not possible to underestimate the role of institutions, which can lead to prejudice, discrimination and racism against Muslim women in various spheres of employment.[58]

Observing closely some of the differences between Muslims from different backgrounds, generally Muslim Pakistanis and Bangladeshis have lower economic activity than Muslims from India – in terms of both employability and earnings. This gives rise to the argument that employers are not discriminating against religion per se:

57 Brown, M.S. (2000) 'Religion and Economic Activity in the South Asian Population', *Ethnic and Racial Studies*, 23(6): 1035–61.
58 Tryer, D. and F. Ahmed (2006) *Muslim Women and Higher Education: Identities, Experiences and Prospects: A Summary Report*, Liverpool: Liverpool John Moores University and European Social Fund.

'Muslims as a group report lowest percentage in full time work (half that of Hindus) [...] the experience of the Indian Muslim minority (hidden in census analysis) challenges any notion of a simple negative association between being Muslim and the likelihood of holding a full-time job'.[59]

Indeed, Muslim Indians have employment rates close to that of the national average (41 per cent compared to the national average of around 44 per cent). When exploring graduate employment profiles, compared with the national average, Muslim employment rates are often lower.[60] Although this variation in the employment rate may be a result of lower levels of higher education, it is to bear in mind questions in relation to Muslims persistently scoring lower degree scores than the average. That is, Muslim undergraduates tend to opt for certain degree disciplines such as law, medicine, dentistry, pharmacy, finance, information technology and business-related degrees, and these are often competitive sectors. Women graduates make up around 39 per cent of the Muslim graduates but have only a 64 per cent employment rate, compared with 83 per cent for Muslim men.[61] Muslim women's employment rate is as low as their level of participation in the labour market, i.e. there are more women from the Muslim community not actively seeking work than there are for other women. Of those that do attain a degree and manage to find work, 78 per cent of Muslim graduates are employed in the professional or technical fields. Even this high rate is lower than the national average for graduates.

One of the biggest problems facing the Muslim community with respect to employment is the level of economic inactivity. This is a measure of all those who are aged sixteen or above but who are not working. The high rate could be for a number of reasons, such as that people are enrolled in full-time education, permanently sick, disabled, unemployed and looking for work, or engaged in other activities. Muslims in general have lower participation in employment and therefore have a higher economic inactivity rate. Muslim women have a lower participation level than the general population. In relation to men, Pakistanis and Bangladeshis have on average one-third lower participation levels than those from other religions (38–9 per cent compared with 56–9 per cent). Economic participation is low for Muslim women, even as graduates, and this may reflect cultural issues within the home and the community, with women often perceived to be the 'home-keeper'. It may appear to be a reflection on the religion, but Islam does not

59 Brown (2000), op. cit., p. 1039.
60 Conner, H., C. Tyers and T. Modood (2004) *Why the Difference? A Closer Look at Higher Education Minority Ethnic Students and Graduates*, London: Department for Education and Skills Research Report RR552.
61 Ethnic Minority Employment Taskforce (2005) *Muslim Graduates in the Labour Market: Seminar Report*, London: Department of Work and Pensions.

prohibit women from the workplace, and cultural and family-based decisions are taken after graduation or the end of formal education. They are, however, still classified as economically inactive. As Pakistani and Bangladeshi ethnicity is taken as a strong proxy for Muslims, there is a strong correlation between religion and the non-participation of Muslim women in the workforce. Causality is assumed but cannot be deduced as the example of Muslim Indian women participation in full-time work suggests, which is not too dissimilar to the overall average.[62]

The question of the 'ethnic penalty' is worth exploring, and it is important to consider whether, if at all, there is a further 'Muslim penalty'. It is suggested that there are numerous factors that affect unemployment, and religion may act as a proxy for one or all of them. These include lack of professional qualifications, lack of fluency in English and high unemployment rates in particular locations.[63] Even when other factors that affect employment are controlled, religion still plays a part: Pakistani and Bangladeshi Muslims are more than three times as likely to be unemployed as those who report no or other religion. Certainly, 'Muslims are the most disadvantaged of all the [ethnic] groups […] how much [it] is the result of […] factors such as anti-Islamic discrimination' is not entirely clear.[64] But when analysing factors affecting labour-market participation using mathematical modelling, there is 'evidence of unemployment disadvantages to British-born non-whites and above [average] differences in religious affiliation'.[65]

In relation to educational qualifications prior to employment, there is evidence to show that Muslims are underperforming compared with white Britons, but Muslim graduates are increasing in number faster than the non-Muslim indigenous population. There is, however, little clarity on the perception that ethnic penalties generally increase as one moves up the educational ladder.[66] Income data seem to show more evidence of disadvantage for Muslims, especially those from Pakistani and Bangladeshi backgrounds. The overriding factor that appears to remain consistent with all groups in this instance is language proficiency and ethnicity, with foreign-born non-white men experiencing the greatest earnings penalty. In terms of unemployment rates, there has been no real fall among the second generations in the extent of the 'ethnic penalty'. In fact, there is reasonably

62   Peach, C. (2006c) 'South Asian Migration and Settlement in Great Britain, 1951–2001', *Contemporary South Asia*, 15(2): 133–46
63   Fieldhouse, E. and M. Gould (1998) 'Ethnic Minority Unemployment and Local Labour Market Conditions in Great Britain', *Environment and Planning A*, 30(5): 833–53.
64   Lindley, J. (2002) 'Race or Religion? The Impact of Religion on the Employment and Earnings of Britain's Ethnic Communities', *Journal of Ethnic and Migration Studies*, 28(3): 427–42.
65   Ibid.
66   Heath et al. (2008), op. cit.

clear evidence to suggest that second-generation men experience a greater disadvantage than the first generations. This is surprising as second-generation Muslims will be fluent in the language whereas the first generations may not have been. What is more, second generations will not have the human capital issues in relation to the undervaluing of overseas qualifications, and therefore it contradicts somewhat the argument that language proficiency is a dominant factor in unemployment. Without doubt, Muslims in Britain (along with some Sikhs) have lower economic activity rates, and are more likely to be unemployed and less well paid than the average. There is an observable distinction between Indian, Pakistani and Bangladeshi Muslims, and it is possible to conclude that Bangladeshis and Pakistanis are under-represented in the top income bands and certain employment sectors as opposed to Indian Muslims. Interestingly, there is some data pointing to religious discrimination, as those who classify themselves as white Muslim graduates have a lower than average employment rate after graduation; 'it's even the case that a white Muslim faces a higher employment penalty than a Pakistani of no religion'.[67]

Therefore, evidence seems to point towards a 'Muslim penalty', such that those of Muslim background, especially Pakistani and Bangladeshi, will be less economically active, more likely to be unemployed and may well be earning less. It may be statistically significant; causality, however, cannot be confirmed, and, therefore, religion cannot be held entirely responsible for all the discrepancies in labour-market outcomes. Other factors such as the informal economy, self-employment rates, the collapse of the traditional industries (a main source of employment for many South Asians and Muslims), leading to continued structural unemployment, as well as issues concerning female employment patterns, are also important to consider.

One route out of disadvantage in the labour market is self-employment. During the late 1980s, ongoing de-industrialisation and globalisation led policy-makers to presuppose that 'ethnic small businesses may offer an alternative and possibly more viable route to upward mobility' for those groups losing employment as a result of shifting industrial processes.[68] In the 1980s, with the advent of monetary policy and the collapse of the engineering and manufacturing sectors, the predominant view was that growing numbers of ethnic minorities entering into business would not only make a radical difference to economic growth but would also provide a means for ethnic minorities to achieve rapid upward social mobility.

67 Secretary of State for Work and Pensions Rt Hon. John Hutton (2007) 'Ethnic Minority Employment in Britain: Recognising Women's Potential, Women's Enterprise Project – Bethnal Green', speech delivered 28 February.

68 Waldinger, R., R. Ward and H. Aldrich (1985) 'Ethnic Business and Occupational Mobility in Advanced Societies, *Sociology*, 19(4): 586–97, p. 587.

South Asian Muslim entrepreneurs were thought to be following the Jewish 'rags-to-riches' success story that has exemplified their economic profile in the diaspora. In reality, this outcome did not materialise. South Asian Muslim businesses tended to be in the independent retailing sector, which had largely been in significant decline in the post-war period. Business activity was also concentrated in smaller and more localised retailing, which provided the least in marginal gains. In addition, the long hours spent in work were hidden in accounting terms. This South Asian Muslim entrepreneurialism was more a factor of a lack of opportunities rather than taking advantage of specific opportunities. The experience has been an adaptation to structural disadvantage rather than a route out of it, and is based on a dedicated work ethic which taught the view that there is no substitute for hard work.

For Pakistanis under study in Bradford in the early 1990s, it was found that the reasons to enter into business were largely a function of social class. The finding has some validity as it is the case that, generally, South Asians are known to possess a tendency towards business, but Muslims are more likely to enter business because of unemployment.[69] In seeking to determine the combined effects of the cultural and structural to conceptualise the general opportunity structure, a range of factors can be identified: market conditions; favouring of co-ethnic workers, suppliers and producers; routes to obtaining businesses; pre-migration circumstances and group characteristics; reaction to the host society; and resource mobilisation through particular features of the ethnic-minority community.[70] Consequently, strategies are formed to adapt to the opportunity structure and to carve out a particular entrepreneurial niche. For many, often located in declining inner-city areas, economic disadvantage as a result of racism re-materialises in the form of economic disadvantage in business activity.[71] In as much as there appears to be growth in the numbers involved in business activity, it is not always reciprocated by respective economic development or success.

Explanations relating to differentiated rates of business success in comparison to other South Asians were explored as part of a study of the independent restaurant sector by the author and colleagues. Of the study sample, many, if not all, that originated from Bangladesh did so from rural areas. The lack of formal education before and after migration limited the educational outcomes available to individuals. As Muslim entrepreneurs tend to be less educationally qualified, it is more likely that they use

69 Rafiq, M. (1992) 'Ethnicity and Enterprise: A Comparison of Muslim and Non-Muslim Owned Asian Businesses in Britain', *New Community*, 19(1): 43–60.
70 Waldinger, R. (1995) 'The "Other Side" of Embeddedness: A Case Study of the Interplay of Economy and Ethnicity', *Ethnic and Racial Studies*, 18(3): 555–80.
71 Barrett, G., T. Jones and D. McEvoy (1996) 'Ethnic Minority Business: Theoretical Discourse in Britain and North America', *Urban Studies*, 33(4/5): 783–809.

members of their own family as labour to begin with but also later on through children.[72] As other Bangladeshis migrate, they can find work within the same enterprises owned and managed by co-ethnic groups. They are able to acquire the necessary skills to familiarise themselves with the basic functions and roles needed to set up similar businesses themselves. Rather, for the Bangladeshis, it is a result of structural marginalisation, alienation in society and the lack of formal training or education that have led to a proliferation of so many Bangladeshi-run restaurants. It is indicative of the lack of the opportunities available to this group in society in general. But irrespective of the structural and racialised disadvantage and despite the constraints imposed by the free-market economy, Muslim minority businesses continue to grow in numbers.[73]

The inner-city areas in which many Muslims live provide such facilities as accountants, solicitors, travel agencies, clothes shops, craft shops, jewellery shops, barber shops and beauty salons. Indeed, the availability of relatively cheap labour to work within such businesses is a genuine basis for their existence. It is also argued that the common bond of culture (and religion) between workers creates the basis for solidarity, as social-capital theory suggests.[74] This results in a personalised environment for individuals in which to work, and it gives reason for people to avoid the deleterious conditions and often impersonal nature of work in other occupational spheres. In order to accommodate workers, the personal and cultural requirements of work hours are often flexible. Employment in such settings is certainly an opportunity in which individuals are able to acquire the necessary skills and experience with which to eventually run, own or manage their own enterprises.

Over time, it is possible that local businesses become suited to the needs of the local community, where the extent of identification within an ethnic and religious community serves to facilitate the notion of local businesses meeting the demands of (co-ethnic and co-religious) local people. The reasons for such developments are said to be a function of the ability to serve specific ethnic, religious and cultural preferences, cemented by social and cultural capital. 'White flight' leaves opportunities for co-ethnic-minority

72 Ram, M., T. Abbas, B. Sanghera, G. Barlow and T. Jones (2001a) '"Apprentice Entrepreneurs"? Ethnic Minority Workers in the Independent Restaurant Sector', *Work Employment and Society*, 15(2): 353–72; Ram, M., T. Abbas, B. Sanghera, G. Barlow and T. Jones (2001b) 'Making the Link: Households and Ethnic Minority Business Activity', *Community Work and Family*, 4(3): 327–48; Ram, M., T. Jones, T. Abbas and B. Sanghera (2002) 'Ethnic Enterprise in Its Urban Context: South Asian Restaurants in Birmingham', *International Journal of Urban and Regional Research*, 26(1): 26–40.

73 Portes, A. and M. Zhou (1992) 'Gaining the Upper Hand: Economic Mobility Among Immigrant and Domestic Minorities', *Ethnic and Racial Studies*, 15(4): 491–522.

74 Putnam, R. (2001) *Bowling Alone: The Collapse and Revival of American Community*, New York: Simon & Schuster.

consumers and producers to enter the area, and the extent of the loyalty of co-ethnic customers tightens bonds between community and enterprise. However, a 1980s study based on research in three British cities found that ethnicity is a resource for surviving in a hostile economic environment rather than a force for genuine upward social mobility among the South Asian community.[75]

As a result of choice and constraints, the Muslim business community is thus highly dependent upon the minority market for patronage, which ultimately determines the level of business activity. Therefore, the emergence of a small number of ethnic businesses in tightly knit locations can quickly lead to other businesses following in the hope of taking advantage of the number and type of other Muslims that live, work or visit the locality. Often these can develop into regional ethnic shopping centres (e.g. in Leicester and Birmingham). These 'agglomeration economies' spur others to develop businesses in related ethno-religious niche markets as well in the provision of mainstream goods and services to co-ethnic customers (more recent examples include Islamic gift and book shops).[76] Prior ethnic, religious and cultural ties are significant features in this regard. The association becomes the preferred method of economic and cultural interaction.[77]

Differences emerge in the extent to which ethnic minorities are able to take advantage of such networks as, invariably, every network has its own social and cultural *raison d'être*. For example, in the British case, Gujerati Ismailis are international in their desire to develop commercial enterprises and capital bases in a variety of localities. East African Asian Muslim groups are essentially 'twice migrants' bringing with them the acumen for business and an experience of the colonial system.[78] In comparison, working-class Indian, Pakistani and Bangladeshi South Asian Muslims had little or no entrepreneurial experience before migration. Therefore, some groups have been more productive and efficient in generating the necessary economic and social networks than others. There emerges a pecking order of how different Muslim groups are successful in business spheres. Bangladeshis originate from rural areas where poverty is high and educational attainments are low. This impacts upon what they choose to do or are able to do given the limitations faced. The example of Sikh groups is somewhere in between, with Pakistanis tending more towards

75 Aldrich, H., C. Zimmer and D. McEvoy (1989) 'Continuities in the Study of Ecological Succession: Asian Businesses in Three English Cities', *Social Forces*, 67(4): 920–44.
76 Waldinger, R., H. Aldrich and R. Ward (1990) (eds) *Ethnic Entrepreneurs: Immigrants Business in Industrial Societies*, Thousand Oaks, CA: Sage.
77 Waldinger, R., I. Light, G. Sabagh, M. Bozorgmehr and C. Der-Martirosian (1993) 'Internal Ethnicity in the Ethnic Economy', *Ethnic and Racial Studies*, 16(4): 581–97.
78 Bhachu, P. (1985) *Twice Migrants: East African Sikh Settlers in Britain*, London and New York: Tavistock.

the experiences of Bangladeshis and the Sikhs more towards those of Gujerati Hindus.

In reality, the potential of any group to enter into business is remarkably similar. There are little differences between Muslims and the white British in their experiences of small businesses, particularly in relation to the accumulation of initial start-up capital, use of family labour and general survival rates. And, so, it is important not to examine ethnic-minority firms in isolation as characteristics observed may appear distinctive, 'but, in fact, many traits are common to all small-business owners, given the turbulent environment they face'.[79] For example, in relation to African-Caribbean self-employment experiences, the reasons given for their limited rates of success are that this group is not as spatially segregated as communities of South Asian Muslim origin. Thus, it is argued, certain African-Caribbean groups are not able to take advantage of social and cultural networks that provide means of support and exchange. African-Caribbeans have not been able to successfully develop niche markets along the lines of the more successful South Asians. Here, South Asian Muslims are able to commodify that part of their colonial history, with the inception, expansion and growth of enterprises in certain economic sectors, in particular the manufacture, wholesale and retail of clothing, arts, crafts and foods. There are also instances of horizontal economic integration that can be recognised in particular settings (i.e. greengrocers, butchers, Islamic bookshops, barbers, audio, print and DVD outlets, travel agencies, foreign-exchange bureaus, solicitors, insurers and accountants). This experience is, of course, conditioned by wider micro- and macro-economic forces, but the roles that ethnicity, culture and religion play in this regard cannot be entirely eliminated.

There are certain patterns in the education, employment and entrepreneurial experiences of various British Muslim minorities that demonstrate acute fragmentation and various outcomes in relation to the formation of social, cultural and economic capital. Educational achievement is conspicuously low for Muslims, but there are strong ethnic variations within particular patterns of underachievement found among the sons and daughters of rural–urban first-generation Muslim economic migrants. The experience of marginalisation in education is often translated into problems of limited higher-educational outcomes, followed by high graduate unemployment, but it is noticeable that the role of community cultural values is important when exploring the education of young Muslim women. Statistical analysis suggests that Muslims suffer a 'Muslim penalty' in the labour market over and above that of an 'ethnic penalty'. For Muslims entering the world of self-employment, often the decision to do so originates out of

79 Zimmer, C. and H. Aldrich (1987) 'Resource Mobilization through Ethnic Networks: Kinship and Friendship Ties of Shopkeepers in England', *Sociological Perspectives*, 30(4): 422–55.

structural constraints rather than the positive mobilisation of ethnic or cultural resources.[80]

In the post-9/11 and post-7/7 period, there has been a sharp focus on the identities of Muslim minorities, with little or no appreciation of the structural constraints often facing many communities. A negative politicisation of the debate in the light of media and political discourses can impact on the perceptions of both the individual or group of interest as well as from the point of those who form majority society. 'Islamophobia' is an observable cultural phenomenon, and it invariably compounds an already highly problematic social world experienced by many Muslim minorities.

---

80 Clark, K. and S. Drinkwater (2007) *Ethnic Minorities in the Labour Market: Dynamics and Diversity*, London: Joseph Rowntree Foundation.

5 Neo-Orientalism and Islamophobia
Media and print news

Notions of cultural and social identification of the 'Muslim other' emerge from an understanding and experience of imperialism and colonialism, and this 'fear or dread of Islam or Muslims' is described as Islamophobia. Since the emergence of Islam in the year 622, the general representation of Muslims in Europe has been largely negative. Throughout the history of Western European contact with Islam, it has been convenient for the established powers to portray Islam and Muslims in the worst possible light in order to prevent conversions as well as to encourage Europeans to resist Muslim forces at their borders. There have been periods of learning and understanding on the part of the British and Europeans, but there has also been ignorance, conflict and the demonisation of Islam.[1] Periodically, Muslims have been portrayed as 'barbaric', 'ignorant', 'narrow-minded' or 'intolerant religious zealots'. This characterisation of Islam is still present today in the sometimes damaging representation and treatment of the 'Muslim other', which exists as part of an effort to aggrandise established powers and, in the process, to legitimise existing modes of domination and subordination. It is important to explore how Muslims and Islam have come to be represented in such destructive terms through an analysis of the concept of Orientalism and Islamophobia, and, in particular, the intersection between media and politics, and using case study examples to illustrate the case being made.

As much as present-day Islamophobia relies on history to fill the essence of its stereotypes, the present fears of Islam and Muslims have their own idiosyncratic features that connect them with more recent experiences of colonialism, decolonisation, immigration and racism. The Runnymede Trust stated that Islamophobia is created analogously to xenophobia, which is the disdain or dislike of all things 'foreign'. Seven features of Islamophobia were identified in the initial Runnymede Trust report of 1997, and they are still relevant today:

1. Muslim cultures are seen as monolithic.
2. Islamic cultures are substantially different from other cultures.

---

1 Bennett, C. (1992) *Victorian Images of Islam*, London: Grey Seal.

3. Islam is perceived as implacably threatening.
4. Adherents of Islam use their faith to gain political or military advantage.
5. Muslim criticism of Western cultures and societies is rejected out of hand.
6. The fear of Islam is mixed with racist hostility to immigration.
7. Islamophobia is assumed to be natural and unproblematic.[2]

Although it is important not to treat Muslims as an undifferentiated mass as there are very many ethnic, cultural, social, economic and political differences between individuals and groups, as has been discussed, the above profile of Islamophobia nevertheless remains relevant. While racism on the basis of 'race' continues, the anti-Muslim shift suggests markers of difference of a social and religio-culture nature. Furthermore, while traditional descriptors of 'race' have been afforded legislative protection, the same does not hold true for 'religious' identifiers, where protection is restricted only to ethnically defined religious communities through case law, namely people from the Jewish and Sikh communities in Britain. (However, a European directorate outlawing religious discrimination in employment came into effect in December 2003 and the Equalities Act 2006 makes it unlawful to discriminate on the ground of religion, and supports the notion of a single equality duty.) Despite Muslims being targeted by right-wing groups, with more subtle forms of racist prejudice and hatred after 9/11 and 7/7, Muslims remain outside the domain of domestic anti-racist legislation. The social and religious foundations of Islam, as well as of Muslims in general, have attained such a degree of notoriety that their 'visibility' is immediately associated with entirely negative and detrimental frames of reference. Since 9/11, the situation has both deteriorated and intensified. Islamophobia has gained a greater discursive prevalence to the extent that much of Western European society has become uncritically receptive to an array of negative images, perceptions, attitudes and behaviours in relation to Islam and Muslims.[3] Moreover, it seems a painfully convenient way in which to paint the picture of Muslim culture as somehow at the centre of issues of the apparent breakdown of multiculturalism.[4]

Towards the end of the nineteenth century, British newspapers were established in order to generate and disseminate printed news. These newspapers were thought to provide a mechanism for the workings of political systems and parliament to be checked. When revenue generated from the

2 Runnymede Trust (1997) *Islamophobia: A Challenge for Us All: Report of the Runnymede Trust Commission on British Muslims and Islamophobia*, London: Runnymede Trust.
3 Allen, C. and J.S. Nielsen (2001) *Summary Report on Islamophobia in the EU15 after 11 September 2001*, Vienna: European Monitoring Centre for Racism and Xenophobia.
4 Marranci, G. (2004) 'Multiculturalism, Islam and the Clash of Civilisations Theory: Rethinking Islamophobia', *Culture and Religion*, 5(1): 105–17.

sale of advertising injected an explosion of capital into the industry, it permitted other newspapers to enter into the market and flourish. Further developments led to the eventual liberalisation of the press from direct political party association. The newspaper industry began to produce news for the objective of news dissemination, but it also reaped profits from the sale of newspapers through commercialisation.[5] A range of politically leaning newspapers – the *Daily Mail* (1896), the *Daily Express* (1900) and the *Daily Mirror* (1903) – were all created around the same time and they still exist today. The freedom of capital and the eagerness of the industry to appeal to an ever-growing readership have altered the shape of newspaper reporting ever since then. It has resulted in a move away from an exclusive check on political systems and parliament to one that now provides a more information-orientated approach towards news dissemination. The impact has been that working-class consumption of newspapers has been separated from control over its production. Press commercialisation, the impact of advertising, sensationalism as the dominant framework, dominance in relation to the control of media outlets, and the limitation of coverage of actual politics have a contemporary feel about them.[6]

High costs associated with large-scale presses invariably restricted the ownership of newspapers. As such, control over the production and distribution of ideas has become concentrated in the hands of a small number of wealthy capitalists who have sufficient ownership of the means of production to first generate entry into the market and then to achieve subsequent growth. It leads to the views of a powerful few receiving considerable exposure and publicity, which ultimately impacts on the perceptions, attitudes and behaviours of mass consumers. This ideological and economic domination also plays a prevailing role in maintaining class inequalities. The reality today is that large multinational conglomerates are found to be in control of a number of mainstream daily newspapers. Often a single person or dynasty can head these transnational organisations, for example Rupert Murdoch and News International. Because of the ways in which news and media organisations tend to be vertically and horizontally integrated with other forms of media, a great deal of influence and authority rests in the hands of a very few. It is the views and opinions representing the least powerful social groups that are systematically excluded in the process of concentration of ownership. Furthermore, political parties can work with newspaper owners to gain support at times of need. When the *Sun* switched to New Labour months before the general election of 1997, it made a significant impact in encouraging its mainly conservative

5 Curran, J. (1988) 'Whig Press History as Political Myth', in J. Curran and J. Seaton (eds), *Power Without Responsibility: The Press and Broadcasting in Britain*, London: Routledge, pp. 7–10.
6 Negrine, R. (1989) (ed.) *Politics and the Mass Media in Britain*, London: Routledge.

voters to change allegiance, arguably having a direct bearing on electoral outcomes.[7]

News media is central in providing people in society with a portrayal of encounters and events that exist far beyond the immediate lived experience. It has a powerful role in relation to the ways in which social content is included or excluded. Newspapers are also produced and marketed to consumers based largely on the composition and political predilection of newspaper owners and certain columnists. They are also in the business of improving sales. As Anthony Giddens argues, news content 'doesn't happen, it is made, it is a socially manufactured product'.[8] Stuart Hall et al. express the view that the media does not present news that might be considered '"naturally" newsworthy' itself, rather 'news' 'is the end-product of a complex process which begins with a systematic sorting and selection of events and topics according to a socially constructed set of categories'.[9] Such is the influence of media upon society that it is argued to be responsible for the creation of 'folk devils' around which 'moral panics' are created. Here, it is groups in marginal positions that are targets for stereotyping as their actions are placed outside defined cultural boundaries.[10] Furthermore, journalistic criteria and editorial subjectivity are not always open to question. Through gatekeepers and agenda-setters within various news-production outlets, the selection of news topics, which are presented as being in the interest of readers, is controlled and managed. In effect, 'news media in general and the press in particular are clearly involved in the reproduction of elite [discourse and] racism'.[11] Newspapers and television as well as individual journalists may themselves be partially dependent upon other elite groups in the definition of the ethnic (and religious) question. News stories and overall journalistic criteria are inherently white, English, male and middle-class, and 'a dominant white view and perspective pervades in the news, with the white group systematically presented in a more favourable light'.[12]

Muslims across the globe today are ill-prepared to defend themselves from this onslaught. With the advent of YouTube, Facebook, Twitter, internet blogging and a proliferation of new media and communication technologies, it becomes ever more difficult for Muslims to compete for effective representation on the global media stage. Muslims who are prevalent in

7   Rawnsley, A. (2000) *Servants of the People: The Inside Story of New Labour*, London: Hamish Hamilton.
8   Giddens, A. (1989) *Sociology*, Cambridge: Polity.
9   Hall, S., C. Critcher, T. Jefferson, J. Clark and B. Roberts (1978) *Policing the Crisis: Mugging the State, and Law and Order*, Basingstoke: Macmillan, p. 53.
10 Cohen, S. (1972) *Folk Devils and Moral Panics: The Creation of the Mods and the Rockers*, London: MacGibbon & Cohen, S. (2000) 'Some Thoroughly Modern Monsters', *Index on Censorship*, 29(5): 36–42.
11 Van Dijk, T. (1993) *Elite Discourse and Racism*, London: Sage, p. 10.
12 Ibid., p. 7.

less-developed countries often suffer from a lack of knowledge in relation to the intention of the Western media or indeed the physical means to counter it. Western media seeks to reinforce popular stereotypes of the 'Muslim other', constantly highlighting areas of conflict and confusion. The offensive is one that is based on history and on a re-emerging disdain for Islam and Muslims. For some, Islam is the new ideological enemy of the West now that the Cold War no longer persists.[13] Middle Eastern states are persistently 'given the rough treatment' by Western media in general and by the print press in particular.[14] Little reference is given to the historical context of ethnic relations in Britain or in other parts of the world. The economic exploitation or imperial and post-colonial domination of the Caribbean, India, Africa and the Middle East are rarely mentioned.[15] Newspapers have tremendous opportunities to do good or harm to the situations they are reporting: they cannot escape a critical position in current ethnic and cultural relations.

The position of the print media is omnipotent in the rationalisation of anti-Muslim sentiment and expression in society. In particular, simplifications and generalisations can lead to narrow reporting, for example in the concentration on 'extremists' with blanket solutions prescribed to problems usually attributed to Islam or 'Islamic fundamentalism'. It emerges in the absence of genuine expertise on Islam to best explain events and to prevent further misunderstanding (the use of genuine experts is eschewed in favour of the self-promoting few who are selected by senior editors). Images of 'bearded mullahs' and angry Muslims holding weapons, too great a focus on political instability in Muslim lands and, in particular, the constant focus on the treatment of Muslim women are all pre-existing cultural stereotypes dressed up as newsworthy stories. It is what is described as the 'echoes of the medieval polemic'.[16]

In relation to news on British Muslims, there has been widespread misrepresentation and negative reporting in both the broadsheet and tabloid presses, with a heightened period after 9/11 and 7/7 that has not quite abated, although it was evident enough in news media well before the events of 9/11 and the 'War on Terror'.[17] In television news, the language has

13 Halliday, F. (1996) *Islam and the Myth of Confrontation: Religion and Politics in the Middle East*, London: I.B. Tauris.
14 Ahmed, A.S. (2004) *Postmodernism and Islam: Predicament and Promise*, London: Routledge.
15 Sikand, Y. (1994) 'Muslims and the Mass Media', *Economic and Political Weekly*, 29(33): 2134–5.
16 Kabbani, R. (1989) *A Letter to Christendom*, London: Virago, p. 9.
17 Abbas, T. (2000) 'Images of Islam', *Index on Censorship*, 29(5): 64–8; Abbas, T. (2001) 'Media Capital and the Representation of South Asian Muslims in the British Press: an Ideological Analysis', *Journal of Muslim Minority Affairs*, 21(2): 245–57; Ahmed, A.S. and D. Hastings (1994) (eds) *Islam, Globalisation and Postmodernity*, London: Routledge; Poole, E. (2002) *Reporting Islam: Media Representations of British Muslims*, London and New York: I.B. Tauris.

altered substantially, with 'Islamic terrorism' or 'Muslim extremist' becoming everyday parlance. The portrayal of British Muslims in the current period is described as a 'new racist discourse'.[18] This new racism differs from the 'old' in that it is more subtle but at the same time explicit in the direction it takes. In the post-9/11 era, some British parliamentarians have used the fears people have of Islam for their own ends; by focusing on the 'War on Terror' politicians used the existing anti-Muslim frame of reference but have replaced it with the idea of 'terror'. The reporting is compounded by a concentration on the 'enemy within' or the loyalty of Muslims to Britain. Reasons for the increase in these themes in news reporting are symptomatic of the increased fear of the 'Muslim terrorist' since the 9/11 attacks on New York and Washington (and, subsequently, 11 March 2004 in Madrid, 2 November 2004 in Amsterdam, 7 July 2005 in London, 10 August 2006 and the 'transatlantic terror plot', 30 June 2007 in Glasgow and, more recently, in relation to the 'underpants bomber' of Christmas Day 2009).

News and entertainment media can present similarly negative cultural stereotypes of Muslims. In Hollywood films, before 9/11 there was a demonstrable demonisation of Muslims, for example *Delta Force* (1986, dir. Menahem Golan), *True Lies* (1993, dir. James Cameron) and *The Siege* (1999, dir. Edward Zwick). However, Hollywood was more sensitive immediately after 9/11, and even provided a nuanced account of issues of Middle Eastern politics in *Syriana* (2005, dir. Stephen Gaghen) and *Body of Lies* (2008, dir. Ridley Scott), and other films more critical of the 'War on Terror' itself, such as *Lion for Lambs* (2007, dir. Robert Redford) and *Kingdom* (2007, dir. Peter Berg).[19] In television documentaries, there has been a negative trend with only recent positive developments, in particular *The Power of Nightmares* (2004, BBC), which explained how the US neo-conservatives and the Islamists in the form of Osama bin Laden of Saudi Arabia and Dr Ayman al-Zawahiri of Egypt have used their respective political capital to generate the idea of a battle between 'good' and 'evil', and how each side rationalises its existence through the demonisation of the other. However, such nuance in relation to reporting has remained varied. The renowned journalist Peter Taylor presented a three-part series on *Generation Jihad* (2010, BBC). In detail, the processes of radicalisation and the significance of the policy response were presented; however, the imagery and video-editing perpetuated a very negative impression of Islam and young British Muslims, perpetuating the myth that there were countless

---

18   Van Dijk, T. (2000) 'New(s) Racism: A Discourse Analytical Approach', in S. Cottle (ed.), *Ethnic Minorities and the Media: Changing Cultural Boundaries*, Buckingham: Open University Press, pp. 33–49.

19   Shaheen, J.G. (2001) *Reel Bad Arabs: How Hollywood Vilifies a People*, Northam: Roundhouse.

young men who were but a short step away from jihadi-salafism, using the Internet as a way in which to communicate and organise against the state. Moreover, in an effort to present a more dramatised account of radicalism, a number of programmes have been somewhat controversial. Episodes of *Spooks* (BBC) and *24* (Fox) routinely carry plot themes associated with 'global Islamic terrorism'. *The Hamburg Cell* (2004, Channel 4), *Dirty War* (2004, BBC), *Yasmin* (2006, Channel 4), *The Road to Guantanamo* (2006, ITV) and *Britz* (2007, ITV) are all stylised visual projects, where issues of Muslim masculinity feature heavily.[20] They portray how sophisticated and seemingly integrated Muslims, of various national and ethnic origins, are able to come together with the single intent of destroying human and economic targets in the West. None contain positive Muslim characters. All these attempts at news reporting and media manufacturing, particularly in television, could be described as 'weapons of mass distraction'.[21] The point being emphasised here is that media and politics are inextricably linked to Orientalism and Islamophobia.

In the past, the word 'fundamentalism' or 'fundamentalist' has been attached to various religious groups; however, the word is a relatively new addition to the English language. The 1932 edition of *The Universal Dictionary of the English Language* includes a definition of 'fundamentalist' by relating it to the strict adherence of religious principles, especially the belief in creation.[22] In the 1930s, it was principally used in relation to certain US Protestant movements, as a reference to their insistence on the literal truth of Scripture. These groups came into existence after the First World War and were directly associated with the Ku Klux Klan in the USA. The British press first used the term 'fundamentalist' on 24 May 1932 – the *Daily Mail* using it precisely to refer to US Protestant movements. Over the years, other newspapers began to use the expression. On 25 August 1955, *The Times* referred to 'fundamentalism' as the 'bigoted rejection of all Biblical criticism, a mechanical view of inspiration and an excessively literal interpretation of scripture'. The term was first used in connection with Islam in the press in the UK on 27 September 1981, following the Iranian Revolution of 1979, when the *Observer* referred to 'the phenomenon of the new, or rather old, Islam, the dangerous fundamentalism revived by the ayatollahs and their admirers as a device, indistinguishable from a weapon for running the modern state'. The article referred to the new 'Islamic states' as 'little more than intolerant, bloody [...] incompetent animations of the

20   Ahmed, R. (2009) 'British Muslim Masculinities and Cultural Resistance: Kenny Glenaan and Simon Beaufoy's *Yasmin*', *Journal of Postcolonial Writing*, 4(3): 285–96.

21   Rampton, S. and J. Stauber (2003) *Weapons of Mass Deception: The Uses of Propaganda in Bush's War on Iraq*, New York: Penguin.

22   Wylde, H. (1932) (ed.) *Universal Dictionary of the English Language*, London: Routledge. p. 105.

Holy Book [the Qur'ān]'.[23] Associations between the word 'fundamentalism' and Islam is a recent phenomenon in the press and is predefined by the negative connotations it gained when used in relation to groups in the USA. The development of the term 'fundamentalism' adds to an abundance of existing and historical negativity towards Muslims.

For Bhikhu Parekh, 'religions of the book' focus on certain texts that are thought to be the direct word of God. The three Abrahamic religions all believe in the inherent absolutisms of their faiths.[24] Therefore, an appreciation of 'fundamentalisms' would suggest that these groups accept a particular religious text as the true word of God. 'Islamic fundamentalism', however, is often associated with acts of terrorism or extreme political movements and autocratic, dynastic and theocratic regimes found in countries such as Saudi Arabia, Iran, Egypt, Syria or Libya. Societies experiencing inner political turmoil and actions of vested interests from outside, such as Afghanistan, Pakistan, Algeria and Chechnya, are all associated with radical military activity. Groups are described as 'Islamist', 'Islamic fundamentalists' or related terms implying a literal return to the sacred text. The essential view is that 'Islamic fundamentalists' are often perpetrators of particular 'terrorist' incidents and that this is allied to a literal reading of the Qur'ān. Moreover, 'Islamic fundamentalists' are seen as the true Muslims, and all Muslims are fundamentalists. Some observers and commentators in the West find it unproblematic to infer that the Qur'ān is a violent and extremist text. There is little mention made of or recognition given to the extent of 'war and sex' as found in the other sacred texts, such as in Deuteronomy, Samuel and Zechariah.

The human need for the construction of the 'other' as a way of self-identification and self-assurance is a universal one. Relations between Islam and the West are given additional impetus due to the added existence of a god (e.g. Allah or the Christian God). That is, if it is believed that God is on the side of 'good', then the antagonist must be 'evil'. The process can lead to racism, prejudice, hatred and violence in the most extreme of cases. Repressed desires and frustrations, whether conscious or unconscious, can be projected onto the 'other' as a way in which to deny those 'sinful' thoughts within.[26] Muslims are depicted as corrupt, irrational, barbaric and lecherous as a way of denying the presence of these very impulses in Western societies. In contrast, Muslims emphasise the secularism of the West, its immorality, materialism and delinquency as a way of denying that they too

23   Burgess, A. (1981) 'Islam in the Dark', *The Observer*, 27 September.
24   Parekh, B. (1992) *The Concept of Fundamentalism*, University of Warwick: Centre for Research in Asian Migration and Pepal Tree Press.
25   Goffman, E. (1990) *The Presentation of Self in Everyday Life*, London: Penguin.
26   Saeed, A. (2007) 'Media, Racism and Islamophobia: The Representation of Islam and Muslims in the Media', *Sociology Compass*, 1(2): 443–62.

might have such 'evil' desires. In Britain, the recent immigration and settlement of Muslims, bringing with them their seemingly 'alien' culture, is thought to threaten British or Western European values.[27] It comes at a time when economic and social differences in British society are at their greatest. In order to prevent the dilution of their own identity as well as a response to racism and discrimination, Muslims maintain firmly and conservatively their faith and culture. The more this occurs the less they are seen to be part of wider British society, however lacking in neutrality the debate may be. In the macro-dynamic sense, the collapse of Communism in the Soviet Union and Eastern Europe has left an ideological vacuum which the 'spectre' of Islam has filled. At the time of the fall of the Berlin Wall in 1989, Akbar S. Ahmed commented on an opinion survey that showed 80 per cent of the British population saw 'Islam as the next major enemy after communism'.[28] Since then, an array of polling data is routinely published to highlight the apparent unassimilibility of Muslims in Britain. However, the more robust statistical reality is that in the post-9/11 period Muslims in Britain and in other parts of Western Europe are actively working towards integrating into society, demonstrating positive approaches to citizenship and the construction of hybridised-hyphenated identities.[29]

The seminal work on the Western construction of the Oriental and Islamic 'other' is *Orientalism* by Edward Said. Orientalism is a means of 'cultural domination' by which the Orient and Orientals can be contained and represented. It is constructed through a power relationship in which the West remains unconditionally dominant. Thus, the Orient is a Western construct developed for Western purposes. The ideas of Said in *Orientalism* generate a constructive historical perspective on how the 'other' is perceived and made reference to, particularly in contemporary literature.[30] The 'other' is invariably Middle Eastern and Muslim. The idea of Islamophobia, therefore, is argued to be a more recent incarnation of well established Orientalist traditions. In effect, Orientalism is the study of Near and Far Eastern societies and cultures by Western explorers, scholars and analysts. The converse to this would be Occidentalism, which refers to the study of Western societies and cultures by people of the East. Orientalism can also refer to the negative reproduction or representation of aspects of Eastern cultures in the West by writers, designers and artists. It is the study of the East by North Americans and Western Europeans, shaped by the attitudes inherent during

27 Lawrence, B.B. (2000) *Shattering the Myth: Islam Beyond Violence*, Princeton, NJ: Princeton University Press; Hippler, J. and A. Lueg (1995) (eds) *The Next Threat: Western Perceptions of Islam*, London: Pluto Press; Hunter, S.H. (1998) *The Future of Islam and the West: Clash of Civilizations or Peaceful Coexistence?* Westport, CT: Greenwood.
28 Ahmed (2004), op. cit.
29 Pew Research Center (2006) *The Great Divide: How Westerners and Muslims View Each Other*, Washington, DC: Pew Global Attitude Project.
30 Said, E. (1978) *Orientalism,* London: Routledge & Kegan Paul, p. 36.

the era of Western European imperialism and colonialism in the eighteenth and nineteenth centuries. As a result, the term 'Orientalism' has come to acquire negative connotations, implying outdated and prejudicial outsider interpretations of Eastern cultures and peoples. In *Orientalism,* Said was critical of the work of modern scholars, including the renowned Princeton academic, Bernard Lewis. Said claimed that 'knowledge gives power, more power requires more knowledge, and so on in an increasingly profitable dialectic of information and control'.[31] There remains a fear of confrontation between 'East' and 'West': 'even when the Orient has uniformly been considered an inferior part of the world, it has always been endowed both with greater size and with a greater potential for power (usually destructive) than the west'.[32]

'Oriental culture' is thus argued to be trapped in a state of eternal stagnation. Therefore, 'Orientals' and Muslims are thought to be primitive and backward and so must be challenged for their own good; left to their own devices they would degenerate into despotism and corruption. The main traits of the stereotype of the Orient are its irrationality, violence and cruelty such that it symbolises 'terror, devastation, the demonic, hordes of hated barbarians'.[33] Said claimed that these historical stereotypes are indelibly ingrained into the dominant popular imagination and psyche. Orientalism provides a means for the West to deal with 'otherness' and to define itself against it. Comparisons are drawn between the West in relation to cultural differences and foreign entities, and these embodiments of 'otherness' are natural to Western society as a means of personal identification. Myra MacDonald has argued that the link between the negative construction of 'the Arab' and the anxieties about Muslim expansionism became embedded in Western consciousness at the time of the Crusades in the eleventh to thirteenth century.[34] MacDonald highlights the historical 'denigration' that the West has imposed upon Islam, implying that current Western Orientalism is acting upon negative attitudes towards Islam and Muslims in the light of recent events. After 9/11, MacDonald continued with her research to consider the developments to Orientalist ideology in media discourses, offering a unique insight into the reawakening of 'pre-existing discourses of Islamophobia'.[35] In consideration of the possibilities of these so-called inherent binarisms, Said questions the role of social conformity, discussing the extent to which boundaries between the West and the East are constructed in relation to power. Inherent Orientalism in the West acts

---

31 Ibid.
32 Said, E. (1981) *Covering Islam: How the Media and the Experts Determine How We See the Rest of the World*, London: Routledge & Kegan Paul, p. 4.
33 Ibid., p. 59.
34 MacDonald, M. (2003) *Exploring Media Discourse*, London: Hodder Arnold, p. 154.
35 Ibid., p. 174.

to reaffirm stereotypical associations of the irrational, uncivilised and barbaric East. Consequently, society is manipulated into a dominating role over the East, 'a western style for dominating, reconstructing, and having authority over the Orient'.[36]

Elizabeth Poole identifies social conformity in the actions of certain Muslim–West relations. Linking Muslims with conflict whilst ignoring their victimisation is a characteristic of Western society, and this distortion of the East by the West allows the West to continually assert power and dominance over the East: 'discourse is essential to the maintenance of power relations, acting as a form of social control'.[37] In discussing social conformity, existing literature has focused on the themes of homogenisation and representation of Islam and Muslims. Said identified a progressive denial of the mutual humanity between the West and the East. It would lead to a violent back-lash between the two worlds and the creation of a limited political imagi-nation on each side. Muslims and Islam become homogenised and reaffirmed as an enemy surrounded by blame and suspicion. Said identified this distinction drawn between the West and East in Western media, acknowledging a 'strange revival' of Orientalist ideology. Here, Islam and Muslims are increasingly described in opposition to 'us' and 'our' way of life. Through analyses of media in Western society during the 1970s, Said reflected that in most prime-time television shows in the USA, Muslims were almost always portrayed as a homogenised group – more profoundly, a homogenised enemy. It is through these representations that Muslims learn about themselves through Western eyes.

Reality and representation differ, demonstrating the related theme of inherent Orientalism. Poole recognises divisions in the West and the East through media representation and the consequential effects, and identifies the significant role of media representations in the homogenisation of Islam and Muslims, while MacDonald recognises how the negative con-struction of Islam and Muslims plays an integral role in the creation of harmful social perceptions that have emerged in British society. Through textual analysis, MacDonald ascertains an increasingly distinctive Orient-alist ideology permeating Western media. Like Poole, MacDonald recognises the reaffirmation between (Western) 'good' and (terrorism) 'evil'.[38] What can be seen is how this portrayal of 'evil' in the West, despite attempting to distance itself from accusations of racism, is clearly targeted towards Muslims.

In effect, the roles of the media and politics in the framing of anti-Muslim representation have emerged hand in hand. Muslims in Britain feel that part of the reason for their continued existence as an unaccepted and

---

36 Said (1978), op. cit., p. 3.
37 Poole (2002), op. cit., p. 249.
38 MacDonald (2003), op. cit., p. 175.

often-despised minority is based upon the presence of the 'evil demon': the media.[39] There is a belief that media representation of Muslims is distorted and stereotypical and that the images of Western secularism and materialism menacingly invade their homes: 'in the last two decades [up to 1989] there has been an attempt, quite deliberate and perhaps even [a] co-ordinated attempt, to construct an influential stereotype of contemporary fundamentalist Islam'.[40] Initially, it was media portrayal of the Iranian Revolution of 1979, the last of the 'classical revolutions', and of 2 million Muslims on the streets of Tehran, that caused the West to begin to think hard and look closely at this body of people called 'Muslims'.[41] Dressed in black, seemingly exhibiting violence and aggression, these Muslims were painted as 'radical', 'fanatical' and 'fundamentalist'. In 1989, the Rushdie affair was the first occasion when Britain began to look at its own Muslim population in a critical but also sensationalist manner. With most British Muslims strongly opposing the publication of the novel, *The Satanic Verses*, 'Book Burnings in Bradford' became the dominant headline of the day. British Muslims were presented as intolerant, bigoted, reactionary and regressive, all of which questioned their loyalty to the state as well as their rights and obligations.[42] For Muslims carrying out these acts, theirs was a genuine act of frustration and the feeling of hurt that the book had caused them. To non-Muslim onlookers, however, these scenes, as they appeared on national and international television, came to be regarded as symbols of uncontrollable fury and hatred towards the West. Media reporting at the time was regarded as 'shallow and extravagant',[43] partly because no real Islamic experts were permitted to comment on the situation, and the limits of the debate were defined by the liberal establishment in partnership with the media. Coverage was 'distorted', focusing only on events, with sound bites loaded with emotion and based on reference to death threats, the 'medieval fundamentalists' and their 'fanaticism and militant wrath'.[44]

Images of the 'Bradford book-burnings' were circulated at the expense of the plight of British South Asian Muslims who believed their religion had been 'blasphemed' and that they were being denied their right to freedom of expression. Invariably, these Muslim groups used the Rushdie book to vent their frustration at being alienated and marginalised in society through decades of racist hostility and structural subordination.[45] Talal Asad argued

---

39 Ahmed (2004), op. cit.
40 Akhtar, S. (1989) *Be Careful with Muhammad: The Salman Rushdie Affair*, London: Bedlow, p. 10.
41 Asari, F. (1989) 'Iran in the British Media', *Index on Censorship*, 18(5): 9–13.
42 Modood, T. (1990), 'British Asian Muslims and the Rushdie Affair', *Political Quarterly*, 61(2): 143–60.
43 Akhtar (1989), op. cit., p. 40.
44 Ibid.
45 Modood (1990), op. cit.

that the non-Muslim fear was based on a 'perceived threat to a particular ideological structure, a cultural hierarchy organised by an essential Englishness, which defined British identity'.[46] In the same year, the Berlin Wall came down (and with it the end of the Cold War), and this further enhanced the ideological construction of Muslims and Islam as antithetical to the interests of the West.[47] The outrage that the Rushdie book caused ultimately created long-term implications for the ways in which British Muslims would be recognised for the foreseeable future.[48] They remain to the present day.

A number of events in the 1990s made matters quite complex for British Muslim identities. Increasing ethno-religious tensions across the globe involving Muslims (for example in Kashmir, Chechnya and Bosnia-Herzegovina) affected not only how Muslims regarded themselves but also, more significantly, how they were seen by dominant others. They also occasioned the radicalisation of young British Muslims in the mid-1990s, who a decade earlier had been fighting on the streets to protect their territory from violent fascists and nationalists.[49] It was during the late 1990s that 'Islamophobia' became a popular anti-racist discussion in Britain; increasingly, a focus on Muslims as victims became the dominant discourse, particularly in relation to thinking on religious minorities and race equality. Throughout this period, the concentration at home was cultural, economic and political. In relation to the cultural, there was renewed interest in questions surrounding women in Muslim communities: a return to the age-old spotlight on their treatment at the hands of a male-dominated society and, in particular, the ideas of 'forced marriages' and 'honour-related violence'.[50] There was also some attention being paid to questions relating to 'self-styled segregation' – that is, that Muslims did not wish to integrate with their white British 'hosts' – and, as such, this was an important public issue (see Chapter 3). In relation to the economic, there was a concern that low education, high unemployment, poor housing and health, and limited self-employment success were negatively impacting upon the development of Muslims in society. In all of these spheres, British Muslims were seen to be acutely

46 Asad, T. (1990) 'Multiculturalism and British Identity in the Wake of the Rushdie Affair', *Politics and Society*, 18(4): 455–80.
47 Fukuyama, F. (1993) *The End of History and the Last Man*, New York: Penguin; Huntingdon, S. (2002) *The Clash of Civilizations and the Remaking of World Order*, New York: Free Press.
48 Parekh, B. (1990) 'The Rushdie Affair: Research Agenda for Political Philosophy', *Political Studies*, 38(4): 695–709.
49 Abbas, T. (2007a) 'Ethno-Religious Identities and Islamic Political Radicalism in the UK: A Case Study', *Journal of Muslim Minority Affairs*, 27(3): 356–68.
50 Samad, Y. and J. Eade (2003) *Community Perceptions of Forced Marriage*, London: Foreign and Commonwealth Office; Idriss, M.M. and T. Abbas (2010) (eds) *Honour, Violence, Women and Islam*, London and New York: Routledge.

disadvantaged, but the perceptions of their experience in society were generally negative.[51] Politically, questions were being asked about participation and representation (both local and national), as there were concerns relating to the determination of an effective political voice.[52] These areas became the focus of race-equality thinking, certainly impacting on public policy. Indeed, during the first term of New Labour, race equality and issues of diversity were placed near the top of the domestic political agenda, particularly given the findings of the Macpherson Report of 1999 in relation to institutionalised racism in the Metropolitan Police Service.[53] The events of 2001 would reverse many of the progressive equalities developments of New Labour's first term, and from there on domestic and international issues in relation to ethnic and religious minorities would be intertwined. In the north of England, violent clashes between the police and young British-born South Asian Muslim men caused not only destruction of property but also, more notably, the breakdown of community relations in already relatively poor and isolated areas of the country. Often less understood or accepted, these 'riots' were, to a significant degree, inflamed by the tactics of right-wing political groups.[54]

In the summer of 2001, Britain witnessed some of its worst inner-city disturbances in nearly two decades. Young British South Asian Muslims, living in the deprived inner cities of Bradford, Oldham and Burnley, clashed violently with local police. Their pent-up fury was a result of generations of social and economic exclusion, as well as the targeting of existing sensitised areas by right-wing groups who worked to manufacture ethno-religious ill-feeling between communities. It was the response to the disturbances on the part of the Government, in reports published soon after 9/11, which are important to consider. An illustration of Islamophobia in politics is seen in the idea of 'community cohesion'. The notion, in keeping with the New Labour rhetoric of inclusion, masked what was effectively a case of 'blaming the victim'. The incumbent Home Secretary, David Blunkett, while promoting the idea of 'cohesive communities', announced 'a test of allegiance'. Referring to the problems of the 'excess of cultural diversity and moral relativism' that prevents positive inter-cultural exchange and development. Mention was made of English-language issues and female circumcision in speeches soon after 9/11 – conflating many different non-Islamic behaviours

51 Modood, T., R. Berthoud, J. Lakey, J. Nazroo, P. Smith, S. Virdee and S. Beishon (1997) *Ethnic Minorities in Britain: Diversity and Disadvantage*, London: Policy Studies Institute.

52 Anwar, M. (2001) 'Participation of Ethnic Minorities in British Politics', *Journal of Ethnic and Migration Studies*, 27(3): 533–49.

53 Schuster, L. and J. Solomos (2004) 'Race, Immigration and Asylum: New Labour's Agenda and Its Consequences', *Ethnicities*, 4(2): 267–300.

54 Kundnani, A. (2007) *The End of Tolerance: Racism in 21st Century Britain*, London: Pluto; Bagguley, P. and Y. Hussain (2008) *Riotous Citizens: Ethnic Conflict in Multicultural Britain*, Aldershot: Ashgate.

and cultures with that of specific Muslim communities in the north-west of England. These are important issues in their own right, as well as part of a process of making civil society improve the functionality of democracy, but these were arguably not the factors behind the 'riots'. Segregation of Muslims is thought to be self-imposed and the cause of racism rather than a result of it. British South Asian Muslims are economically disadvantaged and socially marginalised but, on the whole, willing to participate and feel they are part of society with the hope of contributing to it. This is demonstrated in the 2001 Home Office Citizenship Survey which affirms this perspective (this is in the context of ongoing experiences and perceptions of racism and discrimination on the grounds of race and religion).[55] Segregation is largely the result of racism and disadvantage, but identification with Islam is the reason given for the segregation. In British race relations, there has been a tendency to concentrate on the minority groups and their social characteristics rather than to scrutinise and change processes, institutions and wider local area socio-economic and socio-cultural dynamics. It is recognised that some Muslim communities are certainly able to positively mobilise class and ethnic resources to develop religio-cultural, social and economic infrastructures that help to support their existence and determine upward social mobility, but the vast majority remain unable to.

As New Labour made preparations for re-election in May 2010, and while there were genuine shifts in approaches to discussions in relation to multiculturalism, citizenship and social justice during the second (2001–5) and third terms (2005–10), it was the policy of assimilation (or enforced integration) that was rejuvenated towards the end. Where equalities were championed in New Labour's first term, 'cohesion' was the driver of policy in the second term. In the third term the focus was on 'preventing violent extremism', and in the context of the securitisation of immigration, integration and domestic community cohesion policy. Eliminating inequalities, which brings about cohesion, helping to significantly prevent the likelihood of violent extremism, and in both minority and majority communities, is not given the same emphasis. Before the global 'credit crunch' of late 2008, Tony Blair and Gordon Brown were attempting to define a 'new ethnicity': Britishness as opposed to Englishness in an era of globalisation and devolution. Eager to embrace the social-capitalist project, New Labour was unable to offer any real solutions to the economic, political and social anxieties and tensions faced by the poor of Britain, within which are

55 Home Office (2003a) *2001 Home Office Citizenship Survey: people, families and communities*, London: Home Office Research Study 270; Munton, T. and A. Zurawan (2004) *Active Communities: Headline Findings from the 2003 Home Office Citizenship Survey*, London: Home Office Research Development and Statistics; Home Office and Department for Education and Skills (2005) *2003 Home Office Citizenship Survey: Top-level findings from the Children's and Young People's Survey*, London: Crown Copyright.

contained a significant proportion of its ethnic and Muslim minorities. The young South Asian Muslim men of Oldham, Bradford and Burnley, who confronted the police in such dramatic scenes during the summer of 2001, did not suffer the problems of being 'un-assimilated'. Indeed, theirs was a predicament based on a society divided by racism, discrimination and, indeed, Islamophobia. Three months after these 'disturbances', it was the tragic events of 9/11 that led to the beginning of the 'War on Terror'. The ultimate approach taken by the UK Government in relation to international affairs was compounded by domestic issues pertaining to some of the most disaffected groups in society.

The ideological constructions behind these approaches concentrated on the integration and community development of Muslims. As a result of a series of local, national and international events, the situation of British Muslims became even more depressing after the events of 2001, home and abroad. It cemented the notion that apparently being unwilling to integrate into society has something to do with a seemingly increasing radical political Islamism among Muslim youths.[56]

While it is possible to demonstrate Orientalism and Islamophobia in the British press, some observers have interrogated the very notion of Islamophobia itself, contending that use of the term is often an attempt to regulate or censor thought by characterising any unfavourable judgement of Islam or Muslims as pathologising or unreasonable (in the same that the term 'anti-Semitism' could be used to de-legitimise disapproval of Israeli policy). There is the case of the liberal feminist commentator, Polly Toynbee, who was nominated for the award of 'Most Islamophobic Media Personality of the Year' in 2003 at the Annual Islamophobia Awards, overseen by the Islamic Human Rights Commission. Toynbee had penned an article in the *Guardian* less than a month after the events of 9/11, stating that 'religious politics scar India, Kashmir, Northern Ireland, Sri Lanka, Sudan [...] [T]he list of countries wrecked by religion is long. But the present danger is caused by Islamist theocracy [...] There is no point in pretending it is not so'.[57] Toynbee continued, 'wherever Islam either is the government or bears down upon the government, it imposes harsh regimes that deny the most basic human rights'.[58] She spurned the description of 'Islamophobe' and reasoned that her remarks ought to be evaluated on their accuracy or falsehoods, and not based on the umbrage they might create for a few outspoken voices from within the Muslim communities. Kenan Malik, political activist and social commentator, has also rejected, for some, the notion of an

56 Ansari, H. (2005) 'Attitudes to Jihad, Martyrdom and Terrorism among British Muslims', in T. Abbas (ed.), *Muslim Britain: Communities under Pressure*, London and New York: Zed, pp. 144–64.
57 Toynbee, P. (2001) 'Last Chance to Speak Out', *The Guardian*, 5 October.
58 Ibid.

all-encompassing Islamophobia in his influential essay, *The Islamophobia Myth*.[59] Malik argues that caution is required when assigning Islamophobia as the primary reason behind any apparent anti-Muslim event as these charges of Islamophobia could be utilised to suppress argumentation and disapproval of certain negative cultural praxes of Muslims and their cultural attributes. Anti-social activity and delinquency may simply be the foundation of a number of cases acknowledged as examples of Islamophobic violence, Malik adds.

Nevertheless, Islamophobia is not just about the numbers of people who have reported physical violence or the numbers of Muslims who have been stopped and searched by the police. There are clearly wider, historically significant culturally embedded institutional practices and individual and group behaviours which are more significant than the idea of Islamophobia being no more than random but increasingly physical attacks against Muslims and the religion of Islam itself. Contemporary Britain prides itself on its liberal ideologies, encouraging multicultural integration, freedom of speech and equality of opportunity. The Government states that Britain has moved away from its inherently assimilationist principles and has developed a multicultural society in which the term 'British' can simultaneously refer to all cultures. Nonetheless, over the past 20 years, Britain has witnessed struggles between these cultures on several occasions, including protests in 1989 following the publication of *The Satanic Verses* and, more recently, following the publication of several cartoons by Danish right-wing newspaper, *Jyllands-Posten*, negatively depicting Prophet Muhammad, originally published in September 2005 and then again in February 2006.

In *The Satanic Verses*, Rushdie presented a story that directly questioned significant aspects of the Islamic religion. The most controversial elements of the book were the use of the name 'Mahound' to refer to Muhammad, the depiction of the Prophet's wives as courtesans and the suggestion that the Qur'ān lacks authenticity. The novel was written to appeal to Western audiences, presenting an Orientalist understanding of Islam that influences their ideologies; 'sex and violence not only sell books, they can also shape the images of other people, other societies, and other civilisations'.[60] It caused outrage among the global Muslim community, and the book was banned in India and South Africa, with some Muslim groups taking to 'book burning'. In a dramatic development, Ayatollah Khomeini issued a fatwa against Rushdie for his alleged crimes of apostasy punishable by death, which remained in place for a decade. The Western world has seen throughout its history capital punishment inflicted for acts of treason. In Islam there is a similar concept. It is not, as in the West, for treachery

59 Malik, K. (2005) 'The Islamophobia Myth', *Prospect*, 107, February.
60 Sardar, Z. and M. Wyn-Davies (1990) *Distorted Imagination: Lessons from the Rushdie Affair*, London: Grey Seal, p. 34.

towards the state but towards the *ummah*. In the case of treason against the *ummah*, capital punishment is the ultimate penalty (as interpreted). It is within this framework that blasphemy is considered an act of treason and that Rushdie was considered a 'traitor' by Khomeini.

The relationship between law and religion differs considerably between Islam and Christianity. Western Christian societies have witnessed the over-turning of apparently blasphemous texts and the altering of law with regards to issues such as homosexuality. Christianity has developed simultaneously with society accepting the importance of not enforcing laws that attempt to regulate religious belief and inhibit freedom of speech. In contrast, most Muslims believe that the law as revealed to Muhammad is perfect in form and should be abided by and maintained because of this.[61] Many puritan Muslims believe that because 'classical Jurists divided the world into Dar al Islam and Dar al Harb, the abode of Islam and the abode of war',[62] regardless of the rulers, the law should remain the same. If the sovereign alters the law, 'the territory becomes Dar al Harb like the rest of the world outside Dar al Islam'.[63] It is this puritanical understanding that the British media depicts as the general Muslim ideology, when, in fact, the majority of Muslims believe that it is possible to live peacefully in Britain and remain perfectly Muslim, with this position also taking on a more theologically ascribed consensual position.[64]

In a similar vein, the Danish cartoons were arguably an offensive attack on the Islamic religion and, in particular, Muhammad. The newspaper was arguably aware of the fact that depictions of the Prophet of any kind are prohibited in Sunni Islam, and that they are an affront to those Muslims. Five thousand Muslims participated in the 'Unity Rally' in Trafalgar Square: 'United against Islamophobia, united against incitement, united in our love of the Prophet'. The peaceful rally was not only a demonstration against the cartoons but it also acted as an 'antidote' to previous Muslim demonstrations that had resulted in an angered response by civil society and the Government and, ultimately, to the proscription of Al-Ghuraba, who were responsible for the initial angry demonstration consisting of merely two hundred people or so. The portrayal of the Muslim protests primarily focused on volatile attacks on various Danish embassies around the world, thus disseminating the stereotype of Muslims as 'zealots' or 'terrorists'. There was minimal attention given to the reporting of peaceful rallies. It is clear that the processes of globalisation and trans-nationalism played

61 Tibi, B. (1990) *Islam and the Cultural Accommodation of Social Change*, trans. C. Krojzl, Oxford: Westview Press, p. 61.
62 Ruthven, M. (1991) *A Satanic Affair: Salman Rushdie and the Rage of Islam*, London: Hogarth Press, p. 51.
63 Ibid.
64 Sulieman, Y. (2009) *Contextualising Islam in Britain: exploratory perspectives*, Cambridge: University of Cambridge in Association with the Universities of Exeter and Westminster.

significant roles in increasing the importance of *The Satanic Verses* and the caricatures of Muhammad. Following the issuing of the fatwa against Rushdie, Khomeini was portrayed in the West as a 'symbol of evil'. It is similar to how Osama bin Laden is depicted in contemporary Western society (along with Saddam Hussein before his execution). The image represents a particular ideological standpoint, presented to global audiences through dominant news media.

Globalisation has dramatically advanced since the Rushdie affair, and with the introduction of the Internet and twenty-four-hour news the transmission of information is instantaneous. Following the printing of the caricatures of Muhammad, the Muslim reaction was relatively subdued, with small groups peacefully appealing for the censoring of the images. With these calls unsuccessful, the Muslim protest increased with messages rapidly transmitted through the global Muslim community asserting the need to censor the images. After the reprinting of the pictures by newspapers in Germany, Italy, France, Holland and Norway in February 2006, some 'extremist Muslim groups' responded with violent protests, most notably against the Danish embassies in Lebanon and Syria. These aggressive outbursts were then depicted throughout the Western media as the generalised reaction of the Muslim community as a whole.

Much of the broad understanding of Islam in the West is influenced and controlled by various dominant media discourses, many of which tend to focus on Muslims as perpetrators and not always the victims of social injustice and violence. The consequences of this are significant for Muslim representation and ultimately for social cohesion. A media-defined worldview is depicted through a range of global communication technologies and then beamed to every living room in the West and, increasingly, in capitalism-fed Eastern worlds. Since the events of 9/11 and 7/7, this stereotype includes such characterisations as terrorists, 'suicide-bombers', illiberal and anti-democratic. Muslims argue that freedom of speech is essential in society; however, the publicising of deliberately sensationalised imagery and news that misrepresents a religion to an unwary audience does not always constitute free speech for some. There is ultimately no authority protecting the Muslim community from calculatedly provocative material produced by the media, as highlighted in the reporting on the publication of *The Satanic Verses* and the Danish cartoons. The Orientalism of the Middle Ages is as evident in contemporary society.[65]

A recent case in point in relation to the intersection of media, politics, Islam and Muslims was in October 2006, when Jack Straw, former Foreign Secretary (2001–5) and Home Secretary (1997–2001), made a number of comments in relation to the wearing of the face veil (*niqab*) by Muslim women who wished to seek his advice at his constituency surgery

---

65 Sardar and Wyn-Davies (1990), op. cit., p. 34.

in Blackburn. Writing in the *Lancashire Telegraph*, Straw carefully, but simplistically, painted a picture of unwanted difference being exercised by British Muslim women who wished to wear the *niqab* when seeking his counsel. A tremendous kerfuffle was made of the issue, by Muslims and non-Muslims alike, but, interestingly, with many coming together on a number of fronts. Straw argued that it was a 'visible statement of separation and of difference'. His comments created a national debate, which at the time drew other notable political figures to make similar claims, including not only Tony Blair, who was still Prime Minister, Chancellor Gordon Brown and Deputy Prime Minister John Prescott, but also Leader of the Opposition, David Cameron, and his shadow Home Secretary, David Davies. The remarks made by Straw and others reflected the exoticisation of the Muslim woman that was at its height during the colonial period of the nineteenth century, re-emerging in recent neo-Orentialist and neo-conservative periods in history. Anglo-Saxon European men infatuated by the infamous, but principally imaginary, harems of the Mughals or Ottomans regarded Muslim woman as the mysterious but altogether alluring 'captives in need of rescuing'. In reality, for Muslims, the *chador, burqa* or the *niqab* is often an attempt to limit the potential menace to Muslim women posed by non-familiar men, not, as it is argued by many in the West, to prevent women from expressing aspects of their femininity. In the vast majority of cases, Muslim women make their own decisions in relation to covering up. For those who do not do it of their own free will, this is certainly a problem for society as a whole, and one where Muslims are an important constituent. An alternative notion is that British Muslim women, born in a free and open society, consciously don the *niqab* as a backlash to neo-colonialism, particularly in reaction to how Muslims in distant lands are being treated by external antagonists. It is a symbol of defiance and an expression of resistance to attempts to forcibly assimilate Muslim minorities without providing the resources or opportunities to generate the capacities of individuals and communities to integrate on their own.[66]

For some, it is simply not appropriate to determine how people ought to dress in an open, liberal and still relatively tolerant society such as Britain. Even so, there are concerns with the *niqab,* as it literally masks the face, making it difficult to directly communicate with others. In certain circumstances, however, others might argue that it has the potential to create barriers and further isolate the very people that British Muslim minorities need to better engage with. It is a practical argument that has a great deal of purchase, but what was perturbing about Straw is how a well informed person in a position of power and influence should reignite such a sensitive

---

66 Afshar, H., R. Aitken and M. Franks (2005) 'Feminisms, Islamophobia and Identities', *Political Studies*, 53(2): 262–83.

issue (and unwittingly, too). Utterances repeated, reinforced and enhanced by senior politicians and public officials, including Trevor Phillips, as the last CRE chair, bizarrely predicted 'blood on the streets' if matters did not change in relation to Muslim women. This served only to fuel existing and rampant Islamophobia in society, real or perceived. Licence is given to reactionary point-scoring political figures vying for the middle ground, arguing that Muslim practices encourage separate lives, destroy multi-culturalism, breed intolerance and potentially create 'suicide bombers'. There is no sense of how the state continues its assault on the basic liberties enjoyed by all or how it has made a mockery of notions of freedom and democracy (particularly in relation to Afghanistan and Iraq). The state conveys a 'fear psychosis' pertaining to the 'War on Terror', absolving itself from its historical involvement in the problems in the first instance and then, when an opportunity arises, pins it on the 'inward-looking' lives that Muslims seemingly live at home (see Chapter 8).

The problems in Britain have been created by the complete lack of appreciation of the needs of Muslim minority communities in inner cities experiencing deepening economic marginalisation and widening social inequality. Public attention is focused away from structure and towards culture, enforcing a debate in relation to 'Britishness': an attempt to transfer from cultural pluralism (or multiculturalism) towards monoculturalism or (cultural imperialism). Meanwhile, mosques are attacked, Muslim graves are desecrated, *niqab*-clad women are assaulted in public spaces and Muslims feel ever-beleaguered and harassed by the state, media and by society in general. The other facet of this debate is the focus on women: that is, somehow Muslim women are prevented from exercising the freedoms enjoyed by all other women per se. The argument falls when the evidence on Western female emancipation suggests that there is still a need for greater equality of opportunity and equality of outcome, although there have been significant gains in the last two decades. Muslim women argue the uniformity that wearing the *niqab* provides is a source of freedom and empowerment before Allah. In many respects, the *niqab* is a 'symbol of separateness' to most communities in the West, Muslim and non-Muslim. For others, it is clear Muslim women are taking matters into their own hands as a direct response to their own and wider Islamic identity struggles in the diaspora. Many politicians will support the idea that the *niqab* leads to 'segregated communities', 'parallel lives' or 'voluntary apartheid', but what voters will forget is the extent of exclusion and alienation that many Muslim minorities already experience. By appropriating certain religiously inspired garb is a reaction to an ongoing onslaught for some while for others it is an expression of defiance in the light of current hostile discourses. At the same time, this discussion is necessary as within Islam there is tremendous debate on what this means for integration into non-Muslim societies over time, and how the veil is reignited as a sensitive political issue, particularly in places such as France, with its assertions that differences in the public sphere are regarded as intolerable,[67] and even Turkey, which seeks to modernise and secularise as part of efforts to enter the EU.

The charge of media bias needs to be taken seriously as the extent of coverage of 'extremist Muslims' and 'Islamic terrorism' has dramatically increased in recent periods and especially since the events of 9/11 and 7/7. The language used to describe Muslims is often violent, thereby inferring that Islam is also violent. Arabic words have been appropriated into universal journalistic vocabulary and invested with new meaning, which is generally exaggerated and aggressive. 'Jihad', for example, has been used to signify a military war waged by Islamists against the West. The deeper Arabic meaning of the term is, in fact, far broader and refers more to the idea of a 'struggle' (where the struggle against the 'false ego' – *nafs* – is the highest of all jihads). Words such as 'fundamentalist', 'extremist' and 'radical' are regularly used in apocalyptic headlines across all sectors of the British press. In the post-9/11 era, politicians have used the fears people have of Islam for their own ends. By focusing on the 'War on Terror' the existing anti-Muslim frame of reference is replaced with the idea of 'terror'. The reporting is compounded by a concentration on the 'enemy within' or the loyalty of Muslims to Britain. The examples of *The Satanic Verses* affair of 1989, the Danish cartoons of September 2005 and February 2006 and the Jack Straw veil comments of October 2006 all confirm the importance of the media and how it relates to the experiences of contemporary Orientalism and Islamophobia, as well as the important relationship between the media and politics.[68]

67 Bowen, J.R. (2007) *Why the French Don't Like Headscarves: Islam, the State and the Public Space*, Princeton, NJ: Princeton University Press.
68 Afshar, H. (2008) 'Can I See Your Hair? Choice, Agency and Attitudes: The Dilemma of Faith and Feminism for Muslim Women Who Cover', *Ethnic and Racial Studies*, 31(2): 411–27.

6 The political philosophy of multiculturalism and the 'modern Muslim'

The ideas of unity within diversity *and* diversity within unity are broadly typified by the notion of multiculturalism – where ethnic minority and majority groups maintain a set of cultural and social norms and values but, crucially, commit to their roles and responsibilities as citizens of the state. In recent periods, many have argued that developments in British ethnic and cultural relations have seen a return to assimilationist thinking, with observable shifts in policy in relation to ethnic and religious minorities.[1] To explore this issue further, political and philosophical debates that impact on Muslim individuals and groups in society are explored from a socio-historical perspective. It is argued that economic, political and social forces restrict Muslims in structurally disadvantaged positions, providing the context for the current debate, but there is also an interest in the ways in which individual and group norms relate to a wider rationalisation of how 'Britishness' can be considered and developed, locally, nationally and globally. The future of multiculturalism, nevertheless, remains uncertain in England, throughout Britain and elsewhere in Western Europe. The reason for this stems from widening socio-economic divisions coupled with issues in the management of culturally plural societies in an atmosphere of global uncertainty and conflict between people on the basis of their faith, culture and identity, perceived or actual. There are also issues of how it is rationalised and operationalised in local, national and international contexts and the nature of inter-relationships between these different spheres of influence.

Utilising a synthesis of primary research findings in the areas of education, entrepreneurship, media, race equality and identity politics in relation to British South Asian Muslims,[2] it is important to explore the historical and political origins of multiculturalism, which includes a critique of liberal

---

1 Modood, T. and F. Ahmad (2007) 'British Muslim Perspectives on Multiculturalism', *Theory Culture Society*, 24(2): 187–213.
2 Abbas, T. (2001) 'Media Capital and the Representation of South Asian Muslims in the British Press: An Ideological Analysis', *Journal of Muslim Minority Affairs*, 21(2): 245–57; Abbas, T. (2004b) *The Education of British South Asians: Ethnicity, Capital and Class*

and communitarian philosophical debates. This discussion provides a closer examination of the British multiculturalism case, taking into consideration the transition from Empire to post-colonial society, and the historical move from assimilationism to anti-racist legislation. In particular, the recent case of New Labour (1997–2010), and the ways in which it developed its pre- and post-9/11 and 7/7 policies and practices in relation to British ethnic minorities (more specifically, Muslims) is examined. The aim is to provide a wider analysis of ('the rise and fall of') multiculturalism and what it suggests for British Muslim ethno-religious identities and the nature of the lived experience. It is carried out in the context of an ever-evolving political framing of the importance of civil society, local governance, international security and the ever-increasing impact of globalisation.

In its present form, the idea of a return to assimilationism is a viable representation of the situation. It is an inherently unstable one, however, as it requires considerable reconceptualisation in order to satisfy the demands placed upon advanced liberal democracies because of their diverse ethnic, religious and cultural minorities. In the British case, government reaction and the general approach to the 'multicultural question' is fraught with counter-competing tensions, conflating a paradigm of paternalism with the importance of group rights; of liberalising markets while socio-economic inequalities persist; and of celebrating multiculturality at the same time as stigmatising and essentialising the 'other'.[3] Questions of modernity, post-modernity and Islam, and whether or not Muslims can live comfortably and peacefully in a non-Muslim state, based on a developing macro-multiculturalist paradigm, need to be fully explored.

Gordon Betts argues that given the more established theories in the sociology of 'race' and ethnicity of the 1970s and 1980s, there is a view that the experience of late post-modernity helps to produce multiple forms of racism and 'new political subjects' that are not simply observable at the level of 'victims' and 'oppressors'. It reflects part of the reason for the theoretical shift beyond the black–white model of racism (the 'colour paradigm') and towards one in which cultural and religious identities emerge at the forefront. In addition, there are a host of factors related to the apparent decline of British sovereignty, national identity and culture as well as the neglect of

(*Continued*)

Structure, Basingstoke: Palgrave-Macmillan; Abbas, T. (2004c) 'After 9/11: British South Asian Muslims, Islamophobia, Multiculturalism and the State', *American Journal of Islamic Social Sciences*, 21(3): 26–8; Abbas, T. and M. Anwar (2005) 'An Analysis of Race Equality Policy and Practice in the City of Birmingham, UK', *Local Government Studies*, 31(1): 53–68; Ram, M., T. Abbas, T. Jones, and B. Sanghera (2002) 'Ethnic Enterprise in Its Urban Context: South Asian Restaurants in Birmingham', *International Journal of Urban and Regional Research*, 26(1): 26–40.

3 Hall, S. (2000) 'Conclusion: The Multi-cultural Question', in B. Hesse (ed.), *Un/settled Multiculturalisms*, London and New York: Zed, pp. 209–41.

certain histories and traditions, combined with the demoralisation of institutions and public services, that are important to appreciate. With rising political and economic instability across the globe, concerns about the impact of these significant developments have grown at home. The end of Communism in Eastern Europe, the emergence of independence movements throughout the world, and ongoing ethnic and social struggles have given rise to flows of economic migrants, asylum seekers and refugees to Britain and to other parts of Western Europe. These developments have evolved into a wide-ranging and interdisciplinary debate in which the conditions of 'nationalism, [multi]culturalism and [cultural] toleration' are juxtaposed, while there is a case made for the maintenance of 'British cultural hegemony and sovereignty by defending against immigration, multiculturalism, devolution, Europeanisation and its enlargement, together with global cosmopolitanism'.[4] The 're-emergence of global ethno-national conflicts and nationalism are seen as confirmation of the continuing need for a national identity as well as an appeal to nationhood, kinship, patriotism and loyalty to a culturally homogeneous nation-state'.[5]

With the arrival of African-Caribbean and South Asian economic migrants from the late 1940s through to the 1970s, the assumption of various governments was that through the provision of English-language support in schools, ethnic minorities would learn 'to become like us'. That is, they would be 'assimilated'.[6] The assimilationist model, however, was based upon an inadequate understanding of the social psychology of group identity and, in particular, the resilience of ethnic identities when the minority community is marginalised and faces hostility. If a minority community begins to adopt the cultural practices of the dominant ethnic community but is still rejected by majority society, assimilation is hardly a viable political or cultural option. It is not unsurprising that xenophobia and racism present themselves in majority individuals, groups, institutions and structures, in the process reinforcing the need for some minority communities to retain their unique ethnic and cultural norms and values, including those deemed to be outside the accepted dominant multicultural citizenship framework.

Historically, assimilation began, in part, as a policy to reassure indigenous white Britons that the arrival of immigrants would not mean loss of the social, cultural and political identity of the nation or the importance of maintaining the status quo. England, along with Scotland, Wales and Northern Ireland, however, have developed into culturally heterogeneous nations, constantly in a state of flux as a result of population movements

4 Betts, G. (2001) *The Twilight of Britain: Cultural Nationalism, Multiculturalism and the Politics of Toleration*, London: Transaction, p. xvii.
5 Ibid.
6 Grosvenor, I. (1997) *Assimilating Identities: Racism and Educational Policy in Post 1945 Britain*, London: Lawrence & Wishart.

that are combinations of ethno-religious tensions and globalisation. In particular, in the older towns and cities of England, different regional communities now have to the manage the needs and aspirations of diverse immigrant populations as well as the more established existing ethnic-minority communities. In identifying lessons from elsewhere, there are limitations in trying to make direct comparisons between the British, Canadian or Australian cases. The latter have had to come to terms with the history of how they have treated indigenous peoples, but they are unaffected by the complex ethnic and cultural relations of the post-colonial experience found in Britain. There are different starting points for different nation-states as they attempt to manage their diverse populations.

In the late 1960s, Enoch Powell, a member of the shadow cabinet of Edward Heath until 1968, made a number of problematic statements in which, it is argued, he used the language of racism to fuel the hate of ethnic minorities and to whip up anti-immigration frenzy. This period in history is well documented, but suffice to say that the era, which was accompanied by radical social, political and cultural change in many Western liberal democracies, is an important one in defining multicultural societies and the nature of individual and collective identities.[7] Powell was anti-immigration but he also advocated the common concern of the un-assimilability of ethnic-minorities.[8] To Powell, 'immigrants' (as well as those already relatively settled at the time) represented a threat – a body of people alien and antithetical to the interests of dominant society; that is, individuals and groups who lacked the inherent cultural qualities or the desire to 'integrate' with white British 'indigenous society'. The attitudes and prejudices of existing ethnic minority and majority groups are often determined by the forces of racism, discrimination and prejudice. Groups act within their relative positions in the hierarchies of power and influence, all of which exist through various efforts to legitimise a sense of self-aggrandisement that is based on the inherent unequal nature of inter-ethnic social relations.

Responding in part to the failure of assimilation, multiculturalism in Britain emerged as an approach that gave space for the recognition of ethnic diversity. Notions of multiculturalism provided the framework within which ethnic diversity could be recognised by policy-makers and respect for different cultures encouraged between individuals. Thus, through multiculturalism, the identities and needs of ethnic minority communities are shaped, but in a political process where difference is the perceived problem. In the early 1970s, issues in the 'management of diverse societies' led to the development of a 'race relations problematic' – that is, questions of how to manage the experience and treatment of ethnic minorities in theory, policy

---

7 Fryer, P. (1984) *Staying Power: Black People in Britain since 1504*, London: Pluto; Solomos, J. (2003) *Race and Racism in Britain*, Basingstoke: Palgrave-Macmillan.
8 Smithies, B. and P. Fiddick (1969) *Enoch Powell on Immigration*, London: Sphere.

and action. It was the 1970s that marked the emergence of multiculturalism as a dedicated policy approach, at first in Canada and Australia and then in Britain and Germany.[9] What appeared then can still be seen today in that multiculturalism is best conceptualised not as a well defined philosophical approach with a general theory but, rather, as a perspective on or a way in which to view the social world – that is, it is a 'philosophical tool'.[10] The idea of multiculturalism is merely four decades old, in its post-war post-modern conceptualisation and application. For Bhikhu Parekh it has three central tenets. First, human beings are 'culturally embedded'; that is, 'they exist in a culturally structured world and organise their social relations in a culturally derived system of meaning and significance'.[11] Second, 'different cultures represent different systems of meaning and visions of the good life'.[12] Thus, ways of life are likely to be enriched if there is access to others, but, in reality, a culturally self-contained life is virtually impossible for most people in the modern world. Third, 'every culture is internally plural and reflects a continuing conversation between different traditions and strands of thought'.[13] This does not suggest every culture is removed of internal coherence or unique identity, but that they are fluid and open. In effect, multicultural societies are new to the current global age and they give rise to 'theoretical and political problems that have no parallel in history [...] There is a need [...] to find ways of reconciling the legitimate demands of unity and diversity, of achieving political unity without cultural uniformity, being inclusive without being assimilationist, cultivating among their citizens a common sense of belonging while respecting their legitimate cultural differences.'[14]

In the late 1970s and into the mid-1980s, multiculturalism was critiqued by certain ethnic minority communities who deeply resented its implied paternalism. At the beginning of the 1980s, anti-racist strategies emerged as an alternative to multiculturalism. This model recognised the conflicts of interest within multi-ethnic Britain, and of the importance of addressing systematic processes of inequality within British institutions. It developed its insights from the concept of institutional racism which informed the Race Relations Act 1976 and exposed the idea that perfectly ordinary (nice!) people can be involved in generating discriminatory outcomes through their everyday professional practices. In responding to inequalities

---

9 Parekh, B. (2006) *Rethinking Multiculturalism: Cultural Diversity and Political Theory*, Basingstoke: Palgrave-Macmillan.
10 Parekh, B. (2004) 'The Future of Multiculturalism', inaugural address at the launch of the Centre for Research on Nationalism, Ethnicity and Multiculturalism, University of Surrey, 9 June.
11 Parekh, B. (2006), op. cit., p. 336.
12 Ibid.
13 Ibid, p. 337.
14 Ibid, p. 343.

and discrimination within a multi-ethnic society, anti-racism was a direct challenge to dominant white Britons who felt comfortable with Britain's 'tolerant credentials'. It provoked considerable debate in political and governmental circles. It also, however, attracted a range of critiques from many on the left and from ethnic minority communities who found it strong on rhetoric but weak on delivery.[15]

There are important qualifications, nevertheless, with such an idealised view of the 'good multicultural society'. The arguments contained in the ideas of Parekh reflect a left-leaning desire to improve equality. It coheres with other left-multiculturalists such as Will Kymlicka and Iris Marion Young rather than the liberal egalitarianism of John Rawls or Brian Barry.[16] More specifically, for the left-multiculturalists, there is an inherent aspiration to eliminate inequality and to remain removed from the 'cultural turn', which is driven by a wish to extend the notion of egalitarianism beyond the confines of liberal accounts of equality of opportunity. Differences between Barry and Young are a function of how each defines and utilises the concept of egalitarianism, with Barry providing the liberal point of view. The arguments put forward by Young refer to the notion of equality of opportunity as well as outcome. For Barry, outcomes matter less than the idea of the opportunity in the first instance.[17] Nevertheless, Parekh suggests that it is perfectly fine to argue that egalitarian liberalism requires that every citizen should enjoy access to the basic conditions of the 'good life', but nowhere in the Western world do people have equal levels of access to these basic rights.[18] Inequalities persist and remain deeply embedded in many instances. Parekh is also of the view that minority demands carry a limit. There is a general willingness on the part of Muslim minorities to form an active part of modern democracies (even though experiences of democracy are limited in the Muslim world), but, for Parekh, Muslims are required to make greater efforts to adapt to majority society. There is a perspective that supports the notion of integration through social interaction and economic exchange. The concern is that the picture painted here is one where Muslims are required to make greater efforts and to work harder to make stronger claims on citizenship rights, because with rights there are certain obligations, and it has been argued by Parekh that Muslims in Britain have made insufficient efforts to meet these responsibilities.[19]

15 Sarup, M. (1991) *Education and the Ideologies of Racism*, Stoke-on-Trent: Trentham.
16 Kelly, P. (2003) 'Identity, Equality and Power: Tensions in Parekh's Theory of Multiculturalism', in B. Haddock and P. Sutch (eds), *Multiculturalism, Identity and Rights*, London: Routledge, pp. 94–110.
17 Kelly, P. (2002) 'Defending Some Dodos: Equality and/or Liberty', in P. Kelly (ed.), *Multiculturalism Reconsidered*, Cambridge: Polity, p. 62.
18 Parekh, B. (2002) 'Barry and the Dangers of Liberalism', in P. Kelly (ed.), *Multiculturalism Reconsidered*, Cambridge: Polity, pp. 133–50.
19 Parekh, B. (2003) 'Muslims in Britain', *Prospect*, 88, July.

There appears to be no limit to the demands being made by Muslims in Britain, made all the more questionable given their apparent lack of reciprocity through engaging with certain civic responsibilities and in relation to certain obligations to the state. Ultimately, much of new left multiculturalism is entrenched within the paradigm of benign egalitarianism, devoid of crucial attempts to eradicate inequalities in society through redistributive means that ultimately remove economic, social and political barriers erected through differences in power, ethnicity and culture. Multiculturalists who adopt this language of political philosophy have tended to ignore the structural and cultural inequalities embedded in society and promote a cosmopolitanism that caters to the needs and aspirations of already established ethnic minority individuals and groups. Here, this multicultural political philosophy receives criticisms from both the left and the right.[20]

Immediately after a dramatic return to power in 1997, New Labour was keen to embrace the multicultural and ethnically diverse nature of the people of Britain. In its first term, 1997–2001, New Labour dropped the 'primary purpose' clause in immigration rules which prevented UK citizens from marrying a spouse from overseas if the main purpose was to settle in Britain. Les Back et al. have suggested that this was to undermine the 'arranged marriage' system. For others, it opened the way for exploitation of the system.[21] In 1999, the number of admissions of wives, husbands and fiancé(e)s from all countries rose to 30,000 compared to 21,000 in 1996, an increase of almost 50 per cent.[22]

The Human Rights Act 1998, the Macpherson Report (1999) and the Race Relations (Amendment) Act 2000 were all important events and developments in multicultural relations; however, matters began to look unsteady with the publication of the Runnymede Trust Commission report, *The Future of Multi-ethnic Britain* – also known as the 'Parekh Report' – in 2000. The then Home Secretary, Jack Straw, publicly disassociated himself from the findings of the Commission when media focus switched to a particular paragraph problematising the idea of 'Britishness'. Some liberal quarters regarded this as multiculturalism 'gone mad'. There was a strong media backlash against the publication of the report and some of the highly

20 Barry, B. (2002) 'Second Thoughts: Some First Thoughts Revisited', in P. Kelly (ed.), *Multiculturalism Reconsidered*, Cambridge: Polity, pp. 204–38; Kymlicka, W. (2002) *Contemporary Political Philosophy: An Introduction*, Oxford: Oxford University Press, pp. 204–38.

21 Back, L., M. Keith, A. Khan, K. Shukra and J. Solomos (2002a) 'New Labour's White Heart: Politics, Multiculturalism and the Return of Assimilation', *Political Quarterly*, 73(4): 445–54.

22 Migration Watch UK (2004) *Immigration and Marriage: The Problem of Continuous Migration*, Briefing Paper 10.8, Guildford: MWUK, p. 7.

respected members who made up the Commission. Furthermore, in 2001, a number of local and international events had a tremendous impact on British Muslims in particular. The civil unrest in the northern cities during the late summer of 2001 shifted the focus away from a celebration of multi-cultural diversity towards an idea of a 'communities lacking cohesion'.[23] The then Home Secretary, David Blunkett, indicated the changing terms of public debate through his controversial comments on the need for 'immigrants to learn English' as a test of citizenship. The language was a reminder for many of the debates in this area in the 1960s, 1970s and 1980s when the assimilationist rhetoric emerged at times of apparent national crises and important turning points in the history and development of British 'race relations'.[24]

Labour electoral strength is in part a function of ethnic minority strongholds, where loyalty to the Labour Party has historically drawn upon the power of community networks that have defended against the mono-culturalist forces of assimilation. It is now apparent that all three main political parties use ethnic minority candidates who reflect the ethnic base of localities they in part seek to represent, taking comfort in the knowledge that certain South Asian Muslim community elders wield power in encouraging their 'clans people' to vote along certain party political lines when asked to do so. In the 2004 local and European elections, a crucial test for New Labour after the debacle of the Iraq war, worrying concerns emerged in relation to how this system of voting was being exploited, particularly with the use of postal votes in certain areas where ethnic minority groups are concentrated. Questions over citizenship and participation have appeared less relevant to Labour MPs when such bloc votes are mobilised in electoral politics. With increasing instances of international political unrest, asylum-seekers and refugees taking front position in relation to local and national media attention, and the growing terrorist fears since 9/11, a new policy agenda emerged, that of 'community cohesion'.[25] The young Muslim men of Burnley, Bradford and Oldham who took to the streets in the summer of 2001 had grievances which had nothing to do with 'assimilation'. At worst, these developments reinforced existing models of patronage and assimilation policy that left the core issues of discrimination and disadvantage intact. On the politics of 'race', ethnicity and racism, Les Back et al., writing in 2002, a year before the invasion of Iraq, argued, 'the Blair government is a political construction rife with incommensurable

---

23 Bagguley, P. and Y. Hussain (2006) 'Conflict and Cohesion: Official Constructions of "Community" around the 2001 Riots in Britain', *Critical Studies*, 28: 347–65.

24 Schuster, L. and J. Solomos (2001) 'Asylum, Refuge and Public Policy: Current Trends and Future Dilemmas', *Sociological Research Online*, 6(1).

25 Home Office (2002) *Community Cohesion: A Report of the Independent Review Team*, chaired by Ted Cantle, London: Home Office.

commitments and aspirations […] it cannot mourn its imperial ghosts, nor embrace a democratic and truly multicultural future'.[26]

According to Ron Geaves, in attempting to appreciate 'the diversity and the tenuousness, multifarious and situational nature of diaspora identities, both South Asian and Muslim, it is also necessary to acknowledge that citizenship is not straightforward'.[27] To many white Britons, 'participation in citizenship is a non-problematic given, a set of clothing that fits like a glove, put on at birth, taken off at death, viewed uncritically and unchallenged'.[28] British Muslims are required to become citizens, not merely from a legal or political perspective, with a stress on democracy, secularism, individual rights and pluralism, but also to negotiate it in terms of an Islamic legal framework, which is vast, diverse and complex. Muslims have had to determine how to be Muslim in a secular society and to develop the appropriate strategies for living as a minority in a non-Muslim society. It has been essential to reconcile faith-based identity and citizenship, individual rights and community rights in a hostile environment, but without retreating into isolationism. Perhaps, above all, Muslims have had to learn to participate in a society which has no need for Islam in its public life. In addition, as once colonised people of the subcontinent, Muslims have inherited the colonial history of their past relations with Britain. This, when combined with racism, which is seemingly endemic in the new home, creates an environment of suspicion in which many white Britons regard Muslim citizens outside the realm of their own communities, and under a scrutiny that oversimplifies and essentialises, in the process reinforcing reductive views of the 'other'.[29]

For Bhikhu Parekh, to effectively manage a diverse society is a formidable theoretical and political task, and no nation has so far succeeded in achieving it. Affluent, stable and politically mature democracies such as Britain, France and Germany have experienced limited success, with all of these nations showing signs of fervent moral and emotional awkwardness in the face of increasing Muslim minority demands for recognition and equality.[30] In reality, however, empirical research continues to provide evidence of racism, discrimination and general disadvantage and hostility experienced by new and existing ethnic minority groups and, in particular, Muslims, right across the Western European Muslim diaspora.[31] It suggests that economic and social inequalities continue to reveal themselves in relation to the

26 Back, L., M. Keith, A. Khan, K. Shukra and J. Solomos (2002b) 'The Return of Assimilationism: Race, Multiculturalism and New Labour', *Sociological Research Online*, 7(2).
27 Geaves, R. (2005) 'Negotiating British Citizenship and Muslim Identity', in T. Abbas (ed.), *Muslim Britain: Communities under Pressure*, London and New York: Zed, pp. 66–7.
28 Ibid.
29 Ibid.
30 Parekh, B. (2006), op. cit.
31 Open Society Institute (2009) *Muslims in Europe: A Report on 11 EU Cities*, Hungary: OSI.

polarising social and ethnic stratification of Britain, but in the present climate the focus is less on colour and more on religion as the major division in society. Liz Fekete affirms that after the events of 9/11 in the USA, policies of assimilationism have come to dominate in Western Europe, 'which include the recasting of citizenship laws according to security considerations'.[32] It is apparent that throughout Western Europe, existing 'race relations' policies are being steered away from multiculturalism and towards monoculturalism. In Britain, the idea of 'community cohesion' exemplifies this instance. In all the EU member states, including the UK, there is an implicit working belief that *all* Muslims are somehow responsible for the reactionary cultural practices of the few in society (an acute form of Orientalism and Islamophobia). The debate is centred on the idea of an 'us' and 'them' (while playing on the notion of the *ummah*). Progressive Muslim voices from within the community are notably silenced by media and the state apparatus but mobilised by government departments to help project a positive view of Islam in Britain. Fekete argues that when the 'security state' demands 'cultural homogenisation and forces assimilation [...] it spells the death of multiculturalism'.[33] In recent expositions of a multicultural European identity, others have come to the conclusion that to be European is to be a Christian Enlightened liberal who abides by Roman law, where the emphasis is upon a return to a narrower multiculturally exclusive Western European identity.[34]

Will Kymlicka maintains that there are three axes that help to expedite the positions found in various secular Western liberal social-democratic multicultural societies in the current period. If 'illegals' are seen to be advantaged by state apparatus, public reaction is likely to be hostile (moralistic objection). Second, if the particular cultural practices that immigrant groups bring with them are seen as illiberal, then groups will experience opposition (cultural objection). And, third, if immigrant groups are seen to be 'sponging off' the welfare state, the indigenous population, particularly the majority working and middle classes, will regard it as a deliberate misappropriation of their investments (material objection).[35] Veit Bader argues that post-modern liberal nation-states face a series of trade-offs which are important in any attempt to reconcile the dilemmas of immigrant and

---

32 Fekete, L. (2004) 'Anti-Muslim Racism and the European Security State', *Race and Class*, 46(1): 3–29, p. 4.

33 Ibid., p. 21.

34 Amin, A. (2004) 'Multi-Ethnicity and the Idea of Europe', *Theory Culture and Society*, 21(2): 1–24; Marranci, G. (2004) 'Multiculturalism, Islam and the Clash of Civilisations Theory: Rethinking Islamophobia', *Culture and Religion*, 5(1): 105–17.

35 Kymlicka, W. (2004) 'Multiculturalism: Finding or Losing Our Way?' Panel discussant at the Multicultural Futures conference. Convened by Monash University, Australian Multicultural Foundation and the Metropolis Project, Canada, held at Monash University Centre, Prato, Italy, 22–3 September.

minority settlement, adaptation and incorporation.[36] In relation to the British case, there are two areas of concern. First, where the policy of cultural integration is strongly assimilatory there is a moral dilemma as well as the potential for resistance, with incessant stereotyping and stigmatising of immigrant and minority populations who are thought to be unwilling to adapt. Conversely, if the policy is pluralist, there is every chance of it being seen as an obstacle to 'integration' or a threat to 'our common culture'. Second, if the policies in relation to the 'political or public culture' are accommodationist, stressing a political character, then ethnocentric or nationalist reactions are enforced. If, however, they are 'ethno-nationalist and assimilationist they create "fundamentalisms" on both sides'.[37]

Western European governments since the 1960s have shaped policy and practice in relation to ethnic-minority groups based on various strategies of anti-immigration and anti-discrimination legislation, on the one hand, with a programme of assimilation, integration and latterly multiculturalism on the other. What permeates policy and practice each time is the underlying assumption concerning the inevitable assimilability of immigrant and ethnic-minority groups. In relation to British Muslims, this has not occurred to the extent envisaged, partly as a function of racist hostility impacting on individual and group potential to positively integrate into dominant economy and society, but also because of a lack of appreciation of the extent to which ethnic-minority communities have come to rely on specific group class and ethnic resources to mobilise what little economic and social development they can achieve (see Chapter 4). In effect, Muslims have often had little choice but to retreat into their communities. Even before the events of 9/11, questions in relation to 'loyalty' to a cultural–national identity were being asked of British Muslims. The Rushdie affair placed the concerns of British South Asian Muslims firmly on the political landscape, with the 1990s dominated by issues of civic engagement, blasphemy laws, multicultural philosophy, the nature and orientation of certain religio-cultural norms and values, as well socio-economic exclusion and marginalisation.[38]

The broad multicultural citizenship thesis which consists of a rationalisation of the modern world and the interdependencies of different individuals and groups in Western societies, where identities are shaped by the ways in which the nation is articulated, is interesting and relevant to the British case but with the added factor of devolution. Britain consists of three countries, each with its own rich historical and cultural base. It is England and the

---

36 Bader (2004), Panel discussant at the Multicultural Future conference, ibid.
37 Ibid.
38 Modood, T. (1998) 'Anti-essentialism, Multiculturalism and the "Recognition" of Religious Groups', *Journal of Political Philosophy*, 6(4): 378–99; Werbner, P. (2000) 'Divided Loyalties, Empowered Citizenship? Muslims in Britain', *Citizenship Studies*, 4(3): 307–24.

idea of 'Englishness' that suffers in relation to this reconfiguration, whereas the Scots and the Welsh have far more resolute cultural and social national identities, particularly in opposition to this very same evolving 'Englishness'.[39] Undeniably, some of the problems faced by English multiculturalism are precisely linked to the ways in which England sees itself and its position in the world, and at a time of rapid geopolitical change and with the ongoing developments to media and telecommunications industries. England is also where most of the British Muslims live and work, and, in particular, where minority rights are an important aspect of this new English state, but the role, status and conditions of various ethnic minorities are less appreciated. Rather, what is required is the acknowledgement of differences between individuals and groups at the level not only of heritage, language and culture but also, more significantly, religion. Notwithstanding, it is apparent that Islam has little place within this development in liberal societies and, as such, Muslims remain outside of the broad conceptualisation of 'the good multicultural society'. It is important not only to develop a clearer understanding of the ways in which Muslims are culturally, socially, politically and economically ostracised from society but also to consider the nature and orientation of the ways in which modern nations construct themselves in opposition to these 'othered' groups in society. In particular, the British (or rather English) case is especially unique at this juncture in Western European history.

Tariq Modood, an established political philosopher on multiculturalism, has argued that South Asian Muslims suffer from racism not only in the form of direct and indirect colour discrimination but also a cultural racism; 'a certain culture is attributed to them, is vilified, and is even the ground for discrimination'.[40] In effect, the racism experienced by South Asian Muslims is one that 'lies deep in their culture'.[41] In any attempt to determine this assertion empirically there is a sticking point. Measuring cultural racism is problematic, particularly when utilising positivist attempts to gauge the racial disadvantage of South Asians, whom, taken as a whole, are almost always variously marginalised in education, housing, health and employment. What is quite apparent, and as the fourth PSI survey results very much confirm, is that many South Asians are actually quite successful – on average, all Indian groups compared with all Bangladeshis and Pakistanis; however there is a distinct Muslim–non-Muslim divide (although not exclusively, see Chapter 4). These differences became apparent only during the 1990s after the fourth PSI survey and detailed analysis of the 1991 Census.

39 Hussain, A.M. and W.L. Miller (2006) *Multicultural Nationalism: Islamophobia, Anglophobia, and Devolution*, Oxford: Oxford University Press.

40 Modood, T. (2005) *Multicultural Politics: Racism, Ethnicity and Muslims in Britain*, Edinburgh: Edinburgh University Press, p. 7.

41 Ibid.

Throughout the 1970s and 1980s, detailed South Asian differences were simply not discernible from official data. In the current climate, what is quite apparent is that South Asians suffer because of concerns around cultural assimilation and it seems that these distinctions have located Muslims within particular social boundaries determined by dominant society. Cultural racism is a form of neo-Orientalism, and, because of this, Modood was ahead of time in his analysis of the British Muslim experience in the 1980s to early 1990s.

As much as the various equality movements are culpable for marginalising Muslims, central government policy and practice have only fuelled these distinctions. Modood argues that 'if Muslims and other minorities are to be welcomed as a constituent community of Britain, they will need [...] protection against defamation'.[42] How this impacts on an application of multiculturalism is seen when it is argued that 'for the plural state, the challenge of the new multiculturalism is the integration of transplanted cultures, heritages, and peoples into long-established yet ongoing historic national ones [...] [F]or the plural state, then, multiculturalism means re-forming national identity and citizenship'.[43] The discussion of British Muslims since the 'War on Terror' 'is arguably the biggest question facing public policy, and questions around equality incorporating unity and diversity in Britain right now'.[44] Modood provides the solution in terms of a plural 'Britishness' that incorporates the range of religious and cultural minorities as part of the body-politic. It is an encouraging social democratic manifesto that celebrates differences but does not overlook structural inequalities. The Race and Religious Hatred Act 2006 goes only some way towards protecting Muslims, as envisaged by Modood. A significant improvement on the current position, it remains untested in relation to the extent of its true powers. Applying to England and Wales only, the Act seeks to prevent 'acts intended to stir up hatred'. The Criminal Justice and Immigration Act 2008, however, abolished blasphemy and blasphemous libel within its remit.[45]

It is clear that one of the most important factors to appreciate is that Muslims are not one undifferentiated mass. The differences between groups impact on any attempts to analyse the affect of policy and practice in multicultural societies. Since 1997, there have been improvements in certain areas: for example, there are more inclusive dress codes in the Army; the police, health and education sectors are working more sensitively; and greater efforts have been made and successes gained by some religious and

---

42 Ibid., p. 123.
43 Ibid., pp. 140–1.
44 Ibid.
45 Weller, P. (2009) *A Mirror for our Times: 'The Rushdie Affair' and the Future of Multi-culturalism*, London: Continuum.

political Muslim lobby and civil society groups. Islamophobia remains a genuine cause for concern, however.[46] State systems can marginalise Muslims: for example, as noted, under existing anti-racist legislation, ethnically defined Jews and Sikhs are protected against discrimination but Muslims are not (as the religion of Islam incorporates people of diverse ethnicities). More integrated Muslims are often described as 'progressive', 'moderate' or 'liberal' whereas 'less integrated' Muslims are seen as 'fundamentalist', 'reactionary' or as 'outsiders within'.[47] In reality, the experience of most African-Caribbean and South Asian people in Britain is of racism, discrimination and geographical and occupational segregation that persist despite the acknowledgement of a multicultural society and the enactment of binding anti-racist legislation.

Multiculturalism therefore should not be seen to be a 'problem' that impacts on just ethnic-minority groups but, indeed, all groups in society, majority and minority. The notion of linking social justice and community harmony to citizenship and multiculturalism ought to be the end goals for all. The reciprocity of the nation-state is balanced through the maintenance of certain rights, responsibilities and obligations by individuals and groups in society. There are at least three ways in which multiculturalism can move forward effectively. First, any attempt to develop multiculturalism requires the elimination of structural and cultural inequalities that keep 'black' people at the bottom of societies and 'white' people at the top (and, increasingly, a Muslim and non-Muslim division), and in an age where religion increasingly distinguishes differences beyond that of 'race', ethnicity or gender. Second, there is a need to move away from an emphasis upon difference to one of 'sameness'.[48] There is great importance in shifting away from a focus on individual and group identities to issues of power and knowledge.[49] Third, it is important to develop ideas of 'Britishness' or 'Englishness' outside of the accepted norms and values that define being English as being entirely white and Anglo-Saxon. Multiculturalism can refer to shared citizenship based on an allegiance to common values which are universal in nature and where ethnic belonging does not impact on perceived allegiance or loyalty. Finally, there is a need to eliminate discrimination (both racial and religious) which is not just attitudinal but systemic, eradicating poverty and disadvantage which are compounded by cultural and structural racisms.

46   Anwar, M. and Q. Bahksh (2003) *British Muslims and State Policies*, Coventry: Centre for Research in Ethnic Relations University of Warwick; Richardson, R. (2004) (ed.) *Islamophobia: Issues, Challenges and Action: A Report by the Commission on British Muslims and Islamophobia*, Stoke-on-Trent: Trentham.
47   Safi, O. (2003) (ed.) *Progressive Muslims: On Justice, Gender and Pluralism*, Oxford: Oneworld.
48   See Skeggs, B. (2004) *Class, Self, Culture*, London: Routledge.
49   Day, R.J.F. (2004) 'Dialogue and Difference: On the Limits of Liberal Multiculturalism', *Canadian Diversity/Diversité Canadienne* 3(2): 36–8.

To genuinely advance the debates around multiculturalism, there is a need for different ethnic and religious groups, majority and minority, to appreciate its inherent value and the importance it carries for civil society. In the present climate, it is the experiences of British Muslims that are important to consider as they are at the centre of debates in relation to multicultural citizenship. What is clear is that much of multiculturalism is about the political climate of the time. How successful or otherwise the British experience of multiculturalism remains will be revealed through how it deals with the current predicaments facing British Muslims. Apart from immediate post-9/11 and post-7/7 threats to international law and order, Islam and British Muslims have been part of the 'gaze' of the 'other'. Until the Rushdie affair of 1989 they were viewed as relatively peaceful and law-abiding communities (perhaps inward-looking and politically passive, too).[50] The geopolitical dimension of the interaction between Islam and the West is also part of the experience of relations between Muslims and non-Muslims, however. British Muslims are negotiating a set of ethno-religious transnational identities and socio-economic realities that are ever-changing in various globalised economic, cultural, social and political contexts, and how matters in relation to identity, civil society and citizenship develop in the near future is important.

As the first New Labour term (1997–2001) placed diversity near the top of the domestic political agenda, with it significantly strengthening existing anti-discrimination legislation, the second and third New Labour administrations (2001–10) to some extent focused on the integration, adaptation and citizenship of British Muslims, but in the context of anti-terrorism and de- and counter-radicalisation. Many in government policy-making circles might suggest that part of the 'problem' of British Muslims is their unwillingness to relinquish their religio-cultural beliefs and practices which are regarded by some as especially antithetical to the ways and functioning of Western European thought and social behaviour (i.e. relating to 'forced marriages', 'female genital mutilation' and 'honour killings',[51] as well as wider attitudes and behaviours in relation to majority society, namely that the 'War on Terror' is a 'war on Islam'). It is the 'lack of Muslim assimilation' that is questioned and compounded by questions of 'loyalty'. It is, however, not an issue for the vast majority of British Muslims. What is being asked is relevant to a tiny majority but has been applied to many more and framed around issues of citizenship, loyalty, identity and responsibility, while civil liberties are limited and state policing powers increase in the aftermath of the events of 7/7 (see Chapter 8). Efforts to develop a national citizenship framework have emphasised the importance of integration

---

50 Werbner, P. (2004b) personal communication, 15 July.
51 Idriss, M.M. and T. Abbas (2010) (eds) *Honour, Violence, Women and Islam*, London and New York: Routledge-Cavendish.

through active civic engagement and participation, developing positive links with 'other' communities and groups, and the preservation of a British identity whilst maintaining 'communities that need to be more cohesive'. At the same time, elements of the British far right target Muslims as the new 'enemy other'. As the shift towards the right among Western European nation-states intensifies in the light of ongoing acts of violence towards settled Muslims in places such as Germany and Denmark, often carried out by indigenous fascist and ultra-nationalist groups, Muslims will continue to believe they are being wholly victimised. Where a significant majority of Muslims in the West wish to continue to work to abide by the laws of the land as well as they can without it affecting who they are as 'good Muslims', some, mostly young Muslim men and women, will continue to be impacted by forces that exploit vulnerable people as part of their own ideologically motivated political projects. Opportunities, coupled with recognition and acceptance from majority society, are required, but greater confidence and belief is also needed on the part of Muslim minorities. Although important, and a necessary aspect to appreciate, conflicting and conflated identities, both minority and majority, do not emerge in a vacuum.[52]

Internal to the Muslim community, there are important struggles taking place that are not always recognised in clear terms. They are broad-based attempts to develop an *ummah* which is an effective force for good and to challenge different ethnic and cultural traditions that are seen as nostalgic. Majority society is sometimes sympathetic to the needs, aspirations and expectations of its minorities, but some sectors feel that Muslims are receiving too much of the 'cake'; extreme elements of majority society such as the British National Party certainly believe this.[53] Muslims want acceptance of their religion, which is beginning, but also opportunities, which are essentially equality issues that are submerged under the weight of the current anti-Muslim rhetoric. The Muslim population that arrived in the 1950s and 1960s has suffered immensely in the intervening period, and, so, Muslims today are seemingly reacting to their oppression in similar ways to the 1960s civil rights and 'Black Power' movements of the USA. In the present climate, the current Muslim experience could be described as an attempt to exercise 'Muslim Power'.[54] What some of the negative government rhetoric and media representation does is to dismiss genuine attempts

52 Kahani-Hopkins, V. and N. Hopkins (2002) '"Representing" British Muslims: The Strategic Dimension to Identity Construction', *Ethnic and Racial Studies*, 25(2): 288–309.

53 Reeves, F. and E. Seward (2006) *From BUF to BNP*, Birmingham: Race Equality West Midlands.

54 Modood, T. (2004b) 'The Muslims in Britain: An Emerging Community', paper presented to conference 'Muslims in Britain: The Making of a New Underclass?' One-day workshop organised by the Centre for the Study of Democracy, University of Westminster with the Leverhulme Programme on Migration and Citizenship at Bristol University and University College London, 18 November.

made by Muslims to modernise, advance and integrate successfully, however incomplete these experiences have been.

For certain, 'modernity' is a contested and controversial concept. Here, the description of 'modern' is to adapt to contemporary society and its features, with self-progress operating within this environment. It involves the organisation of nation-states and commercialised economies, technological and scientific developments and the cultural and social changes that accompany such phenomena.[55] For older Muslims, collective memories of modernity in the post-war period start with Muslim populations being geographically defined and administered into states by colonial powers, subsequently overthrown, only to be ruled by resented military elites or 'democratic' states that commonly undertake regimes of 'de-Islamisation' while also working with sectors of society who wish to 're-Islamise'. The establishment of nation-states therefore implies the disestablishment of Islam. Elites adopt Western styles of living while the lives of the masses remain disrupted. It is these connotations of modernity that still linger in the memories of Muslims, particularly from the Middle East.

Adopting the concepts of 'good' and 'evil' in a world split into the domains of *Dar al-Islam* and *Dar al-harb* has fuelled anti-Western attitudes for some Muslims who see current characteristics of Western 'modernity' falling into the 'godless' category.[56] Sentiments of anger against the West have manifested themselves as oppositions to symbols of 'modernity', for example, in the antagonisms towards Western symbols significant to the democratic process. In principal, Islamic law is intrinsically progressive in its nature (but in practice it is often problematic), and such claims in the name of Islam could thus be regarded as stemming from a particular resistance to Western authority which is political, economic and cultural in character.

Charles Kurzman affirms how the West has long viewed Islam as primitive. The Islamic faith has been equated with fanaticism, Islamic political authority with despotism, Islamic military practices with terror, and Islamic tradition with backwardness.[57] An ICM poll published in February 2006 suggested that 40 per cent of British Muslims would support the introduction of Shariah in parts of Britain; this was reported in the *Telegraph* newspaper as strictly antithetical to modern society.[58] Cultural and

55 Lapidus, I.M. (1997) 'Islamic Revival and Modernity: The Contemporary Movements and the Historical Paradigms', *Journal of the Economic and Social History of the Orient*, 40(4): 444–60.
56 Macey, M. (2002) 'Interpreting Islam: Young Muslim Men's Involvement in Criminal Activity in Bradford', in B. Spalek (ed.), *Islam, Crime and Criminal Justice*, Uffculme: Willan, pp. 19–49.
57 Kurzman, C. (1998) 'Liberal Islam and Its Islamic Context', in C. Kurzman (ed.), *Liberal Islam: A Sourcebook*, Oxford: Oxford University Press, pp. 3–28.
58 Hennessy, P. and M. Kite (2006) 'Poll Reveals 40pc of Muslims Want Sharia Law in UK', *The Telegraph*, 19 February.

media-driven perceptions reinforce the view that suggests Muslims belong to a 'backward' and 'static' faith whose followers are a burden on the rest of civilised society. Philosophies of Islam are regarded by many as regressive and antagonistic to modern norms and values. Yet, from the very beginning, the development of Islam is indeed regarded by Muslim scholars as a feat of tremendous modernisation. The sixth century of the Christian era is generally accepted as the darkest phase in the history of Western humanity. Social disruption and economic chaos increased in Europe as great civilisations decomposed, with the rest of the world only beginning to learn the rudiments of modern civilised existence. New teachings brought people out of a primitive state of ignorance and gave unprecedented rights to women and enslaved people (from, arguably, a deeply inadequate starting point). For Muslim scholars, the Qur'ān encourages these new rights, including individual human rights, rights of liberty, rights of equality, ownership rights, legal rights, political rights and prisoner rights – as well as stipulation for 'just' cases for and 'just' action during conflicts.[59]

It is essential to appreciate the contribution Muslims made in Spain which appeared to show Europe the light and the historical dawn of what became the Enlightenment. European revival is indebted to Islamic thought and scientific contribution, and Islamic civilisation has had profound influences on Western literary and philosophical traditions, thus playing a part in moulding many Western national and cultural identities (see Chapter 1).[60] In contemporary British society, a small but growing number of Muslims are at the forefront of their fields, whether in science, literature, sport or arts, contributing to many different parts of modern contemporary culture. In Western Europe, social exclusion, 'segregation' and racism, however, also play a clear role.[61] In addition, Western media tends to represent Muslims in a negative light by focusing on and sensationalising problems as resulting from religion, rather than portraying Muslims as ordinary people. In Hollywood, only Arabs are used to represent Islam, and they are generally depicted as symbols of primitivism.[62] Moreover, all 'Arabs are Muslims and all Muslims are Arabs' is the dominant view projected. These Muslims are characterised as brutal and uncivilised religious fanatics who terrorise civilised Westerners; 'not only are they terrorists, but they are inept terrorists'.[63]

59 Hofmann, M. (1997) *Islam: The Alternative*, Beltsville: Amana Publications, pp. 195–6, 234–8.
60 Ramadan, T. (2005) *Western Muslims and the Future of Islam*, Oxford: Oxford University Press.
61 Spalek, B. (2002) 'Conclusion: Religious Diversity and Criminal Justice Policy', in B. Spalek (ed.), *Islam, Crime and Criminal Justice*, Uffculme: Willan, pp. 133–40.
62 Shaheen, J. (2003) '"Reel Bad Arabs": How Hollywood Vilifies a People', *The Annals of the American Academy of Political and Social Science*, 588(1): 171–93.
63 Shaheen, J. (1980) 'The Arab Stereotype on Television', *Americans for Middle East Understanding*, 13(2): 1–16.

Present-day Western European discourses have often overlooked the influence and importance of Islamic contributions to humanity. Dominant ethnicities and cultures in Muslim populations tend to get transposed onto 'Islam', with their destructive characteristics essentially tied to perceptions of Muslims in general. That is, the conceptualisations of the British Muslim population are predominantly of South Asian origin. Similarly, in France, the visible predicament of the North African population approximates 'Muslim' with 'Algerian'. Issues of identity play a role in the vision of an 'us versus them' acting in a multiplicity of directions between Muslims and non-Muslims, both domestically and globally, thus hampering collective development. It is an argument of one of the most popular scholars of Islam in the West, Tariq Ramadan, in his civil-society thesis of positive Muslim action and behaviour in Western European minority contexts.[64] An attempt is made to reconcile Islam and modernity through the concept of 'grafting', which tries to integrate two unconnected worlds into a coherent body of knowledge and experience. Whether traditional discourses are grafted onto a 'new' modern base or 'new' discourses are grafted onto an older content, there are contradictory forces that still exist, and which result in distortion and a 'mutilated outlook'.[65] Tariq Ramadan believes in a progressive enlightened pro-active confident engaged 'Muslimness' in Europe, urging Muslims to emerge from their 'ghetto-mentality'. While this is an amiable message, the analysis does not take into consideration the extent of racism and disadvantage at the heart of the problem, and the issues of entrenched discrimination in a deeply divided society. It also suggests that Muslims have equal agency to determine equal outcomes. The reality is far from this, yet.[66]

Scholars calling for a change in the attitudes of Muslims have taken on varying approaches, but they all point to a need to leave behind current static beliefs and sentiments, which are thought to contribute to the current condition of the Muslims. There have been calls for a return to 'pure' Islamic ideals, where their negligence is regarded as the reason for Muslim suffering. In regard to humanity and scope for flexibility and reason, many ideals are suitable for all time and can return Muslims to their 'modern past' in the contemporary environment, ultimately removing the need for Muslims to pursue a purely Western path for modernity. Renowned scholars such as Ibrahim Mogra from Leicester, a leading Deobandi figure, and Musharraf Hussain from Nottingham, a leading exponent of Sufi Barewli traditions, as well Zakir Abdul Karim Naik from Mumbai and Hamza Yusuf Hanson, a 'revert' from California, have all played an important role

64 Ramadan (2005), op cit.
65 Shayegan, D. (1997) *Cultural Schizophrenia: Islamic Societies Confronting the West*, New York: Syracuse University Press, pp. 76–7.
66 Ramadan, T. (2009) *What I Believe*, Oxford: Oxford University Press.

in encouraging Muslims in Britain to look to the past within an open mind and heart rather than to become apologists for Islam or to regard it as wholly outmoded and dysfunctional, as is the dominant paradigm in the post-9/11 context. Other thinkers concentrate on the notion of modernity for a more 'liberal' and progressive standpoint on Islam, which is argued to be reasonably compatible with Western ideals. Scholars here have called for Muslims, especially those in the West, to allow their identities to be permeated by Western norms while simultaneously returning to a more 'progressive' understanding of 'true Islam'. The renowned British Muslim scholar and social commentator Ziauddin Sardar and former South Asian anthropologist, Akbar Ahmed, fall into this second camp. In relation to white-English 'reverts', no one has more clout or a greater following that Timothy J. Winter, also known as Abdul Hakim Murad, and for whom the successes of a future 'British Islam' are indeed rooted in the religion.[67]

Clearly, differences can be seen in the paths of advancement advocated by these approaches in current Muslim-majority societies and in Muslim-minority instances. They exist across a spectrum, attempting to strike the perfect balance between historical inspiration, contemporary adaptation and the context of how liberal democratic secular nations such as Britain imagines and acts in relation to its ethnic, religious and Muslim minorities. What will bring Muslims and nation-state together is the sharing of a common goal and the advancement of the state and Muslims towards a particular form of modernisation. Across the range, it can be argued, from radical Islamists to Islamic liberals, there is a common normative modernist foundation. While such movements can be seen as reactions to conditions of colonial and post-colonial societies, they are, importantly, products of this very modernity. Each movement sees in its aspirations the epitome of the 'modern'. There is a general acceptance of the adequacy and validity of Islam for modern life, but it is the definition of what constitutes a workable Islam and how to get to this truth that will remain a matter of ongoing discussion.[68] This 'true Islam' is not debated, but it is *ijtihad* (individual reasoning) that emphasises the need to go back to the original and definitive sources of Islam. The importance of positive Islamic history is also applied in other ways, whether to extract inspiration from or to build upon cumulative experiences and lessons from history.[69] The mechanism varies, from the strengthening of the Islamic identities of individuals and groups to outright rejection of Western ideals – the

67 Esposito, J.L. (2010) *The Future of Islam*, New York: Oxford University Press, p. 116.
68 Haddad, Y.Y. (1982) *Contemporary Islam and the Challenge of History*, New York: State University of New York Press.
69 Zaidi, A.H. (2006) 'Muslim Reconstructions of Knowledge and the Re-enchantment of Modernity', *Theory Culture Society*, 23(5): 69–91.

permeation of a Muslim identity in the West to complete adaptation to the prevailing environment.[70]

It is important to realise the extent of inequity in the distribution of power, knowledge and resources. Muslim minorities have suffered because of the impact of imperialism, colonialism, decolonisation, immigration and settlement in the West for 300 years. Much of what happens at present is a function of history, but it is also based on how modern societies confront (or not) the challenges of unity within diversity *and* diversity within unity in an era of rapid globalisation. The problem operates not only at the global macro-level in terms of the 'War on Terror' and its aftermath, but also at the local micro-level in terms of 'community cohesion'. Debates in relation to the rise and fall of multiculturalism have been elaborated upon from the point of view of the role of the nation-state and its citizenry. It is also necessary to explore the ways in which Muslim minorities embrace the idea of living and working in a multicultural society such as Britain and whether there are any specific issues relating to the religion of Islam that need to be further explored. The topic of Islam and modernity opens up a number of questions. Are Muslims required to be 'modern' by their faith and, if so, what constitutes this 'modernity'? How have Muslims been perceived as 'modern' in past societies and in contemporary societies? If Muslims lack 'modernity', what can be done to inspire their progress? In attempting to answer some of these very broad questions, it is argued that Muslims can achieve progress and adapt to contemporary society and that both 'traditionalist' and 'adaptive' approaches have a great deal to offer.

Muslims in society are often perceived as pre-modern, but this is not a true representation of Islam; rather, a conglomeration of negative cultural and structural factors and forces faced by Muslim communities, and which are further problematised by social and economic constraints. The extent to which Muslims have been bystanders to modernity is heavily exaggerated, particularly in Western media discourses. Reactions to the Western European project of modernity and post-modernity do not imply that Islam rejects progress. Islam provides the tools for progress and adaptation, arguably towards both Western approaches to modernity and alternative Eastern paths. 'Modernisation' is a viable aspiration for Muslims through a combination of looking proudly into the past but also looking towards a brighter future for all.

The role of multiculturalism in operationalising reactive and proactive identity politics, but also the potential for violent political radicalism, needs to be analysed further.

---

70 Sajoo, A.B. (2008) (ed.) *Muslim Modernities: Expressions of the Civil Imagination*, London and New York: I.B. Tauris.

7 Islamism through the lens of local and global political identities

Having analysed the wider theological, historical and political concerns in relation to radicalism in the Islamic world and the demographic, economic and (multi-)cultural presence of Islam and Muslims in Britain, it is necessary to elaborate on how radicalism came to the UK. In Britain, many who have been found to be involved in Islamic political radical activities in recent periods have been South Asian Muslim, but not all – a number have been African, and also Caribbeans who subsequently converted, sometimes in prisons.[1] Somali groups in Britain, now forming communities in identifiable neighbourhoods and localities, invariably concentrated in existing Muslim minority economic and social enclaves, also experience disadvantage and exclusion. They encounter a particular form of marginalisation that affects them in three distinct ways. First, English society continues to express strong dislike towards 'foreigners': here, xenophobia remains an important issue in white English groups as well in more established ethnic minority communities. Second, direct racism and discrimination are experienced because of visible skin colour. And, third, this group experiences hostility towards Islam in the same way as other Muslims in Britain. As the trial of the Somalis associated with the 21/7 failed attacks in London demonstrated, this body of people can also become embroiled in the act of preparing and engaging in terrorism.[2] The experience of Islamic political radicalism in Britain is compounded by ethnicity, migration, social class and gender.

For many, alienation and disenfranchisement are significant starting points, but a few of the so-called 'radical-jihadi' leaders have emerged from communities that are not necessarily poor – with some who are graduates

---

1 Spalek, B. and S. El-Hassan (2007) 'Muslim Converts in Prison', *Howard Journal of Criminal Justice*, 46(2): 99–114; Beckford, J.A., D. Joly and F. Khosrokhavar (2005) *Muslims in Prison: Challenge and Change in Britain and France*, Basingstoke: Palgrave-Macmillan.
2 Campbell, D. (2007) '21/7 Bomb Plotters Sentenced to Life as Judge Says They Were Under Control of Al-Qaida', *The Guardian*, 12 July.

and middle class, for example. However, it is important to acknowledge that most have all been born or have grown up in circumstances that have caused them to ultimately seek violent solutions to problems. These individuals and groups have experienced prejudice, racism and discrimination throughout their early lives, and sustained themselves in education in spite of its limitations in relation to Muslims or ethnic minorities in general. By hoping to find the 'truth', they are potentially misdirected by a radicalising Islamism that seeks to convince apparently once-decadent young Muslims, those yearning for a more literal interpretation of the religion, or young people without a firm identity foundation of their own, that the solution is in violent action. By giving the young a sense of belonging, an identity or an association with a struggle that transcends their everyday boundaries and barriers, theologically, metaphysically and spiritually, radical Islamism has moved with a perverse message of individual and group salvation.[3]

The international politics of George W. Bush in the USA and Tony Blair, when Prime Minister of Britain, arguably helped to further radicalise Muslims at home; however, this has always been officially denied.[4] There has remained strong resistance to a independent inquiry into the bombings in public until recently, largely because it might suggest that security, intelligence or security services were culpable,[5] or, indeed, that apart from the four 7/7 bombers, others independently organised themselves, preparing and planning their attacks using information collected from the Internet, now that Al-Qaeda had become a franchise through the role played by global communication technologies.[6] At home, with this radicalisation seen to be a product of the interaction of grievances with ideology, a sharp political divide emerges between those who focus on one at the expense of the other.

Since 9/11, in much of the Western world, changes to international finance, anti-terrorism legislation and debates around identity cards, citizenship rights and obligations have all seen various nation-states tightening their grip on Muslim minorities. The 'War on Terror' revealed itself to be an ideological construction that has helped to maintain the status quo, while Muslims continue to be derided, misrepresented, incarcerated without charge and, in general, made to feel and think they are unwelcome. There has been a perceptible shift towards regarding Muslims as the 'enemy within', as an undifferentiated mass of 'Arab terrorists', as groups who are overly demanding of their religious and cultural rights or as people

3 Malik, A.A. (2006) (ed.) *The State We Are In: Identity, Terror and the Law of Jihad*, Bristol: Amal Press.
4 Ali, T. (2005) *Rough Music: Blair, Bombs, Baghdad, London, Terror*, London: Verso.
5 Ahmed, N.M. (2006) *The London Bombings: An Independent Inquiry*, London: Gerald Duckworth.
6 Townsend, M. (2006) 'Leak Reveals Official Story of London Bombings', *The Observer*, 9 April; Sageman, M. (2008) *Leaderless Jihad: Terror Networks in the Twenty-first Century*, Philadelphia: University of Pennsylvania Press.

unwilling to integrate into majority society. Muslims are looking inside themselves and society is gazing at the British Muslim community at large to determine what might be at fault internally. At the same time, externally, the foreign policies of dominant neo-liberal capitalist nations create havoc in distant lands, historically and in the post-9/11 period.[7]

It is clear that in any analysis of the drivers of Islamic political radicalism there are local, national and international issues at play, which are often working in different combinations and permutations. In particular, there is a focus on the ways in which British Muslims identify themselves and how this has been impacted on by recent local and global events. How these very same forces are turning some towards Islamic political radicalism and others towards making greater efforts towards secularisation, particularly in the post-7/7 climate, is also important to understand. A perennial ideological dichotomy has been exacerbated by the 'clash of civilisation' thesis. It is important to critically explore its historical and contemporary sources of influence, and how since the end of the Cold War and more recent events such as 9/11 and 7/7 have led to sectarianism on the part of some young Muslim Britons, analysing the nature of their seemingly increasing 'radicalisation'. There is a further need to critically explore existing ideas in relation to the problematising of Muslim minority identities and how these debates unfold in the context of an ever-evolving ethno-national multicultural citizenship framework.

In the post-2001 climate, Muslims in Britain have been at the centre of considerable political, media and academic focus. The notion of a radical political Islamism has been at the heart of these discourses. It is defined by debates in relation to identity, multiculturalism and exclusion, as well as security and policing. There has been considerable attention given to the 'threat of terrorism', and the focus has been on the meaning and application of 'jihad', those who undertake 'martyrdom missions' and the role and influence of Islamism in the West. Generally, media coverage and the responses by the state have been disproportionate and, in the process, have forged the amalgamation of a range of 'Islamist' movements, radical, reformist and modernist. Over the years, British Muslims have attained significant media and political interest – the Honeyford Affair in the mid-1980s; the issue of faith schools; headscarves, first in 1989 with the Alevi sisters in Cheshire and then again in 2006 when Jack Straw made his comments; the Rushdie affair of 1989 and the Cartoons affair of 2006; both Gulf wars and the northern disturbances of 2001 – but matters were dramatically transformed, post-9/11 and post-7/7. Philip Lewis affirms that the difference between the Salman Rushdie affair and events post-9/11 and post-7/7 is that, currently, articulate and educated representatives of the South Asian Muslim

---

7 Dreyfuss, R. (2005) *Devil's Game: How the United States Helped Unleash Fundamentalist Islam*, New York: Metropolitan.

diaspora and Muslim communities in general are becoming better organised, but issues of identity are still at the heart of many of the problems,
perceived or actual.[8] Importantly, Lewis supports the view that New Labour
attempted to enforce a variation of assimilation after the general election of
2001, and this momentum was given new impetus following the 'urban disturbances' in the northern towns in the summer of 2001.[9]

Meanwhile, Islamist movements in Britain have generated a great deal of
mass-media attention. The exposure has laid bare the twin terrors of Islamophobia and social exclusion that Muslims encounter daily, which is both
exploited and utilised by Islamist groups as recruiting opportunities.[10] Post
9/11, majority societies in Western Europe and the West in general are
appreciating how best to meet the challenges raised by both their immigrant
and indigenous Muslims.[11] The Muslim presence in Western Europe has
placed multiculturalism, integration, citizenship and national identity, and
their relationships to cultural identity and political allegiances, at the forefront of sociological and political inquiry. Sociologically, the fundamental
questions remain: 'How is Western Europe accommodating its Muslim
citizens?', 'Can Muslims live as Muslims in a non-Muslim state?', 'Does
multiculturalism work?' and 'What is the future direction of social policy and
political strategy?'[12] It is true that Muslims have lived in Europe for centuries
and that they have often been demonised throughout; certainly, the relationship between Islam and the West has been one not only of dialogue but also of
conflict (see Chapters 1 and 2).[13] But the fact that the majority of European
Muslims are born as the children of the diaspora and are permanent and active
citizens participating in liberal democracies remains of particular importance.

These are more challenging questions given the role played by mass-
communication technologies. It is possible for Muslims to live in the West

8 Lewis, P. (2002) *Islamic Britain*, London: I.B. Tauris, pp. 211–12.
9 Lewis, P. (2007) *Young, British and Muslim*, London: Continuum.
10 Al-Sayyed, N. and M. Castells (2002) *Muslim Europe or Euro-Islam: Politics, Culture and
   Citizenship in the Age of Globalization*, Lanham, MD: Lexington; Goody, J. (2004) *Capitalism and Modernity*, Cambridge: Polity; Salvatore, A. (2004) 'Making Public Space:
   Opportunities and Limits of Collective Action Among Muslims in Europe', *Journal of
   Ethnic and Migration Studies*, 30(5): 1013–31.
11 Ramadan, T. (2005) *Western Muslims and the Future of Islam*, Oxford: Oxford University
   Press; Maussen, M. (2007) *The Governance of Islam in Western Europe: A State of the Art
   Report*, Amsterdam: International Migration, Integration and Social Cohesion in Europe
   working paper 16.
12 Modood, T. (2005) *Multicultural Politics: Racism, Ethnicity and Muslims in Britain*,
   Edinburgh: Edinburgh University Press; Modood, T. (2007) *Multiculturalism: A Civic Idea*,
   Cambridge: Polity; Pauly, R.J. (2004) *Islam in Europe: Integration or Marginalization?*
   Aldershot: Ashgate; Tibi, B. (2001) *Islam between Culture and Politics*, Basingstoke:
   Palgrave-Macmillan.
13 Lewis, B. (2003) *The Crisis of Islam: Holy War and Unholy Terror*, London: Weidenfeld &
   Nicolson.

but also to maintain strong spiritual, ideological and political associations with the *ummah*. The media is critical in how it represents Muslims as the 'other' (after Edward Said) and 'folk devils' (after Stanley Cohen) that negatively inform public perceptions of the 'Muslim' (see Chapter 5). The fact that Muslims wish to remain in Western Europe and develop their religious and cultural identities is evident in how some of the most capable developments to Islamic literature emerges from Muslims living in the West making proficient use of Western intellectual institutions and political discourses (such as Tariq Ramadan, Nasr Abu Zayd, Fethullah Gülen, Muhammad AS Abdel Haleem or Muhammad Tahir ul-Qadri).

One of the ironies of Islamism is how similar its analysis and rhetoric is to Marxism on the one hand and the 'right's discourse' on the other, which began with the Enlightenment. For the Islamists, Islamism is a 'new' totalising ideology, as well as a self-sufficient social system based on a grand narrative. For Muslims in Western Europe, Islamism offers a complete solution, as well as a sense of belonging to a 'community of believers'. It is not to say that Islamism does not offer an alternative scenario, quite clearly it does – a social system based on the Shariah, however understood – but the three most respected academics of Western European Islamism, François Burgat, Giles Kepel and Olivier Roy, all make the case that Islamism has essentially failed in the Middle East.[14] It did not attract the support of Muslim majorities because of its use of 'violent jihad' and terror, and Islamists do not offer a credible alternative system of governance. Yet, all three still contend that Islamism continues to have an influence on a minority of Muslim youth born and living in the West.

It is within the context of media coverage of Islamism and jihad, and the policy responses that emerge, and given the material and social realities of Muslims in Britain, that it is possible to delineate an expression of masculinity and a 'coolness' associated with rebelliousness and anti-authoritarianism. The essential question is whether media 'moral panics', the creation of 'folk devils', the simultaneous conceptualisation of draconian anti-terror laws, the decline of civil liberties and a constant focus on a 'new age of terror', which remains undefined in some senses and over-developed in others, have led to the development of this 'jihadi cool' generation and directly contributed to the appeal of Islamism?[15] Mounting Islamophobia

14 Burgat, F. (1999) *Face to Face with Political Islam*, London: I.B. Tauris; Choueiri, Y.M. (1997) *Islamic Fundamentalism*, London: Continuum; Kepel, G. (2005) *The Roots of Radical Islam*, London: Saqi; Roy, O. (2004) *Globalised Islam: The Search for a New Ummah*, London: Hurst.

15 Furedi, F. (2007) *Invitation to Terror: The Expanding Empire of the Unknown*, London: Continuum; Abbas, T. and P. Sanghera (2005) 'British South Asian Muslims and Radicalisation of the Youth: Masculinity, Multiculturalism and "Jihadi Cool"', paper presented to British Association for South Asian Studies Annual Conference, 30 March–1 April, University of Leeds.

and progressively oppressive state policies are compounded by socio-economic exclusion and cultural isolation,[16] which are exacerbated by acute inter-generational differences.[17] All of these factors must be taken into account in order to fully appreciate the nature of what it means to be a 'radical' Muslim in Britain.

As explored in Chapter 2, the roots of contemporary Islamism lie in the eighteenth and nineteenth centuries in the Middle East and South Asia, often emerging in reaction to the debilitating experiences of Western imperialism and colonialism, the decline of religious authority in the aftermath of the First World War and the break-up of the Ottoman Empire.[18] It also exists in response to Arab nationalism and socialism after the Second World War, and the exiles produced in opposition to the 'Westernisation' of the Middle East.[19] The analysis of the decline of Islam and predictions in relation to its revivalism have been at the centre of debate for some contemporary Islamic scholars in the West. Without doubt, throughout the history of Islam, the ideas of revival and renewal are well established. With expansion of the post-war Muslim diaspora, these roots have now spread throughout Western Europe and North America, where 'progressive' Muslims thrive in advanced secular societies that, in spite of the challenges of equality and diversity, preserve religious and intellectual freedoms as a fundamental human right.

There is considerable discussion in relation to the defining principles, organisations and aims of Islamism as much as there is about its origins and trajectories. Gilles Kepel provides a persuasive argument on the rise and fall of Islamism as a political ideology culminating in the 'world changing events' of 9/11 and Olivier Roy speaks of a post-Islamism and the 'neo-fundamentalists'. This latter Islamism remains a significant force in both the Middle East and in the West. First-wave Islamism was a response to colonialism and imperialism. Second-wave Islamism was a reaction to the aftermath of the First World War and the end of the caliphate. Third-wave Islamism takes form and shape in a post-war climate in the Middle East and in the West, and has since developed further. Second-wave Islamism was influenced extensively by the ideas and thoughts of Qutb and Maududi, who drew on the convictions of jurist Ibn Taymiyyah (see Chapter 2). Third-wave Islamism is also inspired by Qutb and Maududi, but is dissimilar because of

16 Fekete, L. (2004) 'Anti-Muslim Racism and the European Security State', *Race and Class*, 46(1): 3–29.
17 Ijaz, I. and T. Abbas (2010) 'The Impact of Inter-generational Change on the Attitudes of Working-class South Asian Muslim Parents on the Education of Their Daughters', *Gender and Education*, 22(3): 313–326.
18 Cemal, K. (2007) *Turkey: Islam and Laicism Between the Interests of State, Politics, and Society*, Frankfurt: Peace Research Institute Frankfurt report 78.
19 Sayyid, B.S. (2003) *A Fundamental Fear: Eurocentrism and the Emergence of Islamism*, London and New York: Zed; Esposito, J.L. (1999) *The Islamic Threat: Myth or Reality?* New York: Oxford University Press.

the forces of globalisation eroding the powers of individual states and with new media technologies disseminating ideas at high speeds. This Islamism is essentially an 'anti-Western', 'anti-colonial' and 'anti-imperialist' ideology, which is a mutation of essentialist characteristics developed since the time of Hassan al-Banna and the formation of the Muslim Brotherhood. The significance of this anti-Western perspective is how it has come to influence a minority of young British Muslim men who are seemingly rejecting Western values and forging an Islamist world view.

The historical experience of inter-civilisational dialogue and exchange between Islam and the West is generally ignored by many Islamists.[20] Islamism offers an essentialist world-view of Islam and it represents a seeking-out of a pure and perfect Islam removed of specific cultural and ethnic characteristics. These Islamists are engaged in a purification process based upon the abandonment of any cultural characteristics. Living in Western Europe, Islamists have the ideal opportunity and know-how to exploit how the experience of diaspora ignites the search for roots in an environment in which it flourishes, as people live in 'placeless cultures'[21] and in a 'deterritorialised age'.[22] It is why Islamism is selective in its interpretation of the Qur'ān, Sunnah and Hadith.[23] In many ways, it is not dissimilar to Orientalism, but it is in different clothing: it condemns and misrepresents the West as amoral or immoral (*jahiliyah*), while promoting it as a monolithic hegemonic structure. To Islamists, the emergence of this new existence in the post-Enlightenment West, now in an era of de-industrialisation, cultural pluralism and relativism, is reviled. It is considered incompatible with being a 'true Muslim'. For the Islamists, the re-establishment of a caliphate is a necessity, and specific social and political activism is required to achieve this aim. To accomplish these objectives, certain Islamists seek to re-establish the Islam of the period of the 'Rightly Guided Caliphs' which is based on the forty years or so following Muhammad (*al-Salaf al-Salih*). These Islamists do not offer a credible alternative to the dominant political economy of global capitalism, however. The institutionalisation of a caliphate is essential for Islamists to replace the sovereignty of people with a Shariah-defined state and, thus, 'in accordance with the commands of Allah'. There are, nevertheless, prominent Muslim intellectuals in Western Europe who believe it is possible to live in the West as perfectly good Muslims and loyal citizens of the state (see Chapter 6).[24]

20 Esposito (1999), op. cit., p. 208.
21 AlSayyad and Castells (2002), op. cit., p. 4.
22 Roy (2004), op. cit., p. 2.
23 Euben, R.L. (1999) *Enemy in the Mirror: Islamic Fundamentalism and the Limits of Modern Rationalism: A Work of Comparative Political Theory*, Princeton, NJ: Princeton University Press.
24 Sardar, Z. (20054 *Desperately Seeking Paradise: Journeys of a Sceptical Musli*, London: Granta.

It is the debate of our times, and it rages within the Muslim diaspora living in the West, as well as between the 'host societies' and their diaspora and ethnic minority populations. While there is considerable variation in practice among Islamists there is a range of characteristics that can be identified. Islamists claim that religion is political. They seek to undo the separation between the private and public, and find Western ideas of secularism and personal freedom 'wholly un-Islamic'. Islamists also seek to disassociate themselves from Western epistemology and morality but, interestingly, not scientific and technological developments (in fact, Muslims, past and present, have never been averse to technology). Islamists believe that the generation of a theoretical and conceptual world-view must only draw upon Islamic sources for intellectual and spiritual development, and that this must always exist in a limited notion of *tahwid* (the oneness of Allah). Islamists in Western Europe seek to revive the notion of the *ummah* through campaigning and *dawa* (the call to Islam). The nature and means of establishing a caliphate and proselytising the idea of the *ummah* have focused upon the understanding and application of jihad. While Islamism itself is not a violent movement, it is within this diaspora space that a separatist violent Islamism is taking place in Britain.[25]

A range of terms has been used to prefix Islam and Islamism in the literature, but there is no consensus. In the context of Islamism in Britain, 'radical' is appropriate in that it is counter-cultural and politically active in promulgating an ideological alternative to neo-liberal global capitalism and secular neo-liberal democracy. Within the localised masculine urban spaces of 'turf' and 'our territory', British Islamism nurtures a particular separatist cultural identity and it can thrive in residentially clustered communities where social exclusion and deprivation remain relatively unchallenged by policy.[26] Separatist Islamism as developed here has a dual but related meaning. It indicates first the 'spatial' separateness of Muslim communities and, second, the political goal of Islamism to separate itself socially and culturally from the conditions of modernity and post-modernity and its moral, cultural, religious and intellectual relativism. Separatist Islamism is thus an evolving and changing social phenomenon as well as a reactive social condition. Pre-9/11, Jessica Jacobson identified an 'assertive Muslim identity' that is counter-cultural because it seeks to separate itself from what it regards as the moral decadence of the West.[27] This perspective has strengthened more recently, with Philip Lewis and Tariq Modood showing

25 Brah, A. (1996) *Cartographies of Diaspora: Contesting Identities*, London and New York: Routledge.
26 Amin, A. (2003) 'Unruly Strangers? The 2001 Urban Riots in Britain', *International Journal of Urban and Regional Research*, 27(2): 460–3; Alexander, C. (2000) *The Asian Gang: Ethnicity, Identity, Masculinity*, Oxford: Berg.
27 Jacobson, J. (1998) *Islam in Transition: Religion and Identity Among British Pakistani Youth*, London: Routledge, p. 33.

that cultural-identity claims are now central, particularly in light of the politics of recognition and the politics of difference associated with multi-culturalism.[28]

It is clear that a minority of young British Muslim men are embracing a 'jihadi' self-identification, which is the outcome of a protest-identity subculture that exists within an Islamist counter-culture. It is also a masculine identity.[29] There is much debate as to what exactly jihad means or presupposes but in its simplest form it essentially translates as the 'exertion' or 'struggle' for a goal in the path of Allah. And as Allah grants humans free will in Islam, the form jihad should take varies greatly in practice. Differences in jihad between the Meccan phase of early Islam and the later Qur'ānic verses in Medina (following the *hijra*, the 'flight') suggests its meaning remains open to interpretation; however, Islamic jurists in the tenth and eleventh centuries played a critical role in how jihad is understood today, particularly Ibn Taymiyyah.[30] But the Qur'ān is forever open to human interpretation; Islam is not a monolithic structure; and all Muslims are not the same. Muslim religiosity, belief and the practice of Islam varies in time and space, especially in the global arena. It is within this global context that it is possible to frame a discussion on jihad that examines the complex, contradictory and often troubled relations between the roles Islamism plays in the cultural identities formed by some young Muslim men and the policies and practices of multiculturalism in which they are enacted. As explored in Chapter 6, multiculturalism is a social condition, a visible political and public policy, and an academic discourse. As a discourse and a social condition, multiculturalism is undergoing a paradigm shift in the light of dramatic social and cultural change. Some argue that the political and policy forms of multiculturalism have ceased to work because multiculturalism has failed to 'integrate' its Muslim diaspora in Britain, even though it has afforded religious identity politics centre stage and allowed communitarian politics to flourish. In the multicultural era following the 'liberal hour' of 'race relations', and the strong public statements by Home Secretary Roy Jenkins in 1966, both the politics of difference and the politics of recognition have shaped an important political period in British social and political history. It is within this context that it has been possible for an Islamic political radical identity as well as Islamist counter-cultural social movement to emerge, develop and potentially prosper.

28 Lewis, P. (2007), op. cit.; Modood (2007), op. cit.
29 Ahmed, A.S. (2003) *Islam Under Siege: Living Dangerously in a Post-Honor World*, Cambridge: Polity; Sanghera, G. and S. Thapar-Bjorkert (2007) '"Because I am Pakistani … and I am Muslim … I am Political": Gendering Political Radicalism – Young Masculinities and Femininities in Bradford', in T. Abbas (ed.), *Islamic Political Radicalism: A European Perspective*, Edinburgh: Edinburgh University Press, pp. 173–91.
30 Euben, R.L. (2002) 'Killing (for) Politics: Jihad, Martyrdom and Political Action', *Political Theory*, 30(1): 4–35.

The emergence of 'new racisms' has seen a move away from a concentration on structure and towards culture.[31] Muslims in Britain and the nature of Islamophobia are increasingly a feature of debates, characterised by 'a complex spectrum of racisms' and a 'resurgence of ethnic, cultural and religious differentiation'.[32] There are many demographic studies of Muslims in Western Europe that highlight Muslim engagement in limited spheres of civil life and in relation to the nature of political and cultural organisations, for example, when seeking to establish mosques, when securing provision of halal meat in prisons, schools and hospitals, and when lobbying for state-funded Islamic schools.[33] The building of mosques is reflective of a continuous public expression of Muslim life.[34] Certain Muslim beliefs and practices are, moreover, characteristic of local contexts in the sending regions of the subcontinent. They are often reproduced by newcomers to Britain as accommodations within multi-ethnic nation-states.[35] These ongoing developments are useful in explaining how Muslims have sought to contain and reproduce certain practices associated with their faith in multicultural societies and at specific times in their settlement and community development. As Steven Vertovec and Ceri Peach have suggested, 'the development of Muslim social organisations in Europe has been quite rapid since the 1970s, doubtless linked with the reunion of immigrant families during this period [...] and thoughts of permanent settlement which, in turn, raised awareness of the need for a variety of forms of communal expression'.[36]

As Muslims enter institutional life, seeking accommodation and continuation of practice and belief associated with their faith, they have also resisted it. Islamic revivalisms, it is argued, are in contrast to these efforts as they seek to assert a particular identity and recognition, often using language or slogans which are characteristically 'Islamic' in the face of injustices targeted at Muslim identity and culture. Islamic revivalisms are emancipatory social movements, manifested in urban Islamic culture as well as political protests, where the language of Islam is used as the dominant mode of expression. These revivalisms are defined by the conscious recognition of an identity that harbours diversity, stretching into new

31 Mac an Ghaill, M. (1999) *Contemporary Racisms and Ethnicities: Social and Cultural Transformations*, Milton Keynes: Open University Press, p. 70.
32 Bulmer, M. and J. Solomos (2004) *Researching Race and Racism*, London: Routledge, p. 7.
33 Klausen, J. (2005) *The Islamic Challenge: Politics and Religion in Western Europe*, New York: Oxford University Press.
34 Cesari, J. (2005) 'Mosque Conflicts in European Cities: Introduction', *Journal of Ethnic and Migration Studies*, 31(6): 1015–24.
35 Amghar, S., A. Boubekeur and M. Emerson (2007) *Islam: Challenges for Society and Public Policy*, Brussels: Centre for European Policy Studies.
36 Vertovec, S. and C. Peach (1997) 'Introduction: Islam in Europe and the Politics of Religion and Community', in S. Vertovec and C. Peach (eds), *Islam in Europe: The Politics of Religion and Community*, Basingstoke: Macmillan, p. 24.

political imaginaries. Discussions on Islamic revivalisms emphasise the primacy of grievances, including barriers to social mobility, lack of political and legal freedoms, economic despair and the Palestine–Israel issue as providing the impetus for such movements. The underlying assumptions are that these grievances are generated by socio-economic and political crises. These grievance-based theories are incomplete; they expose the reasons for suffering, but they do not provide explanations for the range and set of variables that translate particular grievances into revivalist movements, however.[37] They leave room for wider psychological, cultural and social explanations in the context of a range of factors operating at any one point in time depending on the individual and the circumstances at play.

Fred Halliday analyses the role of these other factors and contexts that lead to 'anti-Muslimism' and the image of an 'Islamic threat'.[38] In identifying the issues underlying the rise of Islamic revivalisms in the Western world and the reaction to it by the West foremost is the idea that Islam is under threat and at risk of being corrupted.[39] Muslims, therefore, invoke Islam as a justification for political action. For Halliday, issues such as the intrusion of the state into everyday life, legislation perceived as specifically targeting Muslims, and the fact of external domination and strict immigration controls suggest that Muslim communities may feel that there are under constant threat.[40] Halliday suggests that Islamic revivalisms are reflective of panic reactions by Muslims who fear a threat to their religion and identity: 'theirs is a defensive cry'. The Rushdie affair was an example of Islam 'in danger', not so much from outside but from the loss of belief within (i.e. in relation to Rushdie's apostasy as a former Muslim).[41] For Halliday, at the societal level, Islamist movements have developed as a cultural and nationalist response to contemporary problems facing Muslim communities. It is the inability of the nation-state to meet the economic expectations or cultural aspirations of groups that provides the context for Islamic revivalisms to develop. As Talal Asad argues, the response of the British state to the anger expressed by Muslims in relation to the publication of *The Satanic Verses*, 'should be seen primarily as yet another symptom of British, post imperial identity in crisis, and not [...] as an unhappy instance of some immigrants with difficulties in adjusting to a new and more civilized world'.[42]

37 Wiktorowicz, Q. (2004b) *Islamic Activism: A Social Movement Theory Approach*, Bloomington: Indiana University Press.
38 Halliday, F. (2003) *Islam and the Myth of Confrontation: Religion and Politics in the Middle East*, London: I.B. Tauris, p. 107.
39 Ibid., p. 120.
40 Ibid.
41 Ibid., p. 127.
42 Asad, T. (1990) 'Multiculturalism and British Identity in the Wake of the Rushdie Affair', *Politics and Society*, 18(4): 455–80.

Benjamin Barber engages this debate with a narrative on the paradoxical effects of the interaction between a 'McWorld' culture, representing 'soft imperialism', through to the homogenisation of global markets and jihad as the rights of difference being reinvented and ethno-religious sentiments revived.[43] Barber suggests how a McWorld creates trivialisation and homogenisation of values while eroding cultural diversity, creating a facilitating environment for jihad (which for Barber can also denote Christian, Jewish and other types of fundamentalist movements). Barber focuses on some of the underlying features of both phenomena and offers an account that relays an asymmetry between the worlds of jihad and McWorld, yet also interdependence. They 'create a world in which our only choices are to secular universalism of the cosmopolitan market and everyday particularism of the fractious tribe'.[44] The complex interplay between the particular and the universal is crucial in understanding the connections between contemporary racisms and the increasing appeal of Islamic revivalisms. For Barber, jihad is not so much in stark opposition to McWorld, it is a 'dialectical response to modernity', whose 'virtues and vices' are embodied in the McWorld.[45] As a result, McWorld is a symbol of modernity with 'the nation as an imagined political community' and the 'driving engine of Jihad'.[46] Jihadists seek ethnic and cultural particularism derived from the English liberal idea of the nation that perceives self-determination as a condition for the progress of liberty. For Barber, this was mutated in the nineteenth century, when ideas such as pluralism became incorporated into national identity politics and an emphasis upon belonging and loyalty began to take hold. In illustrating this, reference is made to imperialism and how 'empires repressed the political expression of cultural identity and enforced mutuality'.[47]

Aziz Al-Azmeh explains this as a form of 'cultural differentialism [...] premised on irreducible and impermeable difference', which contains a libertarian streak coupled with segregationism.[48] For Al-Azmeh, there is an historical continuation of the imperialist tradition and how a dominant culture 'invigilates ideological processes that oversee the constitution of specific identities under specific conditions of socio-economic confinement, buttressed by what is known, in the "host" society, as multiculturalism'.[49]

43 Barber, B. (1996) *Jihad vs. McWorld: Terrorism's Challenge to Democracy*, New York: Balantine; Barber, B. (2004) 'Jihad vs. McWorld', in F. Lechner and J. Boli (eds), *The Globalization Reader*, second edition, Oxford: Blackwell, pp. 29–36; Barber, B. (2003), *Fear's Empire*, New York; Norton.
44 Barber (2004), op. cit., p. 31.
45 Barber (1996), op. cit., p. 157
46 Ibid., (1996), p. 7.
47 Ibid., p. 167.
48 Al-Azmeh, A. (1993) *Islams and Modernities*, London: Verso, p. 4.
49 Ibid., p. 5.

According to Barber, the globalising processes of McWorld, its homogenising tendencies and the resulting inequalities in relation to power create a context for the emergence and negotiation of Islamic revivalisms as cultural forms, underlying the interdependent worlds of McWorld and jihad. Asad argues that '[Western] Europe [...] is ideologically constructed in such a way that Muslim immigrants cannot be satisfactorily represented in it'.[50] For Asad, this is the result of anxiety felt by most Europeans about the presence of Muslims and Islamic traditions within the borders of Western Europe. Muslims are considered 'external to the essence of Europe', resulting in a reluctant 'coexistence' between an 'us' and 'them'.[51] Western Europe is represented in narratives that express a civilisational difference between Islam and Muslims, the effect being to exclude Islam. The history of the encounter of Europe with Muslims can be seen as cultural encounters, marked by European efforts to 'contain, subdue or incorporate what lies beyond it and what consequently comes to be within it'.[52] The Rushdie affair and the response by the British Government in relation to the Muslim mobilisation associated with it served as further illustration of this. For Asad, while European identity concerns are exclusions for Muslims, identity has come to depend upon how the 'other' recognises itself. Social (mis) representations of Muslims have acted as an objectifying process, subordinating individuals and groups to the status of 'other' and resulting in various dynamics of oppression, i.e. cultural domination, Euro-centrism and mis-recognition.

Charles Taylor provides a conceptualisation of these cultural and symbolic injustices, arguing 'non recognition or misrecognition [...] can be a form of oppression, imprisoning someone in a false, distorted, reduced mode of being'.[53] As Asad has shown, Islam and Muslims, as a result of being excluded from the 'Idea of Europe' and recognised as 'others', have been devalued, and in the process encountering the 'stigmatising gaze of a culturally dominant' other. It hinders the development of their own cultural identity.[54]

Ultimately, it is important to discuss the significance of representation for Muslims in the construction of Islamic revivalisms as negotiated subjectivities and social identities in response to contemporary racisms and

50 Asad, T. (2002) 'Muslims and European Identity: Can Europe Represent Islam?', in A. Pagden (ed.), *The Idea of Europe: From Antiquity to the European Union*, Cambridge: Cambridge University Press, pp. 209–27.

51 Ibid., p. 214.

52 Ibid., p. 218.

53 Taylor, C. (1994) *Multiculturalism: Examining the Politics of Recognition*, Princeton, NJ: Princeton University Press, pp. 25–6.

54 Asad, T. (1999) 'Religion, Nation-state, Secularism', in P. van der Veer and H. Lehman (eds) *Nation and Religion: Perspectives on Europe and Asia*, Princeton, NJ: Princeton University Press, pp. 178–96; Asad (2002), op. cit., p. 209

multiculturalism. Islamic revivalisms are minority demands for recognition and equality in the face of government demands for cultural homogenisation, as well as assimilation into dominant society. Rather than merely reacting to racism, cultural domination and subjection to Eurocentric norms, Muslims consciously (re)construct cultural and political identities as Islamic revivalisms. The notions of self-consciousness, subjectivity, diaspora and transnational networks act as 'machineries' and 'regimes of representation' in the connections between contemporary racisms and Islamic revivalisms.[55] Pointing to a decline in secularised tendencies in the Arab and Islamic worlds, Gema Martín-Muñoz argues that a reassertion of cultural identity is a vital issue for Islamist movements where Islam 'endows an identity and ideological autonomy', referring to the historical encounters between Islam and Christianity, and the 'ethnocentric conception of coexistence'.[56] It is considered to be dependent upon the extent to which other cultures are capable of 'Westernising'; this sentiment reaching its maturity with colonial rule at the end of the nineteenth century and how it has subsequently impacted on the processes of modernity in Islamic societies. 'Disdain for non-European others', Martín-Muñoz argues, left Muslims 'bereft of historical and cultural dignity', generating serious confusion for various Muslims in different societies.[57]

The relationship between Islamic societies in the West and the rise of what is called a 'global Muslim subjectivity' is seen as a conscious response to Western hegemony and a defining feature of post-modernism. The idea that identity is consciously formed is also propounded by Paul Gilroy. Using the example of the history of racial slavery and the modern African diaspora in the West to understand the workings of identity, Gilroy suggests 'that work must be done to summon the particularity and feelings of identity that are so often experienced as though they are spontaneous or automatic consequences of some governing culture or tradition that specifies basic and absolute differences between people'.[58] According to Gilroy, the 'interplay of consciousness, territory and place [becomes a] major theme' in the process of identity formation which is 'as an antidote to anxiety and uncertainty associated with economic and political crisis'.[59] Miri Song states how Muslims have to contend with negative dominant representations in the media and popular culture, i.e. 'Muslim fundamentalists', and how this plays a constitutive role in the formation of their identities in wider society. For Song, the formation of minority group identities are part of a wider interaction

---

55 Martín-Muñoz, G. (1999) (ed.) *Islam, Modernism and the West: Cultural and Political Relations at the End of the Millennium*, London and New York: I.B. Tauris, p. 5.
56 Ibid.
57 Ibid., pp. 4–7.
58 Gilroy, P. (2000) *Between Camps: Nations, Cultures and the Allure of Race*, London: Penguin, p. 100.
59 Ibid., p. 101.

between 'assignments' which are imposed by others in wider society, and by 'assertion', which is a claim to ethnicity made by the groups themselves.[60] Song suggests that with increased interconnections of social life, brought about by globalisation, people have the opportunity to be involved with more than one culture. Thus, 'people's sense of their ethnic identities and affiliations are said to be relativised and shaped by their greater consciousness of the interconnections of people and societies around the world'.[61]

Globalisation, therefore, has implications for the ways in which people experience identity. On the one hand, there are the constraints experienced through powerful homogenising forces at work, and Barber's expression of this as McWorld has been discussed earlier. At the same time, globalisation, transnationalism and the diasporic communities associated with them offer Muslims the option of negotiating and forming an 'identity', and, as Gilroy suggests, 'identity is an anchor in globalisation'.[62] Globalisation, however, has implications for the nation-state, which, in turn, has implications for ethnic-minority groups within particular borders. Migration, which is closely related to processes of globalisation, makes it increasingly difficult for states to control the flows of populations, settlements and cultural exchange.[63] It is what Steven Vertovec calls the 'container model' of the state.[64] Multiculturalism, in its conventional form, entails an essentialised understanding of culture. It proposes a top-down perspective on multicultural unity, where ethnic minorities are expected to 'adopt a sense of belonging to the country of reception'.[65] The argument has been covered earlier, when discussing the idea of Europe and how Western European identity involves the exclusion of others, exploring the wider historical and philosophical conceptualisation of multiculturalism (see Chapter 6). Here, it is important to note the historical continuation of this experience in contemporary multicultural societies and its role in (re)producing Islamic revivalisms. The exclusivist and differentialist notion of culture that multiculturalism implies proves problematic for the nation-state in how it perceives and subsequently handles its ethnic and religious-minority communities.

In contemporary notions and applications of multiculturalism, it is possible to see how the nation-state offers ethnic and religious minorities a negotiated space, but what is distinctively marked out within the wider national public sphere is that minority groups are expected to adapt to a

---

60 Song, M. (2003) *Choosing Ethnic Identity*, Cambridge: Polity, pp. 16–21.
61 Gilroy (2000), op. cit., p. 113.
62 Ibid., p. 107.
63 Castles, S. (2000) *Ethnicity and Globalization: From Migrant Worker to Transnational Citizen*, London and New York: Sage.
64 Vertovec, S. (2001) 'Transnational Challenges to the "New" Multiculturalism'. Paper presented to the Association of Social Anthropologists Conference', held at the University of Sussex, 30 March–2 April.
65 Ibid.

predetermined sense of belonging. It can be seen in the 'Idea of Europe' and the subsequent ethnocentric norms that have helped to buttress the concept and, in the process, produce chauvinist and racist outcomes. Individual cultures are homogenised and expected to assimilate into a wider multi-cultural citizenship within an existing national cultural framework, eventually leading to monoculturalism. Cultures are in reality open and porous formations; they interact with mainstream life at a variety of levels; and there should be sensitivity to these differences.[66] Muslims, with their transnational allegiances to their countries of origin and to the concept of *ummah,* potentially pose a problem for multicultural states, which can lead to a paradoxical effect. Global Islamic revivalist movements represented in events such as 9/11 and the resistance to occupation in places such as Palestine, Iraq and Afghanistan lead to objectification of popular assumptions and discourses of Muslims living as 'terrorists' or 'fundamentalists'. The stigmatising process results in a retreat into communities and a continuation of the cycle of racism and revivalism. Vertovec recognises how British Muslim successes in achieving institutional accommodation and modes of public recognition have led to a growth in Islamophobia and suggests that the rise in both these phenomena are interpreted 'through a kind of linked and circular operation'.[67] It is argued that this dilemma can also be understood as part of a wider analysis of Muslim citizens in Western European countries being more self-conscious and the formation of a 'diaspora identity', which, according to Gilroy, 'exists outside and sometimes in opposition to political forms and codes of modern citizenship'.[68]

Clearly, in the wake of 9/11 and the terror attacks in Western Europe, questions in relation to loyalty have come to dominate discussions on Muslim minorities in Western Europe. The policies of assimilation have re-emerged, with citizenship laws developed according to security concerns, creating a fresh climate of Islamophobia in Western Europe. 'The state', Gilroy argues, 'aggravates the feeling of belonging and so people retreat to disaporic identity'.[69] An illustration of this can be found in the case of one of the London bombers in July 2005. Mohammed Sidique Khan declared that his motivation in carrying out the attack was a conscious response to the British state for its 'bombing, gassing, imprisonment and torture of my people across the world'.[70] This was officially confirmed by the Government: that the intervention in Iraq by Britain and the subsequent war indeed

66 Parekh Report (2000) *The Future of Multi-Ethnic Britain*, London: Profile Books, p. 37.
67 Vertovec, S. (2002) 'Islamophobia and Muslim Recognition in Britain', in Y. Haddad (ed.), *Muslims in the West: From Sojourners to Citizens*, New York: Oxford University Press, pp. 19–35, p. 32.
68 Gilroy (2000), op. cit., p. 124.
69 Ibid., p.5.
70 BBC News Online (2005) 'London Bomber: Text in full', available at <news.bbc.co.uk/2/hi/uk_news/4206800.stm>. Accessed 21 July 2009.

motivated the London bombers.[71] In Khan's words it is possible to recognise the professed theoretical diasporic link with an imagined (global) Muslim community based on the idea of the *ummah*. Nation-states can seek to preserve territorial sovereignty by introducing immigration controls, for example; yet this has little effect on the wider processes of globalisation and transnationalism from which flow de-culturated images, ideas and objects circulated with growing speed and intensity. New communication technologies and mass-media developments have transformed the practice and means of organising and strengthening religious movements. Analysis of the diasporic Muslim experience is a valuable contribution to the analysis of intercultural and transcultural processes that shape Islamic revivalisms. Given these criticisms of multiculturalism, thinkers are turning to cosmopolitanism to explain political belonging in the light of transnational communities and relations, and the bearing these have on how individuals conceive of identities, belongings and associations within specific national frameworks, as well as the impact of particular urban and inner city socio-economic contexts in which most Muslim minorities find themselves.[72]

The growth of Islamism has been recognised in the many voices and statements made by populist ideologues. Until recently, in Britain these have included Abu Qatada al-Filistini, Abu Hamza al-Masri and Omar Bakri Mohammed.[73] The latter is self-exiled in Lebanon, while the former two are languishing in maximum-security Belmarsh prison. Without doubt, there is a great deal of anger, frustration and even reactionary feeling among young Muslim men, but the case being made in this analysis is that it is more a function of subordinated socio-economic conditions, political disenfranchisement and cultural dislocation than any recent or specific developments to the religion of Islam itself. A recent focus on Hizb ut-Tahrir (HT) since 7/7 does not detract from the fact that before 7/7 it operated in much the same way. Ironically, in the immediate post-7/7 climate, having had three years to prepare after HT was banned in Germany, members of HT-UK were often the ones to appear as the reasonably acceptable face of British Islam in television representations.

The current local, national and international political climate was wholly concerned with 'international terrorism' and 'radical political Islam', and though the mere association of these areas is in itself an act of oversimplification, there are genuine social, political and economic concerns that amalgamate them. The ideas that relate to radical Islam are, nevertheless,

---

71 House of Commons (2006) *Report of the Official Account of the Bombings in London on 7th July 2005*, London, HC 1087, London: Stationery Office.
72 Hall, S. (2002) 'Political Belonging in a World of Multiple Identities', in S. Vertovec and R. Cohin (eds), *Conceiving Cosmopolitanism*, Oxford: Oxford University Press, pp. 25–31; Keith, M. (2005) *After the Cosmopolitan? Multicultural Cities and the Future of Racism*, London: Routledge.
73 See Jonson, R. (2002) *Them: Adventures with Extremists*, London: Picador, for a journalistic and often witty account of the character of Omar Bakri Mohammed.

genuinely alien to most South Asian Muslims in British society as they are for non-Muslim dominant groups; however, there is a concern that disaffected Western Muslim youth are increasingly succumbing to radicalisation in a setting of permanent disadvantage and the virulent 'othering' of Islam and Muslims. In Britain and throughout Western Europe, there is presently the phenomenon of the indigenous-born, English-speaking Muslim youth politicised by a radicalised Islam. The patterns across Western Europe are remarkably similar. Post-war immigrant groups who were either invited or who came searching for improved economic opportunities found their young growing up in local area contexts that exhibited prejudice, discrimination and racism towards minority Muslim communities. In these localities, educational opportunities have generally been limited, affecting the likelihood of securing effective higher-education or labour-market entry. There are considerable inter-generational tensions as a result of differences to language, culture and attitudes towards majority communities. Invariably, as the process of adaptation begins to evolve, there is an acceptance of the values of majority society by subsequent generations of Muslims who ultimately become ethnic-minority communities. At times there is resistance, as in the case of the few Muslims who see it as a negative feature in their life in liberal secular parliamentary democracies. For these few, this existence is regarded as somewhat antithetical to the life of a 'good Muslim'.

In Britain, many indigenous Muslims experience a complex, dislocated reality. Low social-class positions, coupled with religious and cultural isolation, place the experiences of many young Muslims outside the spheres of wider social life. Where there are intergenerational tensions in relation to tradition – for example, the insistence on consanguineous marriages by some South Asian Muslim parents – many young Muslims object and wish to return to a more literal interpretation of Islam as a way of self-empowerment. The development encourages young Muslim minds to explore Islam further, but parents cannot always provide the knowledge as they frequently lack the linguistic, intellectual and cultural skills to communicate with their children, even though they often experience a reinvigorated approach to Islam later on in their own lives.[74] The mosques, for the most part, provide a limited learning environment, and the knowledge of Islam is presented at a very basic level or is geared within a specific linguistic or cultural framework, largely because of limited knowledge and professional capacity on the part of educators. As a result, the young are encouraged to seek alternative forms of 'empowerment knowledge', whether it is via the Internet, underground reading groups or religious study circles.[75] This latter knowledge is often

74 Anwar, M. (1998) *Between Cultures: Continuity and Change in the Lives of Young Asians*, London: Routledge.
75 Bunt, G.R. (2003) *Islam in the Digital Age: E-Jihad, Online Fatwas and Cyber Islamic Environments*, London: Pluto.

tainted with a radicalising message that promotes intolerance, antipathy and the general disregard of all things Western. The theological nature of these messages stems from outside traditional Sunni Islam, acting more as a function of literalist ideological thought that has been many centuries in the making.[76] Much of this thinking appeals to a small number of young Muslims (mostly men, but not entirely) who see it as a form of liberation – from the traditions, norms and values of their own communities and from states that apparently seek to subjugate Muslim minorities at home while bombing Muslims abroad. What is important to point out is that any notion of reading websites or joining study circles does not itself suggest activities more sinister. With increasing efforts made to de-radicalise young Muslims based on closer working relations between communities, organisations and government departments, many Muslims may even feel the need to explore precisely these concerns on their own but without feeling the actual need to take up 'radical jihadi missions' of any kind.

There were many cases of Salafi organisations influencing impressionable minds throughout the 1990s. Organisations such as Al-Muhajiroun, Supporters of Shariah and HT had much success in 'infiltrating' university Islamic societies all over Britain before their actions began to be viewed with suspicion. Now disbanded, Al-Muhajiroun proved a powerful vehicle for young Muslims who used the Palestinian–Israeli conflict to pursue a pan-Islamism agenda in Britain. Eventually, the forces of mainstream Islam and the negative media profile it received from all sectors of society led to its downfall, although it is clear that the sentiments it articulated still carry weight among many disaffected young Muslims. Omar Bakri Muhammad stated that British Muslims are required by divine law to promote an Islamic state in Britain. His followers therefore rejected democracy on the basis that it enshrines popular rather than divine sovereignty. They also rebuffed the term 'British Muslim' as they are against all forms of nationalism and believe that no loyalty is due to the British state. Loyalty should be to Islam only, and Al-Muhajiroun's ideology encouraged a 'divine duty' to be contentious and to act out against the authorities. Before it was dissolved by Omar Bakri Muhammad in 2004, Al-Muhajiroun was active in nineteen local areas.[77] Supporters of Shariah have been described as a small Salafi group characterised by its uncompromising opposition to the British state,

76 Ansari, H. (2005) 'Attitudes to Jihad, Martyrdom and Terrorism among British Muslims', in T. Abbas (ed.), *Muslim Britain: Communities under Pressure*, London and New York: Zed, pp. 144–63.
77 Conner, K. (2005) '"Islamism" in the West? The Life-span of Al-Muhajiroun in the United Kingdom', *Journal of Muslim Minority Affairs*, 25(1): 117–34; Wiktorowicz, Q. (2004) 'Joining the Cause: Al-Muhajiroun and Radical Islam'. Paper presented to the conference, The Roots of Radicalism, Yale University, 8–9 May; Mukhopadhyay, A.R. (2007) 'Radical Islamic Organisations in Europe: South Asia in Their Discourse', *Strategic Analysis*, 31(2): 267–85.

US foreign policy, mainstream Muslim organisations and democracy itself. It supported international 'jihadi' movements and is explicit about its support for Al-Qaeda. Its leading figure was Abu Hamza and its followers are thought to have worked closely with followers of Omar Bakri Muhammad. Minority Muslim sects such as Shi's and Ahmadiyas are accused of heresy. Hamza has categorically denied despatching British Muslims to jihad in other countries, but, has in the past openly inspired them to do so.

During the 1990s, young British Muslims who watched on their British and foreign satellite channels the events of Bosnia-Herzegovina, Kashmir, Chechnya and Palestine were acutely affected. The 'Seven in Yemen' (1999), the 'Tipton Three' (2001) and the 'Dudley Two' (2003) were almost all British-born South Asian Muslims. Not all necessarily poor – some attended institutes of higher education – but considered born on the 'wrong side of town', they experienced prejudice, racism and discrimination throughout their early lives and sustained themselves in education in spite of its limitations in relation to Muslims and other visible minorities. By hoping to find the 'truth', they were ultimately misdirected by radicalising Islamists seeking to convert once decadent or 'sinful' young Muslims, or those yearning for a more literal interpretation of the religion. Because of this wider geo-political context British Islamism has found greater sustenance. For example, the ways in which Muslim prisoners were found to have been treated in Guantanamo Bay and Abu Ghraib prison at the hands of the North Americans, and the revelations of the extent of the abuse inflicted on Iraqi prisoners and civilians by the British Army, served only to disillusion an already disenfranchised British Muslim community. Since 9/11, in much of the Western world, governments have seemingly tightened their grip on Muslim minorities with changes to international finance, anti-terrorism legislation and debates around identity cards, citizenship, and rights and obligations. The argument here that the 'War on Terror' has revealed itself to be an ideological construction helping to maintain the status quo, while Muslims are derided, misrepresented and illegitimately incarcerated has some validity. It is no accident that it is the same ethnic Muslim groups as those involved in the Rushdie affair when discussing issues of integration, community, identity and 'loyalty' to the state on the one hand and problems of education, employment, housing and health, on the other. Such was the initial post-war economic and social subjugation of these groups of people. Other Muslim groups (the half of British Muslims who are not Kashmiri or Pakistani) are conspicuously absent in the current discourse on the problems of 'Muslim radicalism' in Britain today, although there has been some attention given to the radicalisation of Black African groups in the UK.

Therefore the turn to radical political Islam among a certain subsection of the Muslim male youth population can be explained by issues of identity politics but also the ways in which the British multicultural experience has facilitated a concentration on individual and group norms, values, lifestyle choices and cultural identities, taking it away from a focus on structural inequalities at a time when it was perhaps most pertinent in the history of British 'race relations'. In 1999, the publication of the Macpherson Inquiry into the murder of Stephen Lawrence highlighted the problem of institutionalised racism, which was seen as endemic in the Metropolitan Police Service. It brought the issue of racial violence to the top of the political agenda. The inquiry found that the investigation into Stephen Lawrence's murder by the London Metropolitan Police Service was 'marred by a combination of professional incompetence, institutional racism and a failure of leadership by senior officers'.[78] The report further highlighted the ways in which Dwayne Brooks, a friend of Stephen Lawrence and a witness, were racially stereotyped. Stephen Lawrence's parents were also thought to have been handled rather insensitively. It ultimately underscored an enhancement to the Race Relations (Amendment) Act 2000 which put a statutory duty on nearly 50,000 public sector organisations to measure and act upon improving race equality. It was the 'northern disturbances' of 2001 and the subsequent 'community cohesion' reports less than two years later that led to a focus on identities, communities and behaviours as the central race equality strategy. This effectively placed the onus of responsibility onto the Muslim communities to become better citizens engaged in an evolving multicultural society, taking attention away from the state to provide the resources to create the necessary economic infrastructure to do so. In the summer of 2001, second- and third-generation young Muslim men were fighting with the local police and fascist groups on the streets in five separate locations. Violence and physical destruction emerged in Burnley, Oldham and Bradford, while in Stoke and Leeds the problems were much less severe. Not only did these young men receive heavy sentences for first-time offences, they also experienced intense vilification in the press, especially as at the time the international Pakistani cricket team was on tour, and problems of post-match pitch invasions had raised the profile of young Muslim men. At war in Afghanistan by November 2001, Britain and the coalition of the willing were fully engaged with the 'War on Terror'. There were issues of radicalisation of British Muslim youth in the early 1990s, essentially because of the problems in former Bosnia-Herzegovina,[79] with some young British-born Muslims found to be fighting there. However, it was the 'War on Terror' that led British Muslims to feel further ostracised, and because of experiences of exclusion, alienation and marginalisation, and with the long-term problems of the lack of intellectual, cultural, political and theological leadership of the first generations, many aimless young Muslims, essentially using the Internet and other media communication technologies, became further radicalised.

78 MacPherson, W. (1999) *The Stephen Lawrence Inquiry*, London: Stationery Office, 46.1.
79 Kohlman, E.F. (2004) *Al-Qaida's Jihad in Europe: The Afghan[-}Bosnian Network*, Oxford: Berg; Abbas, T. (2007a) 'Ethno-Religious Identities and Islamic Political Radicalism in the UK: A Case Study', *Journal of Muslim Minority Affairs*, 27(3): 356–68.

Rather than ameliorate the situation, the multicultural context in which these realities materialised potentially problematised the situation. But this is not because of multiculturalism per se, rather it is because of the ways in minorities are treated as part of wider societal processes and the ways in which they are managed from within a centralised state. The experience of anti-Muslim racism, migration and settlement, and Islamophobia itself are inextricably linked.[80]

After 9/11, universities found Muslim student groups unable to deal effectively with identity and political issues, and with little support offered as argued by the Federation of Student Islamic Societies.[81] Instead, attention turned to university campuses as 'hotbeds' of radical activity without any real evidence to support the claims being made.[82] The Muslim Council of Britain (MCB) was ostracised by New Labour for its apparent lack of action after 7/7.[83] The MCB has asserted that the centre of Muslim self-identity in Britain is faith rather than 'race' and, partly as a result of MCB lobbying, the Government agreed to include religion as a category of identity in the 2001 census. The MCB is committed to democracy in a practical way and not only urges Muslims to take part in elections but stresses that it is a religious obligation to do so. The newly formed Communities and Local Government Department placed its trustin new groups such as the British Muslim Forum (BMF) and the Sufi Muslim Council (SMC), while the MCB was dropped from its privileged position. The BMF claims to represent the largest cohort of Barelwi Muslim groups and organisations in Britain. Formally launched in 2005, it represents nine sections of the Sunni Barelwi community. The SMC was established in 2006. Such dialogue represents another attempt to counter the dominance and influence of certain schools of thought and ideologies on British Muslims, particularly from the more puritanical 'Salafi' movements. When it did not produce the immediate outcomes government sought, new forums such as the Muslim Women's Advisory Group and the Young Muslims Advisory Board (both established in 2008) were put together, made up of identified and recognisable achievers from these target groups.

The process of opening up to Muslim communities also encouraged other protest, lobby and pressure groups to mobilise. City Circle is a Muslim professionals group that regularly invites controversial speakers to its sessions, while the Islamic Human Rights Commission is fully committed to

80 Fekete, L. (2009) *A Suitable Enemy: Racism, Migration and Islamophobia in Europe*, London and New York: Pluto.
81 Federation of Student Islamic Societies (2005) *The Voice of Muslim Students: The FOSIS Muslim Student Survey 2005*, London: FOSIS.
82 Glees, A. and C. Pope (2005) *When Students Turn to Terror: Terrorist and Extremist Activity on British Campuses*, London: Social Affairs Unit.
83 McRoy, A. (2005) *From Rushdie to 7/7: The Radicalisation of Islam in Britain*, London: Social Affairs Unit.

identifying human rights abuses against Muslims in Britain. The Forum against Islamophobia and Racism, originally founded by the late Sheikh Zaki Badawi (1922–2006) in the mid-1990s, is concerned with the converging problems of cultural and structural racism against Muslims. The Muslim Public Action Committee has gained headlines because of its rather public 'mosque-bashing' approach to improving the lot of British Muslims. It is argued by some that the Muslim Association of Britain (MAB) has Arab-leaning tendencies, with much criticism of it as potentially the public face of the Muslim Brotherhood in Britain. The MAB was founded in 1997, largely by people of Arab origin. One issue that distinguishes it from other groups is its emphasis on political activism and interaction within wider civil society in Britain. One of its key objectives is to campaign for changes in British policy around the Muslim world. The organisation became an important member of the Stop the War Coalition. It had a central role in the emergence of a Muslim–Leftist alliance with RESPECT (Respect, Equality, Socialism, Peace, Environmentalism, Community and Trade Unionism coalition).[84] The Institute of Islamic Political Thought, led by Palestinian Azzam Tamimi, is considered to have associations with Hamas and the Islamic Association of Britain and the UK Islamic Mission are seen as the face of JI in Britain. Although there is considerable discussion of the apparent Islamising of UK-Muslim organisations and the role of key personnel within them, there is often little, if any, evidence to support the assertions. It needs also to be stated that many of the accusations against newly developed professional Muslim bodies are often based on tenuous links and associations, but the alarmism caused by public discussion gives the impression that the problems are far worse than the reality. Most of these institutions and organisations tend to work independently of each other, and they are often divided by ethno-national and sectarian differences, as well as social class, ethnicity and region.

With emphasis given to popular international figures such as Irshad Manji, author of *The Trouble with Islam* (2005) and Ayaan Hirsi Ali, author of *Infidel* (2007), the latter who denounces Islam altogether while the former sees herself as a 'Muslim Refusenik', government policy has given much credence to liberal organisations, such as the Progressive Muslims Association, Muslims for Secular Democracy and the somewhat incongruous Council of Ex-Muslims of Britain. The Radical Middle Way is funded by the Foreign and Commonwealth Office in conjunction with the Communities and Local Government Department. Its role is to provide training, lectures and seminars to grass-roots Islamic organisations and secular groups in communities across Britain. Also, there are 2,000 or so mainstream mosques and Islamic centres across the country whose capabilities and professionalisms are being

84 Philips, R.S. (2008) 'Standing Together: The Muslim Association of Britain and the Anti-war Movement', *Race and Class*, 50(2): 101–13.

independently developed by an agglomeration of existing umbrella groups, known as the Mosques and Imams National Advisory Board (MINAB). Given all these developments, there still remains a distinct lack of coherence between the different groups and political tendencies, which is perhaps only to be expected. In the process, it limits the potential for a collectivised voice against a well developed series of assaults aimed at an entire community.

Throughout this time, large sections of the media and the political establishment have focused on the British Muslim community as a whole, regarding it in homogenised frames of reference. It has further isolated young Muslims already experiencing a number of deeply impacting exclusions. A particular problem has been in relation to the criminalisation of the Muslim community, the experience of increasingly hard-hitting anti-terror legislation and its impact upon British Muslims and the decline of civil liberties in general.

8 Muslims, crime, terror and the law

Since events of 7/7, the UK Government has developed a range of policies and practices to disentangle the processes of violent extremism, and to help realise appropriate and necessary solutions. When the Preventing Extremism Together (PET) report was put together by independently appointed Muslims two months after the events of 7/7, New Labour responded with a focus on counter-radicalism and de-radicalism.[1] Reducing socio-economic inequalities and building cohesion to eliminate violent extremism are closely related. However the focus in the current period in relation to de-radicalisation has closer associations with policing, security and intelligence initiatives.[2] More recent incarnations of this approach have focused on the idea of 'counter ideology'. Therefore, it is important to analyse the impact of the New Labour response in relation to changes to legislation in the wake of the events of 9/11 and 7/7, and how it has affected Muslims in Britain. There is a need to study the ways in which ethnic minorities are treated within the criminal-justice system in general, followed by a fuller analysis of how Muslims are presently experiencing particular problems. If we consider how young British African-Caribbean men faired in the criminal-justice system in the late 1970s, the parallels with young Muslim men today are remarkably similar. However, what separates the current experience is the intersection of local, national and global factors in the formalisation of the 'Muslim problem' in matters of criminology, the socio-legal realm, various aspects of the criminal-justice system and, the law itself.

Historically, the experience of minorities within the criminal-justice system has been notoriously problematic. Social research on how ethnic minorities are 'processed' by the British criminal-justice system over the past few decades, carried out in academia as well as in government, continues to

---

1 Home Office (2005) *'Preventing Extremism Together' Working Groups: August–October 2005*, London: Home Office.
2 Kundnani, A. (2009) *Spooked! How Not to Prevent Violent Extremism*, London: Institute of Race Relations.

show negativity at the level of enforcement and sentencing.[3] The issue of racial discrimination was first addressed in the Race Relations Act 1965 and then strengthened in the Race Relations Act 1976. Under English law, racial discrimination is defined as treating an individual less favourably than another on the grounds of perceived ethnic or racial difference. Irrespective of the nature of this treatment, the fact that a difference has been identified on the part of the victim is enough to make it unlawful.[4] The Race Relations (Amendment) Act 2000 now makes it unlawful for a public authority, including any government department, to discriminate while carrying out its functions. There is a positive duty on all public bodies to promote race equality, to have due regard for the need to eliminate racial discrimination and to promote equality of opportunity and good relations between people of different ethnicities. Specific duties affecting government departments include publishing a race-equality scheme on how organisations and institutions assess and consult on the impact of policy in relation to the promotion of race equality. In addition, there is a duty to monitor the proportion of staff from ethnic minorities in employment, their appraisal and also promotion.

Interaction with the criminal-justice system begins with the police. The police have more a direct impact on the lives of people than any other enforcement agency of the Home Office. Frustration among certain ethnic-minority groups is based on 'criminalisation and harassment on the one hand and inadequate attention to race crime and behaviour on the other'.[5] The 1999 Stephen Lawrence Inquiry referred to institutional racism in a large public sector organisation, in this case the Metropolitan Police Service. Initially there was an unfavourable reaction to the Inquiry from different police authorities and public policy commentators. In everyday policing situations, however, it did have the immediate impact of dramatically dropping the incidences of 'stop and search' (when a police officer physically searches a person, their clothing and anything they are carrying, in accordance with statutory powers). A decade since the publication of the report, however, both 'stop and searches' and deaths in custody continue to remain disproportionately high for ethnic-minorities.[6] It is clear that as ethnic minorities first became embedded in the inner cities of Britain, the racialisation

3 Hood, R. (1992) *Race and Sentencing: A Study in the Crown Court*, Oxford: Clarendon; See Bowling, B. and C. Phillips (2002a) 'Racism, Ethnicity, Crime, and Criminal Justice', in M. Maguire, R. Morgan and R. Reiner (eds), *The Oxford Criminological Handbook*, Oxford: Oxford University Press, pp. 579–619; Bowling, B. and Phillips, C. (2002b) *Racism, Crime and Justice*, London: Longman.
4 Elliot, C. and F. Quinn (2009) *English Legal System*, tenth edition, London: Pearson.
5 Parekh Report (2000) *The Future of Multi-ethnic Britain*, London: Profile Books, p. 112.
6 Bowling, B. and C. Phillips (2003) 'Racial Victimization in England and Wales', in D.F. Hawkins (ed.), *Violent Crime: Assessing Race and Ethnic Differences*, Cambridge: Cambridge University Press, pp. 154–70.

they experienced also affected the ways in which they were labelled criminals within the 'host society', at one level, and how they became victimised, at another. This experience remains today in relation to young ethnic minorities and the youth justice system.[7]

Until the mid-1970s, South Asian and African-Caribbean groups were not considered to be any more criminally inclined than their white British counterparts. This, however, changed when confrontation between African-Caribbean groups and the police led to increasing rates of arrest. It is from this basis that 'black criminality' became associated with African-Caribbean culture. In contrast, South Asians were originally regarded as passive, 'inward-looking' or 'possessing strong family ties' and therefore potentially less likely to offend. But, there is presently the notion of the 'Asian gang', which is seen as less conformist and more prepared to defend what it regards as territorial rights.[8] The disturbances in the north of England during the summer of 2001 are testimony to the increasing instances of the negative labelling of South Asian Muslim youths as criminals.[9]

A significant factor in how groups are perceived to be criminally inclined or otherwise is the media. Social construction carried out by the press over-emphasises cultural difference and exaggerates rates of criminal activity.[10] Here, the idea of 'folk devils' is not new to British society. In the past, the Irish, Russians and Jews have all been comprehensively criminalised. In the context of news reporting on ethnic minorities, it is not unsurprising that images of conflict, drama, controversy, violence and deviance continue to be generated.[11] At present, it is Muslim Africans, South Asians, poor white Britons and Caribbean converts, as well as the influx of Eastern European workers and 'refugees and asylum-seekers' from Muslims lands, who are considered to be part of a criminal ethnic, religious and immigrant minority 'underclass'. The process of labelling people negatively has the impact of making real the very ideas such characterisations are based upon. The Home Office Citizenship Survey of 2003 found that among people who said there was more prejudice today, 55 per cent cited prejudice

7 May, T., T. Gyateng and M. Hough, with the assistance of B. Bhardwa, I. Boyce and J.-C. Oyanedel (2010) *Differential Treatment in the Youth Justice System*, London: Equality and Human Rights Commission.

8 Alexander, C. E. (2000) The Asian Gang: Ethnicity, Identity, Masculinity. Oxford and New York: Berg.

9 Kundnani, A. (2001) 'From Oldham to Bradford: The Violence of the Violated', in *The Three Faces of British Racism: Race and Class*, 43(3): 41–60.

10 Hall, S. et al. (1978) *Policing the Crisis: Mugging the State and Law and Order*, London: Macmillan.

11 Cottle, S. (ed.) (2000) *Ethnic Minorities and the Media: Changing Cultural Boundaries*, Buckingham: Open University Press; Hallam, E.M. (2000) (ed.) *Cultural Encounters: Representing 'Otherness'*, London: Routledge.

against 'asylum seekers' or 'refugees' and 18 per cent cited prejudice against 'new immigrants'.[12] As African-Caribbeans, South Asians and other ethnic minorities are more likely to be cautioned, stopped-and-searched, arrested and eventually sentenced, it permits the myth to become the reality.[13]

Over the past four decades, there have been many examples of how the police and ethnic-minority communities have come into adversarial contact with each other. Throughout the 1970s and 1980s, the high use of 'stop and search' came to attention. Presently, especially in the post-7/7 climate, ethnic minorities are more likely to be stopped; the stops are more likely to result in searches, which also tend to be more intrusive, including the use of clothing and strip searches.[14] Since the 'War on Terror', it is South Asian Muslim men who seem to have been targeted.[15]

The above experiences impact on the ways in which ethnic minorities are taken through the criminal-justice system and particularly in relation to prosecutions. Once arrests are made, case files are sent to the Crown Prosecution Service (CPS). Based on the strength of the evidence, prosecutors are required to consider whether there is a 'realistic prospect of conviction'. Research has shown that the CPS is often less likely to proceed with prosecutions that concern ethnic minorities than ethnic majorities, as both perpetrator and victim.[16] When cases proceed to court, it is found that ethnic minority groups experience higher acquittal rates compared with ethnic majorities – consistent with termination rates at the CPS. What these findings demonstrate is that the impartiality earlier on in the process is an important aspect.[17] These biases are potentially more a reflection of arrest procedures, and, as the 2001 Denman Inquiry concluded after a formal investigation into issues of race inequality, the CPS was guilty of institutional racism for 'discriminating against ethnic minority defendants by failing to correct the bias in police charging decisions and allowing

12 Home Office (2004) *2003 Home Office Citizenship Survey: People, Families and Communities*, London: Home Office Research Study 289.
13 Gilroy, P. (1987) 'The Myth of Black Criminality', in P. Scraton (ed.) *Law, Order and the Authoritarian State: Readings in Critical Criminology*, Milton Keynes: Open University Press, pp. 107–20; Home Office (2003b) *Statistics on Race and the Criminal-Justice System: A Home Office Publication Under Section 95 of the Criminal Justice Act 1991*, London: Home Office.
14 Newburn, T. and S. Hayman (2001) *Policing, Surveillance and Social Control: CCTV and Police Monitoring of Suspects*, Uffculme: Willan.
15 Kundnani, A. (2004) 'Analysis: The War on Terror Leads to Racial Profiling', *Institute of Race Relations News*. Available at <www.irr.org.uk/2004/july/ ak000006.html>. Accessed 24 July 2009.
16 Phillips, C. and D. Brown (1998) *Entry into the Criminal-justice System: A Survey of Police Arrests and Their Outcomes*, London: Home Office Research Study 185.
17 Mhlanga, B. (1999) *The Colour of English Justice: A Multivariate Analysis*, Aldershot: Avebury.

a disproportionate number of weak cases against ethnic minority defendants go to trial'.[18]

Roger Hood's classic study, *Race and Sentencing*, was one of the first to look at the impact of racism and discrimination on patterns of sentencing.[19] Based on research carried out at the end of the 1980s in five Crown Courts in the West Midlands, it was found that a higher proportion of African-Caribbeans than white Britons or South Asians were being sentenced to custody. The question was whether differential types of criminal activity, prior record or any other factor could account for these differences. It was ascertained that, given these controls, African-Caribbean defendants were up to 23 per cent more likely to be sentenced to custody. This figure holds up to further testing.[20]

To monitor the instances of racism and discrimination the Home Office regularly publishes statistics on sentencing practices in Crown and magistrates' courts. It has been found that ethnic minorities in general are not found to be negatively treated in the magistrates' courts, but South Asians (many of whom are of Muslim origin) are 'significantly more likely' to be sentenced to custody.[21] More recent Home Office published data, termed Section 95 statistics, as required by the Criminal Justice Act 1991, suggest that there is no evidence of difference in the rates of custody between groups. In terms of Crown Court decisions, in relation to violent offending, African-Caribbeans are far more likely to receive custodial sentences. In relation to prison populations, ethnic minorities, in particular African-Caribbeans, are disproportionately represented. In addition, these prisoners are more likely to be younger than white Britons.[22] All of the above facts are evidence of some of the different experiences of minorities in the criminal justice system. These broad observations are important to bear in mind when considering the overall experiences of ethnic and Muslim minorities within the criminal courts as the final stage of a journey full of biases and discriminations towards these minority groups.

18 Denman, S. (2001) *The Denham Report: Race Discrimination in the Crown Prosecution Service*, London: Crown Prosecution Service.
19 Hood (1992), op. cit.
20 Hood's study (ibid.) of sentencing practices in relation to ethnic minorities in five Crown Courts was critiqued for its statistical methods, but Hirsch and Roberts conclude that, 'an adequate threshold of significance was used in the study; that the exclusion of certain status variables did not invalidate the study's findings; and that the choice for which sentencing variables to control for is ultimately a normative matter': von Hirsch, A. and J.V. Roberts (1997) 'Racial Disparity in Sentencing: Reflections on the Hood Study', *Howard Journal of Criminal Justice*, 36(3): 227–36, p. 227.
21 Flood-Page, C. and A. Mackie (1998) *Sentencing Practice: An Examination of Decisions in Magistrates' Courts and the Crown Court in the mid-1990's*, London: Home Office Research Study 180.
22 Cavadino, M. (1999) *Criminal Justice 2000: Strategies for a New Century*, Hampshire: Waterside Press, p. 180.

The confidence of the British Muslim community in the criminal-justice system has been undermined by the perception that it is being unfairly policed and victimised under the existing anti-terrorist legislation. In 2004, Human Rights Watch identified that the powers of arrest under the various anti-terrorism Acts have been used disproportionately against British Muslims, which has harmed race and community relations and 'undermined the willingness of British Muslims to cooperate with police and security services'.[23] As the findings of the 2004 Open Society Institute (OSI) report show, 'there is a perception that the criminal-justice system is concerned more with the political control of Muslim communities than with their safety and protection'.[24] It is also the case that 'there is anxiety that Muslims are being spied on by the authorities, which makes [them] very distrustful of any engagement in civil/public life'.[25] Recently, it has been argued that British Muslims have been subjected to discrimination not only on the grounds of their ethnic origin but also on the basis of their religious identity. The Islamic Human Rights Commission (IHRC) has documented aggressive acts against Muslims since 9/11. According to one IHRC report, produced soon after 9/11, Muslims were on the receiving end of hostile telephone calls, as well as death threats. In particular, women and children received physical and verbal abuse.[26] The IHRC found 188 instances of verbal and written castigation, 20 examples of discrimination, '108 cases of psychological pressure and harassment and 344 serious crimes of violence'.[27] The Home Office conducted its own research in this area immediately after 9/11. The report, *Religious Discrimination in England and Wales*, found that ignorance, apathy, prejudice and discrimination against individuals on the basis of their religious beliefs were regular occurrences for people from an array of different faith groups.[28]

Many British Muslims contend that they are being victimised by the police service, which abuses the powers vested in it. They also assert that the prison service is not sympathetic to the needs of the growing number of Muslim prisoners and that prison staff exacerbate anti-Islamic sentiment in prison establishments. Roger Waters argues that public conceptions of the

23 Human Rights Watch (2004) *Neither Just Nor Effective: Indefinite Detention Without Trial in the United Kingdom Under Part 4 of the Anti-Terrorism, Crime and Security Act 2001*, London: HRW Briefing Paper, 24 June, p. 3.

24 Open Society Institute (2004a) *Muslims in the UK: Policies for Engaged Citizens*, New York: OSI, p. 293.

25 Ibid., p. 293.

26 Islamic Human Rights Commission (2002) *The Hidden Victims of September 11: Prisoners of UK Law*, London: IHRC, p. 4.

27 Open Society Institute (2004a), op. cit., p. 288.

28 Weller, P., A. Feldman and K. Purdam, with contributions from A. Andrews, A. Doswell, J. Hinnells, M. Parker-Jenkins, S. Parmar and M. Wolfe of the University of Derby (2001) *Religious Discrimination in England and Wales*, London: Home Office Research Study 220.

police have traditionally been divided between two contrasting stances. Ethnic minority groups have tended to conform to the 'anti-police' position, which supposes that they are subject to 'verbal abuse, gratuitous violence and arbitrary arrest, plus the fabrication of evidence against them; or that the police refuse to protect [them], either by not responding to their [emergency] calls or by not arresting assailants and those who incite racial hatred'.[29] Conversely, the 'pro-police' position, which has tended to be favoured by the majority, supposes that there are 'only a few "rotten apples" in the police, that ethnic minorities [...] are over involved in crime and [that] they are quick to complain when they misunderstand normal policing methods'.[30]

Nevertheless, ever since the post-war immigration of South Asians and African-Caribbeans from once-colonised lands, there has been a multitude of incidents that lend weight to the argument that there is an inherent institutional bias against ethnic minorities in the criminal-justice system. The Government is at a loss to defend the existing system from mounting accusations of discrimination on racial grounds when empirical data routinely indicates that ethnic minorities are more frequently subject to arbitrary arrest by the police and are over-represented in terms of criminal conviction rates, as well as in the prison population. Muslim communities are increasingly sensitive to the notion that they are being overly marked out by the police, in particular in relation to disproportionate stop and search rates, and that there is also discrimination in responding to telephone calls and harassment of Muslims by members of the police.[31] Allegations of racial discrimination in the criminal-justice system have also been exacerbated by the discernible under-representation of ethnic minority groups at the 'service end' of the system, i.e. personnel occupying positions as police officers, lawyers, judges, and probation and prison officers.

The Prison Act 1952 stipulates that individuals of different religions have the same entitlement to practise as Christian inmates, where the prison chaplain must guarantee that all offenders are able to follow their religion. Statistics reveal that prisoners are now following a wide range of religious beliefs. Between 1975 and 1998, prisoners who belonged to 'other' religions had increased by just under 10 per cent, while those registered as Christian has decreased by 31 per cent.[32] A 2002 prison statistics report indicated that British Muslims formed approximately eight per cent of the total number of prisoners in the UK. From 1993 to 2002, the increase in Muslim inmates

29 Waters, R. (1990) *Ethnic Minorities and the Criminal-justice System*, Aldershot: Avebury, pp. 50–1.
30 Ibid.
31 Commission on British Muslims and Islamophobia (2004) *Islamophobia: Issues, Challenges and Action*, Stoke-on-Trent: Trentham, p. 36.
32 Beckford, J. and S. Gilliat (1998) *Religion in Prison: Equal Rites in a Multi-faith Society*, Cambridge: Cambridge University Press, p. 52.

was 161 per cent.[33] The same Home Office statistics indicate that the total 'number of Muslims in prison doubled between 1993 and 2000, whereas the number of all Christians [decreased] from 75 per cent of the total prison population in 1993 to 59.5 per cent in 2000'. The report also states that 'on 30 June 2002, there were 5,379 male Muslim, compared to 430 Sikh and 256 Hindu male prisoners'.[34] In early 2009 it was reported that,

> '[t]he number of Muslim prisoners in jails doubled in the eleven years to 2007 to reach 8,864 – 11 per cent of the total prison population [with around 6 per cent who are British-born Muslims]. Muslim prisoners make up one third of the population of Whitemoor, 15 per cent of Full Sutton top security prison in Yorkshire and 20 per cent of Belmarsh jail.'[35]

A number of factors are at play in explaining the rising numbers of Muslims in prisons. Age is important, as the average for committing offences for men is around 18 years, while for women it is around 15 years.[36] Recently, there has been significant alarmism in relation to conversion to Islam inside prisons. There is a suggestion that radical Islamist tendencies are merging with the criminal pasts of inmates. Recent research carried out by Basia Spalek and Salah El-Hassan confirms that, in reality, conversion to Islam provides an opportunity for peace and order, as well as spiritual enlightenment for prisoners suffering from the negatives of incarceration, with prison *imam*s potentially providing a dedicated focus for otherwise destabilised prisoners. The process of conversion is often elongated and therefore the role of the *imam* is crucial in providing an effective, balanced and positive moral outlook on life.[37] Prison statistics based on religious classifications do not show numbers who convert to a religion while incarcerated; however, it is apparent that in some prisons conversion rates to Islam are likely to be relatively high and therefore this factor alone directly impacts on rising figures of Muslims in prisons. It is clear that in some prisons there are increasing rates of conversion to Islam, particularly among Black-British groups.[38]

Facilities provided for Muslim prisoners have improved in recent years, but there are a number of areas that continue to cause concern. For example, there is considerable lack of provision for the personal hygiene of Muslim prisoners. There have been reports that prayer halls are far away

---

33 Office for National Statistics (2003) *Prison Statistics: England and Wales 2002*, Home Office Cm 5996, London: Home Office.
34 Ibid., p. 262.
35 Ford, R. (2009) 'Muslim Prison Gangs on the Rise as Inmates Seek Safety in Numbers', *The Times*, 13 January.
36 Cavadino (1999), op. cit.
37 Spalek, B. and S. El-Hassan (2007) 'Muslim Converts in Prison', *The Howard Journal Criminal Justice*, 46(2): 99–114.
38 Quraishi, M. (2005) *Muslims and Crime*, Aldershot: Ashgate.

from facilities for washing in preparation for them, and that many are inadequate in terms of size and design. Muslim prisoners have also questioned the genuineness of *halal* provision they have been offered irrespective of the official view that the food provided is appropriate. Issues have also arisen because of the limited number of officers to escort inmates, Muslims have not been able to go to designated places of worship to attend prayer.[39] In Belmarsh prison, in 2004 there were approximately 150 Muslim prisoners who were served by one full-time *imam*. Also in 2004, at Feltham Young Offenders Institute, one full time *imam* and four temporary *imams* supported around 135 Muslim prisoners.[40] Basia Spalek has suggested that, in reality, the *imams* in prisons experience a number of limitations because of the fact that they are of a non-Christian faith, which is tantamount to a 'form of institutionalised racism'.[41] Respondents in the study stated that not only were they the victims of direct and indirect forms of institutional racism, but that they had to put the prisoners systems to task in order to get them to take action in responding to their specific needs and wants, not just for themselves as *imams,* but also for the Muslim prisoners they served. At the time of the study there was real concern that the power imbalance between themselves and practitioners of a Christian faith in relation to the penal system per se had become entrenched. Basia Spalek and David Wilson found anti-Muslim ill-feeling and institutional racism rife inside prisons. They argue the need to urgently alter the disequilibrium between Christian and non-Christian faiths, generating a more objective position for non-Christian religions, namely Islam. In order to change practices, it is argued that more Muslims need to be recruited into the system in order to provide positive role models.[42] Since this research was published, government-appointed *imams* on civil service salaries are now to be found in a number of prisons.

A 2001 Home Office study suggested that discrimination experienced by Muslims in prisons may well be especially profound. Of the 38 Muslim organisations engaged in the research, 34 identified actual physical ill-treatment meted out by prison staff. There was also inadequate supply of *halal* food and a general problem of white-British positive discrimination. Furthermore, 34 of the Muslim organisations in the study suggested malevolent behaviour by prison staff, while only 21 out of 124 Christian organisations reported this observation. A lack of understanding of the spiritual, theological and indeed practical features of Islam led some prison staff to believe that the Muslim prisoners were 'taking advantage' of them

---

39 Open Society Institute (2004a), op. cit., p. 298.
40 Ibid., pp. 306–7.
41 Ibid.
42 Spalek, B. and D. Wilson (2001) 'Not Just "Visitors" to Prisons: The Experiences of Imams Who Work Inside the Penal System', *Howard Journal of Criminal Justice,* 40(1): 3–13.

rather than simply following a particular religious practice, potentially encouraging inappropriate attention from the non-Muslim inmates. It has led to an increased focus on staff-training needs in relation to increasing their awareness of Islamic issues. Of the prison officers who took part in the study, most were aware of the identity of Muslims and that Muslim prisoners had particular requirements. Nonetheless, some prison officers appeared to be judgemental of Muslim prisoners who broke Ramadan rules or who conversed with friends at times of prayer.

Offenders often utilise a whole host of explanatory factors in order to negate or warrant offending behaviour. By using the services of *imams*, it is possible to provide Muslim offenders with a distinct ethical approach that helps to reconstruct their existence. The positive Islamic scripture and the insight it provides could be made relevant for the everyday lives of offenders. Through this approach, Islamic teachings could help to rehabilitate offenders, thereby potentially discouraging re-offending upon leaving the prison walls. This is beginning to happen in a number of prisons, effectively because of the dedicated efforts of certain full-time *imams*. Nonetheless, more urgent issues relate to support for Muslim prisoners, inside prison but also upon release, and when concerns relating to resettlement become important. Stronger concentration on the religious and spiritual development of Muslim prisoners as part of certain amelioration strategies could perhaps improve the strength of various initiatives. Simultaneously, programmes delivered by *imams* require better resourcing to help improve the chances of a larger number of Muslim prisoners gaining a greater opportunity to take advantage of these initiatives. The Muslim communities from which these Muslim prisoners once originated could also be supported to assist in the resettlement of offenders.[43] All of these issues have become more pertinent in the light of a number of young Muslim men who are entering prisons but also those leaving them after the sentences they received in the post-9/11 period come to an end.

Despite the implementation of improvements to the prison service, which have ostensibly benefited Muslim prisoners, Islamophobia, discrimination, racism and physical violence that involve members of staff as well as prisoners continue to be prominent features of prison life. In March 2000, 19-year-old Muslim prisoner Zahid Mubarek died in hospital, having been clubbed to death by a psychopathic racist cell-mate, Robert Stewart. They were both inmates at Feltham Young Offenders Institute. During the initial stages of the inquiry that followed, Duncan Keys, the Assistant General Secretary of the Prison Officers Association, informed the Commission for Racial Equality of a practice known as 'gladiator'. Prison officers placed

---

43 Weller et al. (2001), op. cit., p. 53; Spalek, B. (n.d.) *Muslims in British Prisons: Pen Picture.* Article 496. Available at <twww.hmprisonservice.gov.uk/assets/documents/100011E4496_ muslims_in_british_prisons.doc>. Accessed 6 March 2010.

bets on the outcome of fights between prisoners in cells, in this case knowing of the persistently violent aggressive and racist nature of one and the relatively minor petty-offending background of the other. In his testimony, Keys contended that the murder of Mubarek occurred because he had been deliberately placed in a cell with a known racist psychopath for the 'perverted pleasure' of officers.[44] The murder of Zahid Mubarek has highlighted the issue of Muslim prisoner safety. More than ever, the position of Muslim prisoners has shown they are at risk from racist anti-Islamic abuse and violent reprisal.

For many British Muslims, the events of 9/11 have marked a shift in the ways in which they are discriminated against in the criminal-justice system. No longer are Muslims simply prejudiced against on the grounds of their ethnic origin; they now increasingly endure a bias on the grounds of their religious identity. Incidents such as the murder of Zahid Mubarek have undermined the alleged objectivity of the system and publicly demonstrated that it continues to be plagued by endemic institutionalised racism.

As a result of the tragic events of 9/11 in New York and Washington, radical political Islamism has perhaps been seen as the single cultural, economic, political and social foe of the West, the chief protagonist in a counter-hegemonic discourse against rampant individual liberalism and social fragmentation in an era of rapid globalisation. Throughout Western Europe and in the USA, anti-terror legalisation has been enacted in an effort to stamp out violent Islamism. However, it has also confirmed trends in neo-Orientalist approaches to the rationalisation of Islam, which have been in ascendancy since the fall of the Berlin Wall and the 'Clash of Civilisations' thesis originally expounded in the early 1990s. Viewpoints that regard Islam as a monolithic entity subsequently inform local, national and global Islamophobia. In the British case, this has led to a gradual decline in civil liberties. The powers of the state to 'police' Muslims have intersected with notions of how these very same Muslims ought to behave in a 'good multicultural society'.

After the events of 9/11, New Labour introduced five pieces of anti-terror legislation: the Terrorism Act 2000, the Anti-Terrorism, Crime and Security Act 2001, the Prevention of Terrorism Act 2005, the Terrorism Act 2006 and the Counter-Terrorism Act 2008. Primarily, it was the situation in Northern Ireland and the perceived threat from the militant Irish Republican Army (IRA) that impacted on the development of the original legislation. Two of the most recent laws were designed to face the threat from 'denationalised' groups with political and religious ideologies that are thought to commit acts of terror but operate globally. It is argued that Al-Qaeda, for example, has no national ties and exists purely through an ideology:

---

44 O'Hara, M. (2005) 'Fatal Flaws', *The Guardian*, 15 June.

the 'idea of Al-Qaeda',[45] with Osama bin Laden as its cha
head and apparent banker. The 'group' does not exist as a
but rather brings together like-minded individuals and g
'ideological struggle'. It is this latter threat that prompte/
to be passed by Parliament in haste, and it is this legisla.
most controversy. The purpose of these laws was to provide a .
tolerant and safe society in which to live, where the threat from ᴎ.
tional terrorism is limited. However, a number of factors have transpireᴜ
that have led to these laws not being the just, democratic and effective
measures that they were intended to be. The knock-on effects of the
increased powers granted to the police have, for example, contributed to
the wider alienation of Muslim communities, and the language and
details surrounding the laws themselves have whipped up the nation into a
deepening sense of fear.

Britain is not a nation that is unfamiliar with threats from terror. The
conflict in Northern Ireland resulted in violent attacks by the IRA and the
Prevention of Terrorism (Temporary Provisions) Act 1974 was in continuous
use from November 1974. The predecessor to this Act, the Prevention of
Violence Act 1939, remained in British law until 1954.[46] The new legislation
is the first time that such a succession of increasingly controversial laws has
been introduced that impinge on civil liberties in such a negative way. The
Terrorism Act 2000 was the first counter-terrorism legislation to be passed
since 1989. Its main focus was to reorganise and bring together the
temporary Acts and provisions that were passed between 1974 and 1989,
and which were initially introduced to deal with the threat from the IRA.
The primary focus was to outlaw terrorist groups in Britain. Nonetheless,
the first assault on civil liberties was introduced when this law gave increased
powers to the police, especially the use of 'wider stop and search powers'
and 'the power to detain suspects after arrest for up to seven days'. The
following Bill passed was the Anti-Terrorism, Crime and Security Act 2001,
and its main features were based on tightening immigration policies and
further widening police powers, primarily increasing their ability to stop and
search UK citizens, with an additional extension to detention laws on suspected terrorists so that they could be incarcerated for up to 14 days. The
controversial Prevention of Terrorism Act was passed in 2005, barely scrap-
ing through Parliament after considerable amendments demanded by the
opposition, backbench MPs and the House of Lords. It allowed the use of
'control orders' to be made against any suspected terrorists and extended the
length of detention without charge for a suspected terrorist to up to 28 days.
The Terrorism Act 2006 was passed by Parliament on 30 March, and was

45 Burke, J. (1994) *Al-Qaeda: The True Story of Radical Islam*, London: Penguin, p. 13.
46 Walker, C. (2002) *Blackstone's Guide to the Anti-terrorism Legislation*, Oxford: Oxford
    University Press, p. 1.

ared after the events of 7/7. This legislation was even more controversial cause it proposed an increase to a 90-day pre-charge detention, seriously mpacting on the principles of habeas corpus. After considerable debate, New Labour suffered the heaviest defeat any government had faced since 1978. Notwithstanding, the legislation introduced an offence of acts in preparation for terrorism and a law against giving or receiving terror training. It also made indirect incitement of terrorism an offence. The Counter-Terrorism Act 2008 re-engaged with the issue of detention without charge, and this time for 42 days. The measure was defeated by the House of Lords and left out of the Bill. The Government then dropped the idea of increasing the time limit for detention without charge from 28 to 48 days. It now allows for post-charge questioning of terror suspects, permits certain police officers to take fingerprints and DNA from persons under a 'control order', and it allows the use of intercepted material during certain specified proceedings. In January 2010, the European Court of Human Rights in Strasbourg ruled the stop and search power under the Terrorism Act 2000 was indeed illegal and an invasion of the right to liberty and privacy.[47]

A 2006 report published by the IHRC focused on Muslim attitudes towards Government anti-terror legislation based on a survey sample of 1,125 and an interview sample of 47 Muslims from across the country. It found that most respondents felt that the law was unfair towards Muslims in Britain, but around one-third, irrespective of stated religiosity, agreed that it was wholly important to abide by the laws of the country. Only seven of the 47 interviewees felt protected by the law.[48] On 30 March 2006, after much heated discussion, three measures were approved. They were the Terrorism Act 2006, the Immigration, Asylum and Nationality Act 2006 and the Identity Cards Act 2006. The new standards introduced by the Acts now bestow otherwise unimaginable powers on various law-enforcement agencies to help in countering terrorism, and they have essentially removed the limited civil liberties that existed in the UK. Some of the new measures introduced the offences of directly or indirectly encouraging or motivating terrorism by glorifying terrorist acts, preparing for terrorist acts, having attended a terrorist training camp in any part of the world, and the apparent transmission or distribution of terrorist literature or other paraphernalia. The Acts also extended the maximum period of pre-charge detention from 14 days to 28 days, as well as widening the grounds to proscribe a range of organisations, in particular those who apparently proclaim terrorism. Moreover, the definition of terrorism is overtly broad and potentially

47 Travis, A. (2010) Stop and Search Powers Illegal, European Court Rules, *The Guardian*, 12 January.
48 Ameli, S.R., B. Faridi, K. Lindahl and A. Merali (2006) *Law and British Muslims: Domination of the Majority or Process of Balance?* London: IHRC.

includes a whole host of activities previously regarded as lawful: 'for the purpose of advancing a political, religious or ideological cause', the use or threat of action 'designed to influence a government or to intimidate the public or a section of the public' which involves any violence against any person or serious damage to property, endangers the life of any person, or 'creates a serious risk to the health or safety of the public or a section of the public, or is designed seriously to interfere with or seriously to disrupt an electronic system'.[49]

In essence, the law 'makes a criminal offence out of a belief shared by almost every society, religion or philosophy throughout history: namely that people have the right to take up arms against tyranny and foreign occupation'.[50] Furthermore, proof of intention is not required on the part of the person alleged to be committing the offence. A person can now be seen to be committing the offence by giving or publishing a statement believing, or having reasonable grounds to believe, that it will encourage others to commit terrorist acts. No requirement is needed by the authorities to establish the objectives on the part of the person committing the offence. It is deemed an offence if a person who disseminates any message with a specific view or if there is adequate grounds to believe that people will regard it as a direct or indirect incitement to engage in acts of terrorism.[51]

On 8 November 2007, Samina Malik, a young British-born Muslim woman, was the first individual to be convicted under the act for 'possessing records likely to be useful in terrorism'. The jury heard how Malik had penned radical verses praising Osama Bin Laden, supported martyrdom and discussed beheading on internet sites, and under the name 'Lyrical Terrorist'. Investigators discovered a range of problematic material written by her, and a number of other dubious publications when they carried out a search at her home, including *The Al-Qaeda Manual*, *The Mujahidin Poisons Handbook*, as well as other literary compositions that she had written. Malik refuted the allegations, claiming she was 'not a terrorist', and her *nom de guerre* was used only because 'it sounded cool'.

In Britain, the Human Rights Act 1998 'guarantees the right to life, freedom from torture, freedom from slavery and forced labour, the right to liberty and security, the right to a fair trial, the right to privacy, freedom of conscience, freedom of expression, freedom of assembly and association and the right to marry and have a family'. There are also the freedoms that protect the individual from arbitrary government interference, which include freedom of speech, freedom of assembly and trial by jury – usually created

49 Terrorism Act 2000, Section 1(1).
50 Milne, S. (2005) 'This Law Won't Fight Terror – It Is an Incitement to Terrorism', *The Guardian*, 13 October.
51 Ansari, F. (2006) *British Anti-terrorism: A Modern Day Witch-hunt*, London: IHRC.

and protected by a constitution. However, in the aftermath of 9/11, the Anti-Terrorism, Crime and Security Act 2001 was rushed through Parliament. It gave powers to hold without charge foreign nationals suspected of terrorism. To do this meant 'opting out' of Article 5 of the European Convention on Human Rights, allowing for this in time of war or other public emergency 'threatening the life of the nation'. Britain was the only nation to take this route. Pressure mounted to alter the ways in which this legislation seemingly impacted on Muslim groups, and in December 2004 the Law Lords ruled eight-to-one in favour of the All-Party Human Rights Commission to repeal internment powers in the legislation. It did so when the Court of Appeal, under Lord Woolf, reversed the decision of a Special Immigration Appeals Commission ruling that detention without trial was incompatible with British and international law. Lord Hoffman said, 'the real threat of this life of the nation, in the sense of a people in accordance with its traditional laws and political values, comes not from terrorism but from laws such as these'.[52] Rather than instantly repealing the Act, it was suggested by the Home Office that the 'control order' would be adopted: this is a non-custodial response, applicable to both foreign and British subjects, without charge and for an indefinite period if an individual is suspected of being involved in domestic or international terrorism. Measures included electronic tagging, curfews, a ban on the use of the internet and 'house arrest' (this term was not used by the incumbent Home Secretary, Charles Clarke). While some minor concessions were made, it was still felt necessary to derogate from the European Convention on Human Rights.

The state now has more powers than ever to hold people without charge, a function of the current climate of fear generated by political crisis and the media focus, the constitutional crisis raised by the Law Lords judgement, and the availability of technology in relation to constraining.[53] The erosion of the principle of habeas corpus severely undermines the civil liberties that have traditionally made this nation 'great' in the eyes of many. The continued racialised profiling of asylum seekers and immigrants is another feature in the negativity experienced by recently arriving Muslim groups, shown also in the attempt made by New Labour to evade the 1951 UN Convention on Refugees. In 1948, the General Assembly of the United Nations adopted and proclaimed the Universal Declaration of Human

---

52 House of Lords (2004) *Opinions of The Lords of Appeal for Judgement in the Cause A (FC) and Others (FC) (Appellants) v. Secretary of State for the Home Department (Respondent) and X (FC) and another (FC) (Appellants) v. Secretary of State for the Home Department (Respondent), on Thursday 16 December*, Paragraph 97, London: UKHL 56.

53 Nellis, M. and R. North (2005) 'Electronic Monitoring and the Creation of Control Orders for Terrorists Suspects in Britain', unpublished paper, University of Birmingham.

Rights and declared to the world that these rights ar
'as a common standard of achievement for all peoӷ
'that human rights should be protected by the rule
cornerstones of modern society and is founded /
alistic principles necessary for a healthy democrӟ
use the full power of these laws there would haˀ
from Article 5 of the European Convention fc
Rights and Fundamental Freedoms (ECHR)'.
edged breach of these rights by any governmeıı.
believes the new UK laws have breached a further six funɑɑ
'respect for private and family life; freedom of thought, consciencɛ ⸗
religion; freedom of expression; freedom of assembly and association; freedom of movement; and right to a fair trial'.[55]

Sentiments in relation to the targeting of young Muslims by the police
were exacerbated by comments made by Hazel Blears in 2005, then minister
responsible for counter-terrorism, who said that Muslims would have to
accept as a 'reality' that they will be stopped and searched by the police
more often than the rest of society. Never has a minister previously declared
that particular laws could be used in this potentially discriminatory way,
contradicting the Race Relations Act (Amendment) 2000 and the other
equalities legislation currently in effect. The Special Powers Act 1972 in
Northern Ireland was the previous occasion when a government exhibited
such derision for the administration of justice. Blears stated that the 'threat
is most likely to come from those people associated with an extreme
form of Islam, or falsely hiding behind Islam, if you like'. She added
'inevitably [it] means that some of our counter-terrorist powers will be disproportionately experienced by people in the Muslim community. That is
the reality of the situation, we should acknowledge that reality'.[56] Statistics
published by the Home Office in 2007 revealed that 1,166 people were
detained between 11 September 2001 and 31 December 2006 on suspicion of
involvement in terrorism. A total of 652 were released without charge. These
arrests led to 221 charges under the anti-terror legislation, but with only
40 convictions, although many other prosecutions are still awaiting a
court hearing. In 2008 and 2009 a number of high-profile convictions were
made.[57] Figures released in mid-2009 by the Home Office showed that
the number of detained suspects had risen to 1,471 – an increase of 305
in the space of the 16 months to April 2008. 'Of those arrested, 102 were

54 United Nations (1948) *Universal Declaration of Human Rights*, New York: UN.
55 Amnesty International (2005) *UK: The Prevention of Terrorism Bill is a Grave Threat to Human Rights and the Rule of Llaw*, EUR 45/006/2005, London: AI.
56 BBC News Online (2005) 'Muslim Police Stops "more likely"'. Available at <http://news.bbc.co.uk/1/hi/uk/4309961.stm>. Accessed 25 July 2009.
57 Morris, N. (2007) 'Less Than One in 20 Held under Anti-terror Laws is Charged', *The Independent*, 6 March.

terror offences and 94 were convicted on terror-related

On

1 March 2008, there were some 125 terrorist prisoners in England and Wales. Of these, 62% were UK nationals and 91% classed themselves as Muslim. According to the figures, there were 231 terrorism arrests in 2007/8 compared with a yearly average of 227 since 1 April 2002. Of those arrested under section 41 of the Terrorism Act 2000, 46% were held in pre-charge detention for one day and 66% for less that two days. The figures also show that six suspects were detained for a full 28 days since the maximum period of pre-charge detention was raised in July 2006. Of the six, three were released and three were charged'.[59]

Arrests under the anti-terrorist laws have attracted widespread media coverage while convictions of non-Muslims in court have not been widely reported: for example, six members of the British National Party who were charged with terrorism offences in late 2009, many with links to ultra-far-right groups who espouse violence towards Muslims and Jews.[60] Most people are therefore left with the impression that the criminal-justice system is successfully prosecuting 'Muslim terrorists' in Britain. An illustration is the dramatic arrest of twelve Muslim students who were in British universities in April 2009. Statements made by senior political figures, including the then-Prime Minister Gordon Brown, suggested these were serious and credible arrests, but within a matter of weeks they were all released without charge.[61] Since the events of 9/11, large numbers of ultimately exonerated Muslims are being arrested, questioned and released. In the post-7/7 period, it seems this pattern has remained.

There are important intersections between matters of civil law and Muslims, and in 2006 the issue of the veil was again put onto the socio-legal landscape of British Islam, and this time in relation to the House of Lords ruling on Shabina Begum, who was then a pupil at Denbigh High School in Luton. Initially arguing her right to wear the *jilbab* (a long gown, without the face veil) to school, it was ultimately said to be against the existing school dress policy. As a result, Begum refused to attend school. With her brother acting as her guardian for the purposes of legal action, Begum asserted the right for a judicial review based on her view that the school had

58 BBC News Online (2005) 'Terror Arrest Conviction Rate 13%'. Available at <http://news.bbc.co.uk/1/hi/uk/8047477.stm>. Accessed 25 July 2009.

59 Ibid.

60 Buaras, E.A. (2009) 'Terror Conviction Shows BNP True Colours, Says Anti-fascist Group', *Muslim News*, Issue 249, Friday 29 January 2010. Available at <www.muslimnews.co.uk/paper/index.php?article=4478>. Accessed 9 April 2010.

61 Laville, S., R. Norton-Taylor and S. Bates (2009) 'All 12 men Arrested During Anti-terror Raids Released Without Charge', *The Guardian*, 22 April.

obstructed certain religious obligations and consequently her right to an education (both rights safeguarded in Article 9 of the European Convention on Human Rights). Begum was unsuccessful in the High Court, but later won at the Court of Appeal. In appealing against this ruling the school was able to get the case heard by the Judicial Committee of the House of Lords. After submissions were made by the Department for Education and Skills, the House of Lords decided in the school's favour.

It was felt that the school already possessed a liberal policy in relation to dress code, where there was a Muslim head teacher, and nearly four in five pupils were of Muslim background. Moreover, Pakistani pupils would often wear the *shalwar kameez* (traditional dress worn by men and women of South Asian origin). Local mosques and community groups were closely consulted in relation to planning this school dress policy. Begum and her counsel, however, were of the view that the *shalwar kameez* was too fitting to the body as a form of dress, and it therefore contravened essential Islamic codes in relation to modesty. It was also argued that the *shalwar kameez* was a culturally specific dress worn by Pakistanis and not Bangladeshis. Those who supported the school argued that Begum was under the influence of the Islamist political party Hizb ut-Tahrir (HT), because Shuweb Rahman, her brother and member of her legal team, was a known follower. The school also argued that if Begum was permitted to wear the stricter form of Muslim dress, it would encourage others to follow, with problems of radicalisation possibly emerging among a sub-section of the pupils.

Lord Bingham made it clear at the start of his decision 'this case concerns a particular pupil and a particular school in a particular place at a particular time'.[62] Lord Cornhill added that 'the House is not, and could not be, invited to rule on whether Islamic dress, or any feature of Islamic dress, should or should not be permitted in the schools of this country'.[63] The Law Lords suggested that the right of an individual to possess certain religious beliefs was inviolable, however the manifestation of a particular religious belief of a person had to be legitimate (i.e. there could be reasonable ground for its interference if justified). Three of the five Law Lords argued that the rights of Begum were not impeded in any way (Lord Bingham, Lord Scott of Foscote and Lord Hoffmann), but two viewed that they were (Lord Nicholls and Baroness Hale). However, they were all in agreement that there were reasonable bases for intervention in this case, in particular in relation to safeguarding the interests of other pupils at the school who did not want to be seemingly forced into wearing particular forms of religious dress. Ian Ward argues that there is a wider context in which the Shabina Begum case must be viewed. It revolves around the question of what Muslim women

---

62 Idriss, M.M. (2006a) 'The Defeat of Shabina Begum in the House of Lords', *Liverpool Law Review*, 27(3): 417–26.
63 Ibid.

should wear or not wear. It also shows the 'tensions that exist between liberal and multicultural or communitarian political visions'.[64] The idea of veiled women is problematic for feminists as much as it is for secularists, and it becomes difficult to determine a position in relation to Muslim women who, potentially, may or may not always have a significant say in the matters of whether to wear a headscarf (or a *jilbab*). It is clear that this problem is reflective of wider perceptions in Western Europe, as well as the effects of changes to the legislation on community relations but also individuals.[65] Notwithstanding, there is a genuine feeling that the Law Lords skirted around the essential issues.[66] Although Lord Bingham was careful to note that the House of Lords was not ruling specifically on the matter of Islamic clothing in schools, it was also stated that it would be impossible to ignore how the 'War on Terror' has been closely aligned to a political project to delimit the problem of extremist interpretation. Lieve Gies notes,

> 'it seems unusual for bodies to be perceived as this offensive and threatening in a largely non-sexual way: while the bodies of young Muslim men have become signifiers of lethal destructiveness, those of young Muslim women are associated with aggressive proselytization'.[67]

In essence, Begum's desire to change her dress was felt to be one that she did not make on her own and that in the current period it has particular implications for society as a whole. It relates closely to the 'fear of the headscarf' that re-emerged not only in Turkey but also in Germany in 2005 and France, where legislation was enacted to prevent 'conspicuous religious symbols' in public institutions, namely in schools and universities.[68] In the end, the result of the case was founded on traditional lines of liberalism – to avoid a focus on freedom of religion, the House of Lords concentrated on personal choice and acquiescence – but the crucial issue of whether faith can be construed as only a matter of consent was left untouched.[69] The fact that Begum had to go to a different school was deemed less significant than having to realign the school dress policy of Denbigh High School to meet certain needs. Omitted was the nature of the equilibrium between 'individual rights and collective welfare' and how proscribing the *jilbab* may have perhaps

---

64 Ward, I. (2006) 'Shabina Begum and the Headscarf Girls', *Journal of Gender Studies*, 15(2): 119–31.

65 Motha, S. (2007) 'Veiled Women and the Affect of Religion in Democracy', *Journal of Law and Society*, 34(1): 139–62.

66 Gies, L. (2007) 'What Not To Wear: Islamic Dress and School Uniforms', *Feminist Legal Studies*, 14(3): 377–89.

67 Ibid., pp. 387–8.

68 vorn Bruck, G. (2008) 'Naturalising, Neutralising Women's Bodies: The "Headscarf Affair" and the Politics of Representation', *Identities*, 15(1): 51–79; Silverman, M. (2007) 'The French Republic Unveiled', *Ethnic and Racial Studies*, 30(4): 628–42.

69 Gies (2007), op. cit., p. 388.

caused an already vilified and excluded minority to feel further persecuted. And, certainly, the irony is that there are other schools that permit both the wearing of the *hijab* and *jilbab*.[70] The ruling in relation to Begum is conclusive enough, but it will certainly not prevent other Muslim women making similar requests.[71] It is argued that the law is in urgent need of revision to take into consideration approaches based on human rights and also anti-discrimination principles. This is especially important to consider given the roles that schools play in the socialisation of young people and in the development of societal norms. Ann Blair and Will Aps contend, 'if the school's authority in matters that are spiritual are recognized to be limited in cases of RE [religious education] and collective worship, there is no logical reason why they should not be limited in terms of religious dress'.[72]

The predominant argument is that state schools should not be seen to be imposing particular religious values onto other people, but when it comes to staff there are specific problems in relation to effective communication that might emerge, as was stated in the case of Aishah Azmi in late 2006. Losing a discrimination case against the school that employed her because of failure to remove her face veil, she won £1,100 for victimisation for the way the dispute was handled.[73] Blair and Aps conclude, 'it is our view that schools should not be required to deal with inconsistency and complexity of this order and that fundamental non-discrimination rights deserve much clearer and more consistent protection'.[74] The other important issue here is that the courts have been able to maintain a ban on the *jilbab* in a state Muslim-majority school where the pressure to wear it is perhaps greater, but there is a possibility that in a school where Muslims are the minority, the courts may actually be in breach of Article 9 of the ECHR and Section 49 of the Equality Act 2006.[75] For Haleh Afshar, the reawakening of an interest in what Muslim women place over their hair reveals an Orientalism and Islamophobia reinvented for the modern era.[76]

A 'climate of fear' has not come into being without some context or history. Frank Furedi argues the existing uncertainties in liberal Western societies disproportionately affect the enactment of anti-terror legislation,

---

70 Idriss, M.M. (2006b) 'Jilbaabs in Schools', *Nottingham Law Journal*, 15(1): 19–27.
71 Idriss, M.M. (2006c) 'The House of Lords, Shabina Begum and Proportionality', *Judicial Review*, 11(3): 239–45.
72 Blair, A. and W. Aps (2005) 'What Not to Wear and Other Stories: Addressing Religious Diversity in Schools', *Education and the Law*, 17(1–2): 1–22, p. 16.
73 Wainright, M. (2006) 'Tribunal Dismisses Case of Muslim Woman Ordered Not to Teach in Veil', *The Guardian*, 20 October.
74 Blair and Aps (2005), op. cit., p. 17.
75 Carney, D. and A. Sinclair (2006) 'School Uniform Revisited: Procedure, Pressure and Equality', *Education and the Law*, 18(2/3): 131–48.
76 Afshar, H. (2008) 'Can I See Your Hair? Choice, Agency and Attitudes: The Dilemma of Faith and Feminism for Muslim Women Who Cover', *Ethnic and Racial Studies*, 31(2): 411–27.

and, subsequently, the impact is highly exaggerated.[77] The 'climate of fear' permits controversial measures to be passed by Parliament without significant initial public outcry, or even forced through as a response to public demand. They in turn sustain the very same 'climate of fear'. With the increased awareness of the threat from global terrorists since 9/11, there has been a proportional increase in Islamophobic feeling and sentiment, with many Muslims suffering verbal and physical abuse, harassment, and aggressive threat levels that are often reprehensible. Increasingly, the British media has associated Islam with terror. It is this assumed association between Muslims and terrorism that is also perpetuated by Hollywood films, television adaptations, sub-plots in popular crime or hospital drama series and, most recently, in the satirical cartoons that were published in Denmark (see Chapter 5). It has created the upsurge in aggressive Islamophobic attacks and has led to many Muslims living in a new 'climate of fear', purely because their religious beliefs are so mistrusted.[78]

Much of UK Government justification for its action is based upon the idea of Islamic political terrorist acts being carried out on British soil, but the approach taken by central government has been in excess of the needs of the lived reality. The Government originally focused on outside would-be terrorists and how they might work with groups here, but the post-7/7 reality suggests that the terrorists who carried out the recent attacks were in fact 'home-grown'. Even so, what remains true is the decline of civil liberties and personal freedoms. The following question should be asked by political analysts and social scientists. Did government reaction to 9/11, namely the 'War on Terror', play a role in motivating these young British-born men to attack their very country of birth, utilising violent politico-ideological abstraction of Islamic scripture, as a number of leftist commentators have suggested or, indeed, was there a sinister enemy called radical political Islamism at its root? The conceptual, ideological and policy-orientated solutions to Islamic political radicalism in Britain are discussed in the conclusion.

---

77 Furedi, F. (2007) *Invitation to Terror: The Expanding Empire of the Unknown*, London: Continuum.
78 Sheridan, L.P. (2006) 'Islamophobia Pre- and Post-September 11th, 2001', *Journal of Interpersonal Violence*, 21(3): 317–36.

9 British Islam tomorrow and the battle ahead

At a time of ever-increasing global economic, social and political inter-dependence on the one hand, with uncertainty on the other, questions in relation to what it means to be a Muslim minority are at the forefront of debates in policy, government, media and the academy in Britain. A range of discussions emerge on radicalisation, secularisation, modernisation, identity conflicts, intergenerational change, cultural relativism and social and economic alienation. A particular phenomenon to emerge is that of Islamic political radicalism. Arguably, those on the left of the political spectrum believe the 'War on Terror' and structural inequalities are at the heart of the problem, while those on the right argue it is more about the very essence of a religion that is seen as alien, barbaric or ill-adjusted to the expectations and aspirations of a post-Enlightenment Western Europe. Blame does not lie exclusively with the religion of Islam, the material reali-ties of already-isolated British Muslims or indeed British foreign policy. They are all equally relevant in this sensitive equation.

While the current focus has been on post-9/11 and post-7/7 experiences, there have been earlier periods in the so-called radicalisation of Islam and Muslims; in particular, through the writings of Muslim ideologues in the 1940s, 1950s or 1960s, namely Sayyid Qutb and Maulana Sayyid Abul Ala Maududi; the actions of the Palestinian Liberation Organisation and its wings, the Popular Front for the Liberation of Palestine and Fateh, in the 1960s and 1970s; and the activities of the Libyans, Iraqis, Iranians or the Lebanese, including Hamas and Hezbollah, since the 1980s. There is a per-ceptible pattern where Muslims in Islamic lands have reacted against the 'double standards' and the prevailing interests of Western capitalistic economies vying for power and domination. In the decades since the Iranian Revolution of 1979, the Muslim world has been in turmoil while Muslim minorities in the Western world have faced economic, social, political and cultural marginalisation. It is these harsh experiences that continue to characterise the current sociological, anthropological, cultural-studies and political-science interests in the study of Muslims in the West.

Muslims across the globe have become the focus of particularly negative attention ever since the Iranian Revolution of 1979. Images of 2 million men and women on the streets of Tehran, shown on television screens all over the world, shocked many in Western Europe. The Rushdie affair of 1989 highlighted the extent to which the media and British Muslims (who vociferously opposed the publication of the book) became 'emotionally unhinged' over the issue, and how the South Asian Muslims of Britain were shown to be weak and intolerant when, in fact, they were expressing their opinions in relation to a publication that was to them profoundly offensive. This piece of magical realism deeply upset Muslims at the time, and it gave rise to discussions of freedom of speech, blasphemy laws and the protection of non-Christian religions in Britain.[1] The first Gulf War (1990–1), the atrocities in Bosnia-Herzegovina (1993–6), the Taliban in Afghanistan (1997–present), Grozny and Kosovo (1999), the recent Palestinian Intifada (September 2000), the War on Iraq (2003–present) and the attack on Lebanon by Israel (2006) have all played a part in fostering a transnational Muslim political identity: a genuine and conscious identification with others sharing the same religion even though there are vast ethnic, cultural and social differences between groups.[2]

The 'Clash of Civilisations' thesis propounded by Samuel Huntington – positioning East and West, Islam and Christianity, as diametrically opposed with irreconcilable differences – has served only to build upon growing anti-US sentiment and increased Orientalism through over-simplification and generalisation. Few, however, could have prepared the world for the 9/11 attacks on the World Trade Center and the Pentagon in the USA. Reactions were swift, and associations between Islam, terrorism and the notion of a Christian versus Islamic conflict only served to further fuel anti-Islamic views on the one hand, and anti-US feeling on the other. The attacks gave rise to efforts by British far-right groups to paint Muslims as epitomising unwanted difference and to almost excuse anti-Islamic violence. In the days following the the 9/11 attacks, an Afghan taxi driver was assaulted and left paralysed in London, while a Sikh petrol-station owner was shot dead in Arizona, USA. To the assassins, the beard and attire of these men resembled those of Osama bin Laden. Since then, political, cultural and social interest, with infinite books, television programmes and films on Muslims, Islam, the Qur'ān, jihad, international terrorism, international security, moderate Islam, political Islam, radical Islam and Islamic militancy have been extensively published and disseminated, exploring and discussing many elaborated and often conflated debates. There appears to be a genuine desire to learn more and deliberate the issues in relation to a

---

1 Weller, P. (2009) *A Mirror for Our Times: 'The Rushdie Affair' and the Future of Multiculturalism*, London: Continuum; McGhee, D. (2008) *The End of Multiculturalism? Terrorism, Integration and Human Rights*, Milton Keynes: Open University Press.

2 Bowen, J.R. (2004) 'Beyond Migration: Islam as a Transnational Public Space', *Journal of Ethnic and Migration Studies*, 30(5): 879–94.

religion and a body of people that, for many, have remained relatively unfamiliar, but this is not always carried out without a value-, power- or honour-free (after Akbar S. Ahmed) agenda. Attempts have been crude and simplistic, without any effort to present seriousness or detail. They played on existing Orientalist and Islamophobic stereotypes found in film, television, drama and literature. There has emerged a trend to satirise the issues of radicalism, difference and identity by acclaimed UK writers of comedy in the films *Four Lions* (2010, dir. Christopher Morris) and *The Infidel* (2010, dir. Josh Appignanesi), both in the British tradition of self-deprecation and irony.

In the aftermath of the 9/11 attacks, the then British Prime Minister, Tony Blair, was keen to present the imminent action against Al-Qaeda as not a war on Islam (while comments made by President George W. Bush that the 'War on Terror' would be a 'crusade' left little doubt in the minds of British Muslims that political Islam was his main target). The dilemma Tony Blair had was how 'to balance the bombing of Muslims abroad with wooing them at home'.[3] On Friday 28 September 2001, a few hours after the attacks on Afghanistan, a delegation from the Muslim Council of Britain (MCB) was invited to Downing Street. Paraded to the media were smiles and shaking hands. On 9 October 2001, the MCB issued a press release strongly denouncing the war. It led to the beginning of the end of the cosy relationship the MCB had with Number 10. In addition, pressure was applied to the five British Muslim parliamentarians at the time, namely MPs Khalid Mahmood and Mohammed Sarwar and the peers, Lord Ahmed, Lord Patel and Baroness Uddin: they were apparently 'encouraged' to sign a letter denouncing the events of 11 September partly justifying the retaliatory bombings in Afghanistan.[4] Placing British Muslim communities at the centre of what would be regarded as the 'problems' but, crucially, also the 'solutions' was integral to how New Labour began to present its case in relation to the 'War on Terror' to UK audiences, and right up until the general election of May 2010.

Since the 7/7 bombings, a variety of labels and definitions has been used in an attempt to explain and describe the individuals and groups involved in acts of terrorism. Terminology used here includes 'extremists', 'violent extremism', 'Islamic fundamentalism', 'Islamists', 'political Islam', 'radical Islam', 'Salafists', 'jihadi-Salafists' and 'Islamic political radicalism'. Terms with widely different meanings are used interchangeably, but within Islam there exists a diverse range of groups, movements, organisations and schools of political and theological thought. It is important to understand how the

3 Saghal, G. (2002) 'Blair's Jihad, Blunkett's Crusade: The Battle for the Hearts and Minds of Britain's Muslims', *Radical Philosophy*, 112 (March/April): 2–5.
4 Birt, J. (2005) 'Lobbying and Marching: British Muslims and the State', in T. Abbas (ed.), *Muslim Britain: Communities under Pressure*, London and New York: Zed, pp. 92–106.

sometimes nuanced differences of this diversity impact upon policy development and the delivery of interventions at the local level. For the purposes of 'naming' the issue it is suggested that the specific challenge that has emerged from 7/7 is the rise of jihadi-salafi ideology and its support amongst a very small section of British Muslim men. Jihadi-salafism is a form of radical political Islam, or militant Islam, that advocates the use of violence to achieve its ends. As has been explored in Chapter 2, the term 'salafi' can be used to describe either the largely non-political nineteenth-century reform movements or the twentieth-century revivalist movements, where some of which developed a consciously political character. The form of 'salafism' that mutated into jihadi-salafism is thought to be influenced by a number of the political concerns. However, it needs to be noted that neither 'salafism' nor 'wahhabism' is necessarily violent or political. The term 'jihadi', in this context refers to the use of violent struggle to defend Islam against attack. It is worth remembering that the word 'jihad' translates as 'striving', and in Islam its non-violent meaning has greater emphasis. Indeed, *jihad an-nafs*, which is the struggle to master one's ego, is considered the most important of all jihads, and arguably the most difficult. Since the end of the Soviet–Afghan war, the term 'jihadi' has been used to describe the actions of a range of nationalist and opposition movements in a number of Muslim countries, with some led by ex-Afghan international or Arab fighters. The current 'jihadi-salafi' ideology, therefore, has its origins in the Islamist successes in the Soviet–Afghan war, and they developed further during the course of the 1990s when a global interest group emerged, whose practical manifestation was the network or movement called 'Al-Qaeda'. The story of the emergence of jihadi-salafi ideology intersects with Britain through the presence of exiled Islamists granted refugee status in the UK during the 1990s, including some of the clerics and ex-Mujahidin who had been involved in nationalist and oppositional 'jihadi' movements in Muslim countries.[5]

From the late 1990s to the early 2000s, the key figures promoting jihadi-salafism in Britain were Abu Hamza al-Masri, Omar Bakri Muhammad, and Abu Qatada, the latter termed 'al-Qaeda's spiritual ambassador in Europe'. The influence of Abu Hamza al-Masri, Omar Bakri Muhammad and other clerics has been pivotal in the development of radical Islamist groups in Britain and, in turn, their influence on some young British Muslims. Understanding the reasons and causes of why some young Muslims may be attracted to the ideology of these groups and are willing to act in their name is part of the solution to devising appropriate prevention strategies. However, it should be realised that there is nothing intrinsically wrong with people showing an interest in 'radical politics' per se. From a national-security perspective, the problem lies with particular and known

---

5 Phillips, M. (2008) *Londonistan: How Britain Is Creating a Terror State Within*, London: Gibson.

radical groups that promote the use of violence towards the objective of a global vision. To conflate all radical Islamist groups with political violence in Britain risks targeting and labelling as possible 'terrorists' a whole host of non-violent people and interests. This is popularly known as the 'Londonistan' thesis.

This exploration of Islamic political radicalism has explored issues of youth, culture and local, national and international multicultural politics. In the final analysis, as a result of 'structural racisms' (post-war immigration, patterns of social demography and structural disadvantage) and 'cultural racisms' (Islamophobia, negative representation of Muslims in the media, changing concepts of citizenship and multiculturalism, and the impact of anti-terror laws), British Muslims are increasingly at odds with an 'English' or 'British' as opposed to an 'Islamic' way of life. This has genuine implications for a multicultural citizenry. Of particular theoretical and empirical interest are questions pertaining to national and international Islamic political radicalism. Muslims outside London are more likely to be living in some of the worst housing stock, possess the poorest health, significantly underachieve in education, and are more likely to be 'underemployed' or unemployed in the labour market compared with their non-Muslim counterparts. Many of the Muslims in Britain, specifically those originating from the rural areas of Azad Kashmir in Pakistan and Sylhet in north-west Bangladesh, are working in the declining or highly competitive globalised manufacturing, textile or catering sectors, and residing in inner-city housing of poor condition built at the turn of the twentieth century. They live as joint and extended families in restricted spatialities of ethnic and cultural life. They remain close to kith and kin, extending their religious and cultural social identities, which directly helps to shape their presence in Britain. As part of their adaptation to society, which is limited through constrained opportunity structures, younger generations of British Muslims have begun to question the religious and cultural values of their parents. De-industrialisation, technological innovation and the internationalisation of capital and labour have helped to ensure that many British people, including a disproportionately high percentage of Muslims, remain at the bottom of society. These patterns emerged early on in the immigration and settlement of Muslims from the late 1950s right through to the late 1970s and early 1980s, but the social divisions very much remain at present – largely as a function of pernicious structural and cultural social divisions as well as the increasingly competitive labour, education, housing and health markets.

It is true that British multiculturalism is a 'distinctive philosophy that legitimises demands upon unity and diversity', with the aim of achieving 'political unity without cultural uniformity', and ensuring all the citizens of the state have both a 'common sense of belonging' and a willingness to 'respect and cherish deep cultural differences' (after Bhikhu Parekh 2004). It is an amiable ambition but one that is not easy to achieve. In fact, there are few international examples that can be used to verify its success, but Canada and, in more recent periods, Australia, are looked to as notable cases. After 1997, the New Labour experiment had both successes and failures: the Race Relations (Amendment) Act 2000, the Human Rights Act 1998 and the Stephen Lawrence Report (1999) were positive steps, but, as a result of the 9/11 attacks and the 'northern riots', public-policy focus was on culture *and* values, integration through adaptation (assimilation), domestic security, and the war against international terrorism. All of these policy agendas have had significant impact upon British Muslims. Developments to this philosophy suggest that while the categories of British and English are being formed and reformed, Muslims in Britain are considered (and do identify themselves) by their religion, first and foremost, thereby completing the cycle. Furthermore, there are issues that exist at the level of intergenerational change, particularly in the climate of globalisation, and how they relate to the ways in which Islam and Muslims are being recognised, treated and appreciated. In the post-9/11 and post-7/7 era, British Muslims are at the forefront of questions in relation to what it means to be British or English. The basis of these concerns rests on issues on the global agenda, national dilemmas around multicultural citizenship, philosophy, policy and practice, as well as local area concerns in relation to 'community cohesion'.

The 9/11 and 7/7 attacks and the reactions that followed have permeated many areas of everyday life for Muslims the world over, and nowhere less so than in Britain. As events, they had far-reaching implications, which go beyond merely 'international terrorism'; they are linked to politics, religion, and issues of cultural difference in societies and democracies in Western Europe, which contain a significant number of Muslim minorities.[6] In the Middle East, as revealed in the aftermath of the war on Iraq, further unrest, political turmoil and violent action and reaction are the main features of the current climate. In the future, if further Western locations become targeted by young European- or British-born extremists who claim to have their motivations supported by their faith in Islam, relations between Muslims and their Western hosts will continue to remain problematic, with discussions dominated by a focus on citizenship, civil society, multiculturalism, political representation and participation (as components of democracy) and identity, gender, intergenerational development and radicalism versus liberalism (as components of the individual).

As British South Asian Muslims (Bangladeshis, Indians and Pakistanis) are reaching the third and fourth generations, matters of concern have shifted away from cultural assimilation and towards social integration, religious identity politics and discrimination. The study of Islam and Muslims has become vigorous, with a greater emphasis upon attempting to understand

6 Bader, V. (2007) 'The Governance of Islam in Europe: The Perils of Modelling', *Journal of Ethnic and Migration Studies*, 33(6): 871–86.

the nature and orientation of British Muslims from more historical, anthropological, sociological, cultural, theological and political-science perspectives. The first generations of South Asian Muslims expressed their religious values and traditions within their private or kinship spheres. Subsequent generations struggled with issues of integration and racism in the early 1960s, cultural pluralism in the 1970s, economic determinism and the free market of the 1980s to the mid-1990s, through to the 'third way' centre-left politics of assimilationist New Labour. At the same time, identification with Islam is strengthening amongst some of the current generation of Muslims, both as a reaction to racist hostility as well as a desire to understand the religion in more precise and in, perhaps, more literal detail, too. This faith identity is different from a political identity, but it is the pull of the latter which can afflict those with motivations for more immediate ideological outcomes.

The 'War on Terror' is a war that has no singular defined enemy, only a set of ideologies, appropriated and actualised by the 'clash of fundamentalisms' thesis, promulgated by a 'fear psychosis'.[7] But this globalising scenario is merely part of the experience of Islam and Muslims in Britain. More immediate concerns are the everyday social and economic challenges that are faced by most. Based on a classical neo-Marxian notion, the more British South Asian Muslims establish a determined economic and social foothold in society, the more their needs and aspirations will be met. The question is the path they take given the constraints faced by all: to be in a viable position to reach this objective, elimination of pernicious structural and cultural racisms is crucial. Furthermore, the nature and orientation of British multiculturalism is under severe test, and how Muslims experience the next few years and decades will be important to observe. What is apparent, however, is that 9/11 and 7/7 did not change the world, but what did transform was the political reaction and rhetoric in relation to 'the Muslim'. It will undoubtedly impact on how Muslims will be considered and treated for the foreseeable future, possibly for the remainder of the twenty-first century, as Akbar S. Ahmed has recently argued.[8]

The direction this new lived world experience will take is a function of dominant nation-states, their policies towards different Muslim migrants, minorities and citizens, as well as how Muslims work to adapt to majority society, closely adopting some of the more central norms and values, while sufficiently challenging others to make their new home a more peaceful, interdependent and secure place. British society has become sensitive to the threat of 'Islamic terrorism', while at the same time wider events in the

---

7 Ali, T. (2003) *The Clash of Fundamentalisms: Crusades, Jihads and Modernity*, London: Verso; Furedi, Frank (2006) *Culture of Fear*, London: Continuum.

8 Ahmed, A.S. (2003) *Islam under Siege: Living Dangerously in a Post-honor World*, Cambridge: Polity.

world, including the 'War on Terror', have continued to shape government attitudes towards Muslim citizens, as well as being important foci for political, social and policy discussions. In reality, Muslims in the East have favourable views towards the West, and Muslims in the West are more likely to have favourable views of the non-Muslims in the non-Muslim majority states they find themselves in.[9] Muslims are at an important juncture in their history of immigration to and settlement within Britain.

The following question is often put to Muslims in Britain. 'Are you Muslim first or are you British first?' It is a question which has received much attention recently, but it presupposes that there is an incompatibility between the two, that they are mutually exclusive, that there is an irreconcilable difference between one set of norms and values in relation to the 'other', or that the two are in never-ending historical conflict. This simple question is in fact symptomatic of how much of the West sees Islam and Muslim minorities, and how some Muslims see the West. Western Muslims are perceived to be different from the norm. It is not possible to remove the context of history from this question as the past 500 years have led to an imbalance of world power – the growth of the Western civilisations while others have fallen, arguably at the hands of these very new civilisations. A force for good during the early period, Islam has now either remained static or, more critically, has retreated into sectarianism and ethno-culturally specific practice.[10] A circular process emerges when the dominant hegemonic powers of the West exploit the resources of the East, which can create resistance and instability. These grievances are ideologically nurtured into violent fury vented at the external dominant powers, which then over-react. This starts the process of legitimising the 'othering of the other' to maintain the status quo, and the circle is complete. As part of the process, external agents help shape the political, economic and cultural dominance within respective hosts. This ensures internal discord, and the constant competition for access to higher echelons of power and influence only adds to the internal system of subservience. The West has extensively utilised the science, knowledge and technology of historical European Islam to determine a social, political and economic hegemony, but, today, it acts as the arbiter of all knowledge, truth and legitimacy.

Capitalism exists to retain economic and political power in the hands of the few at the expense of the many. Since the seventeenth century, this relationship has been racialised, with white Europeans thought to be at the top of the biological hierarchy with 'black others' at the bottom. In the past three hundred years or so, ever since the imperial and colonial project

9 Esposito, J.L. and D. Mogahed (2008) *Who Speaks for Islam? What a Billion Muslims Really Think*, New York: Gallup Press.
10 Allawi, A.A. (2009) *The Crisis of Islamic Civilisation*, New Haven, CT: Yale University Press.

accelerated, Muslim lands and their peoples have been subjected to widening inequalities. Over time, racialisation on the basis of colour has shifted to one on the basis of religion and culture. It is not an absolute, however, as testified by the case of African-Caribbean teenager Anthony Walker, brutally killed in July 2005 by white-English youths because of his skin colour. The ongoing concerns of death in custody and the general problems faced by African-Caribbeans in the education and criminal-justice systems confirm that 'race' and racism remain in existence.

All the same, there is a perceptible movement in relation to the major 'race relations' problems of this country. When it comes to crime, education, health, housing, unemployment, graduate employment, local area tensions in relation to regeneration, vilification in the media, national and international focus on terror, violence, extremism, and, indeed, multiculturalism, Muslims as well as the religion of Islam remain in sharp focus. And, undoubtedly, this has occurred at least since the Rushdie affair of 1989 but particularly since the events of 9/11 and, more recently, since 7/7. There is, as such, a persuasive economic and sociological context that needs to be appreciated in any effort to understand why Muslims are in the position they are and why the Western world is where it is, and, further, the political context in which questions such as the one put above can flourish. The question as to whether Muslims see themselves as more British or more Islamic is ever-evolving, but a British Muslim identity is an ever-changing conceptualisation determined by a whole host of endogenous and exogenous forces.

To be a perfectly good British Muslim is to be a loyal British citizen (see Chapter 6).[11] The two are not mutually exclusive, far from it. The concept of *ummah* is important for Muslims, as it stipulates a global solidarity, but it is not necessarily an effective political or social movement on its own. There are many shared bonds between Muslims and non-Muslims in Britain – for example, in relation to attitudes towards welfare, charity, neighbourliness, reciprocity, kindness to children and elders, voting, property rights, inheritance rights and divorce rights – but most people, Muslims and non-Muslims, are not always aware of these basic commonalities. The concept of being a Muslim transcends nation and ethnicity. What differentiates Muslims is language, culture, history: the nation-state is a relatively recent development. Christianity experienced a reformation around 500 years ago with people either having to align with the King or the Pope, but there is no separation between church and state in Islam. (The Mutazlites of Abbasid Baghdad were keen to make that division in the ninth century and Ibn Taymiyyah was a reformer in the Martin Luther sense.) Some Muslims are fighting with non-Muslims because they regard Islam as under siege, and historically there has been theological justification to carry out military jihad

11 Afshar, H. with commentaries from B. Barry, M. Bunting and I. Sacranie (2006) *Democracy and Islam*, London: Hansard Society.

(reactive and proactive defence of Islam). However, in the current period, this action is political, as it was during the time of the Khawarij. The concerns of the present day emerge because of the experience of colonialism in the past and systematic economic, political and social oppression more recently.

The development of the system of Western liberal democracy, as it is presently understood and applied, took a bloody struggle. For human society to reach this stage, it remains imperfect and under constant development. According to the Western concept, democratic governments enjoy absolute powers and infinite freedom, whereas Islamic power is bound by the commandments of Allah. Even so, the concept of modern democracy is not alien to Islam.[12] In the Medinan phase of the origins of Islam, Muhammad signed important pacts with the Christians, Jews and other minorities. In present times, Iran, Syria, Turkey, Kuwait, Lebanon, Egypt and Tunisia, for example, are democracies (although weak), and there is no separation of 'mosque and state'. The misconception that Islam cherishes dictatorships has its roots in the history of ancient Muslim rulers. The Mughals in India, the Abbasids of Baghdad, the Mamluks of Ayyubid Egypt, the Umayads of Muslim Spain (Al-Andalus) and the Ottomans of Turkey, despite their contributions to Islamic civilisations over the millennia, were all relatively dynastic rulers, especially towards their various ends.

What do the issues of radicalisation and multiculturalism mean for British Muslims in the current period and what solutions can be identified in relation to the present malaise faced by a significant proportion? There is indeed a need to move beyond 'British Muslim' navel-gazing, although there are important critiques of this experience providing useful personalised insights into the challenges of 'coming of age' as a 'Muslim Briton'.[13] But it is also true that Muslims need to engage with wider British society far more in the process of moving every community forward. Indeed, it is incumbent upon the whole of society to change together and, in particular, of the state to determine the necessary policies that genuinely advance the positions of those in a hugely divided society, a significant proportion of which are Muslims in Britain. Therefore, it is important to spell out a number of recognisable factors for future thinking, many of which relate to the need for community-led solutions to wider social problems.[14] They relate to five

---

12 Masud, M.M., A. Salvatore and M.v. Bruinessen (2009) (eds) *Islam and Modernity: Key Issues and Debates*, Edinburgh: Edinburgh Univesity Press.

13 Ahmad, I. (2007) *Unimagined: A Muslim Boy Meets the West*, London: Aurum; Aziz, S. (2007) *In the Land of the Ayatollahs Tupac Shakur Is King: Reflections from Iran and the Arab World*, Bristol: Amal Press; Husain, E. (2007) *The Islamist: Why I Joined Radical Islam in Britain, What I Saw Inside and Why I Left*, London: Penguin; Manzoor, S. (2007) *Greetings from Bury Park: Race, Religion and Rock'n'Roll*, London: Bloomsbury; Omaar, R. (2007) *Only Half of Me: Being a Muslim in Britain*, London: Penguin.

14 Briggs, R., C. Fieschi and H. Lownsbrough (2006) *Bringing It Home: Community-based Approaches to Counter-terrorism*, London: DEMOS.

themes: socio-economic exclusion, a crisis of masculinity, intergenerational conflict, interpretation of theology, local and global Islamophobia, and UK and US foreign policy. While hopes are high, the reality tends to be more of despair.[15] In an initial attempt to bring enlightened Muslims together to work out solutions, the Home Office appointed seven working groups immediately after the 7/7 attacks, and they focused on issues such as 'Muslim youth; education; women's issues; regional, local and community projects; the training of imams and the role of mosques; community security and police relations; and, finally, tackling extremism and radicalisation'.[16] Published in the autumn of 2005, the groups reports provided an initial review of the perceived problems, many of which, as argued here, have been in play for quite a considerable period of time.[17]

There is little doubt that social, economic and political exclusion features significantly in this analysis. Many young Muslims live in poverty, in overcrowded homes, in segregated declining inner-city areas and they face educational underachievement, high unemployment, and low graduate employment and poor health. This has significant implications for young people growing up in society, experiencing limiting horizons, fuelling distrust, generating disdain towards the nation-state, and in fostering an acute sense of isolation. These structural factors are wholly significant to the sense of alienation that young people feel. With issues of economic marginalisation, young Muslim men feel increasingly impotent in an ever-competitive and globalising marketplace in relation to employment, social mobility and cultural acceptance. Related are the issues of racism and discrimination that continue to permeate many of the structural problems affecting Muslim minorities, particularly in the Midlands and the north. Young Muslim men, invariably of South Asian origin, are also experiencing a sense of displacement because of the presence of increasingly aspirational and committed women in society in general, and women within the South Asian community in particular. Men of South Asian origin show bewilderment and exude a view that their position in communities and society at large is being undermined as women seek and attain equal status. In educational terms at least, Muslim women are outperforming Muslim men; however, their representation in further and higher education is sometimes left wanting, although improving.[18]

15 Abbas, T. and A. Siddique (2010) 'Perceptions on the Processes of Radicalisation and De-radicalisation among British South Asian Muslims in a Post-industrial City', *Social Identities: Journal for the Study of Race, Nation and Culture*, in press.

16 Brighton, S. (2007) 'British Muslims, Multiculturalism and UK Foreign Policy: "Integration" and "Cohesion" in and Beyond the State', *International Affairs*, 83(1): 1–17.

17 Home Office (2005) *'Preventing Extremism Together' Working Group Reports: August–September 2005*, London: Home Office.

18 Hussain, Y. and P. Bagguley (2007) *Moving On Up: South Asian Women and Higher Education*, Stoke-on-Trent: Trentham.

These experiences can fuel the 'jihadi cool' expressions of aggressive masculinity that affect some.

The crisis of masculinity, where it particularly affects Muslim men, relates to issues of patriarchy. British-born Muslim men often desire to integrate into or resists society far more than early generations. As a result, certain intergenerational tensions can emerge. Parents have a particular set of expectations and children another. In the context of South Asian patriarchy, tensions and rifts emerge, especially with young Pakistani men, who are sometimes unable to effectively channel their energies in a productive way. The bridge between the generations is not always traversed, with young men distracted and parents unaware.[19] A particular problem then emerges in relation to the political religiosity of this intergenerational divide. Some younger Muslims want a stricter and more literal interpretation of the Qur'ān, Sunnah and Hadith because it gives them a sense of identity in an ever-fractured world. It locates these individuals within the context of struggles at home, and in other parts of the Muslim world, with the liberal multicultural freedoms provided in their new homes to take on those challenges. The Islam of the first generation and the second generation of South Asians, and in particular in relation to Kashmiris and Pakistanis, tends to be inflexible. The fissure exposed has been unable to accommodate the interests and anxieties of current generations. As a consequence, younger Muslims turn to a set of 'radicalised' messages that stem from outside their community. It positions them in reaction to their parents, existing Muslim community elders, and in relation to the wider dominant society. Islamophobia essentially refers to the 'fear or dread' of Islam. It has an historical narrative that stretches back to the dawn of Islam, but it displays modern-day equivalents. It is demonstrated daily in the press, news media, documentaries, docu-dramas and various crime-detective series. It is also seen in politics, certainly in relation to how references are made to 'evil ideology' or 'good Muslims are with us and bad Muslims are against us', homogenising and standardising a very diverse world religion. What all this does is to further isolate marginalised young Muslim men who perceive that they are ever-beleaguered by a popular culture that regards Islam and with it Muslims in antithetical and monolithic terms. A re-framed neo-Orientalism places Islam as the bogey of society, perpetuated by negative media and popular discourses. Furthermore, it exhibits no boundaries, as Islamophobia has both local and global reach and impact.

An important question to ask is were the events of 7/7 a direct consequence of the war on Iraq. The answer is clearly no, because there had been young Muslim men involved in Islamic political radicalism before

---

19 Macey, M. (2007) 'Islamic Political Radicalism in Britain: Muslim Men in Bradford', in T. Abbas (ed.), *Islamic Political Radicalism: A European Perspective*, Edinburgh: Edinburgh University Press, pp. 160–72.

7/7 and 9/11. It is true that Iraq has been the single biggest British foreign-policy disaster of recent times, however. While Britain has withdrawn from the front lines, the war has undoubtedly destabilised the region and has concerned Muslims throughout the globe. It is not the central cause of current Islamic political radicalism. In fact, the phenomenon has been long in the making, well before the events in Bosnia, Chechnya, Yemen, Afghanistan and Iraq. The problems of radicalism are multi-layered and multi-faceted. For young Muslims to make the final jump to 'suicide-bomber' they have first to experience complete social, cultural, generational, political and economic marginalisation compounded by a distorted theological outlook on life. It is the nature of the interaction between grievances and ideology. The irony is that those who might regard what they are doing as acceptable would probably state the opposite, i.e. what they do is for Muslims, for social justice and for the rest of humanity. It is a rare combination for any young British Muslim man to take that ultimate path but, regrettably, it has been shown to be the case, with many more apparently willing or preparing to do the same. British Muslims consistently believe that foreign policy does not recognise their concerns and believe that the USA strongly dictates UK policy directions, and all of this in the context of rising Islamophobia and anti-Muslim racism.[20]

The notion that there is something inherently problematical about British multiculturalism because of Muslims has been presented for some time, namely since the Rushdie affair, the 'northern disturbances' in the former mill towns in 2001, and more recently since 7/7. A critique of multiculturalism has been expressed by certain liberal commentators, but it fails to appreciate that France has an assimilationist notion of integration and the Netherlands works towards a culturally pluralist framework, but both countries have suffered attacks by 'home-grown' radical Islamists. The problem has more to do with that which intersects the local and global in how disaffected Muslims determine their relations with others (see Chapter 7). This dislocation has been accelerated by the advance of communication technologies. The belief that the problem is one of Muslims per se is a function of over-pandering to difference, and an exaggeration of the debate that returns to a culturalist socio-pathological argument, which suggests that Muslims are not working hard enough to better integrate into society, ultimately ignoring the structural context in which many Muslims find themselves. However, it is important to acknowledge that the British model of multiculturalism is arguably the most advanced in Western Europe, but it is still under development. It is both embraced and hotly contested by wide sections of society.

---

20 The 1990 Trust (2006) *Muslim Views: Foreign Policy and Its Effects*, London: The 1990 Trust; Esposito and Mogahed (2008), op. cit.

Without doubt it is in the inner cities where most British Muslims are still concentrated. Invariably, neglect will remain on the part of the nation-state and the political establishment, until, of course, something tragic happens. The British people have been witnessing troubling events and, in relation to ethnic-minority communities, sometimes the same lacklustre responses since the 1980s (i.e. Brixton, Broadwater Farm or Handsworth). In 2001, Muslims in Britain needed a 'Scarman Report', not a 'Cantle Report': the former suggested the important link between racism, discrimination, structural disadvantage and poor police–community relations, while the latter stressed the need for changes to culture and values, under-emphasising the importance of structural inequalities.[21] This is precisely where the multiculturalism model in Britain works least well. In celebrating differences and being culturally sensitive to minority interests, the notion of a universal national identity has not been determined to permit the different ethno-cultural characteristics in various minorities of Britain to sufficiently coalesce around. Meanwhile, in the inner cities, different poor minority and majority groups effectively compete directly with each other for what are often the crumbs of society. At a policy level, in the current era, the promotion of cultural identity politics have superseded those concerns relating to the need to eliminate deep-seated structural inequalities.

Muslims have a considerable role to play in being confident about their roles and responsibilities in Western European nation-states.[22] As immigrant and now minority communities, Muslims are in a relatively opportunistic position, living and working in advanced economies and receiving the relative protection they do (of course, more could always be done). What Muslims do with that freedom, however, is crucial. Majority society needs to work purposively for Muslims *and* Muslims need to work resolutely with majority society. The teachings of Islam in relation to equality, morality, ethics, social justice, compassion and humanity are for all to learn. With nation-states making moves through the empowerment and incorporation of a burgeoning professional, and, more importantly, what are regarded as a 'moderate' class of Muslims, there have been some gains in how the process has positively engaged young professional people and Muslim women in particular, but it is important to bear in the mind the limitations of a top-down highly engineered approach. Rather, a bottom-up, community-inspired, self-reliant and forward-looking concept of integration and multiculturalism is the key to success. In Britain, at the level of the community,

21 Scarman, Lord (1982) *The Scarman Report: The Brixton Disorders, 10–12 April 1981*, London: Penguin; Home Office (2002) *Community Cohesion: Report of the Independent Review Team*, chaired by Ted Cantle, London: Home Office.
22 Sinno, A.H. (2009) (ed.) *Muslims in Western Politics*, Bloomington: Indiana University Press.

which is differentiated by ethnicity, culture, social class, region and sect, a number of Muslim faith-based, civil society and community organisations are working with government and these projects are delivering valuable outcomes. As structural preconditions emerge to permit equal opportunities and outcomes, Muslim groups will be able to value more their presence in society, becoming engaged citizens in the context of an ever-evolving national politico-cultural framework.

At the level of the state, popular discourses have been focusing on the culturally essentialist notion of 'the Muslim'. It can be a blame-the-victim philosophy that is imperceptibly instilled into majority society. In such a hostile local, national and international climate, radical Islamism can easily target susceptible young Muslim men, directly and indirectly. The violent radical Islamist ideology appeals because of its political and ideological context, however improperly appropriated. It is also fuelled by the actions of certain global powers and their approaches to foreign policy, as well as how they go about effectively incorporating Muslim minorities at home, or not, as the case may be.

In mid-2010, various Western European nation-states continue to maintain their legal, social and cultural engagement with Muslims in relation to issues of extremism, in particular with attempts to strengthen anti-terror legislation at home while fighting Muslim 'insurgents' abroad. Meanwhile, with ongoing harmful discourses that vilify, stigmatise and homogenise Muslims and Islam, many more young Muslim men are vulnerable to radicalisation. Unless there are greater efforts to tackle the structural issues and politico-ideological constructions in relation to 'being Muslim', among Muslims but crucially non-Muslim majorities, too, the potential threat of violent Islamic political radicalism will linger. Local area efforts are compounded by national and international issues, leaving many Muslims disempowered. The status quo cannot remain if liberal economies wish for stable and prosperous multicultural futures, confident of inter-cultural and inter-faith relations as globalisation bites harder and individual freedoms erode in the face of rampant capitalism and insidious post-9/11 invasions into basic freedoms in (relatively) progressive post-modern Western-European societies, and, in particular, in Britain. In relation to the religion of Islam itself, Muslims need to appreciate the importance of the oneness of humanity as is stipulated in the core doctrines while not falling foul of immediate political gratifications. The test is to evoke the beauty, excellence and stability of advanced Islamic culture, where faith, logic, reasoning and human progress go hand in hand. In the present climate, embattled Muslim minorities in Western Europe constantly have to defend themselves against violence, terror and various negative cultural associations. However, it is hoped that in the near future it will be possible to move beyond these immediate concerns and determine a positive image of Islam, where family, community, knowledge, nature and technology exist for the good of humanity as a whole, and not just the few. It needs to be an Islam that demonstrates responsibility for all in a world where Muslims and non-Muslims are interdependent human beings striving for collective efficacy in the face of challenges for scarce resources and the inevitable fallibility as well as frailty of humankind. This is the radical British Islam of the future.

Bibliography

Abbas, T. (2000) 'Images of Islam', *Index on Censorship*, 29(5): 64–8.

——(2001) 'Media Capital and the Representation of South Asian Muslims in the British Press: an Ideological Analysis', *Journal of Muslim Minority Affairs*, 21(2): 245–57.

——(2004a) 'Structural and Cultural Racism in the Educational Underachievement of British South Asian Muslims', in K. Jacobson and P. Kumar (eds), *South Asians in Diaspora: Histories and Religious Traditions*, Leiden: Brill, pp. 269–93.

——(2004b) *The Education of British South Asians: Ethnicity, Capital and Class Structure*, Basingstoke: Palgrave-Macmillan.

——(2004c) 'After 9/11: British South Asian Muslims, Islamophobia, Multiculturalism and the State', *American Journal of Islamic Social Sciences*, 21(3): 26–8.

——(2007a) 'Ethno-religious Identities and Islamic Political Radicalism in the UK: A Case Study', *Journal of Muslim Minority Affairs*, 27(3): 356–68.

——(2007b) (ed.) *Islamic Political Radicalism: A European Perspective*, Edinburgh: Edinburgh University Press.

——(2009) 'United Kingdom and Northern Ireland', in J.S. Nielsen, S. Akgönül, A. Alibašić, B. Maréchal and C. Moe (eds) *Yearbook of Muslims in Europe 2009*, Leiden: Brill, pp. 363–73.

——(2010) 'Muslim-on-Muslim Social Research: Knowledge, Power and Religiocultural Identities', *Social Epistemology: A Journal of Knowledge, Culture and Policy*, 24(2): 123–36.

Abbas, T. and M. Anwar (2005) 'An Analysis of Race Equality Policy and Practice in the City of Birmingham, UK', *Local Government Studies*, 31(1): 53–68.

Abbas, T. and P. Sanghera (2005) 'British South Asian Muslims and Radicalisation of the Youth: Masculinity, Multiculturalism and "Jihadi Cool"', paper presented to British Association for South Asian Studies Annual Conference, 30 March–1 April, University of Leeds.

Abbas, T. and A. Siddique (2010) 'Perceptions on the Processes of Radicalisation and De-radicalisation among British South Asian Muslims in a Post-industrial City', *Social Identities: Journal for the Study of Race, Nation and Culture*, in press.

Afshar, H. (2008) 'Can I See Your Hair? Choice, Agency and Attitudes: the Dilemma of Faith and Feminism for Muslim Women Who Cover', *Ethnic and Racial Studies*, 31(2): 411–27.

Afshar, H. R. Aitken and M. Franks (2005) 'Feminisms, Islamophobia and Identities', *Political Studies*, 53(2): 262–83.

Afshar, H. with commentaries from B. Barry, M. Bunting and I. Sacranie (2006) *Democracy and Islam*, London: Hansard Society.

Ahmad, A. (1967) *Islamic Modernism in India and Pakistan 1857–1964*, Oxford: Oxford University Press.

Ahmad, I. (2007) *Unimagined: A Muslim Boy Meets the West*, London: Aurum.

Ahmad, W.I.U. and R. Walker (1997) 'Asian Older People: Housing, Health and Access to Services', *Ageing and Society*, 17(2): 141–65.

Ahmed, A.S. (1995) '"Ethnic Cleansing": A Metaphor for Our Time', *Ethnic and Racial Studies*, 18(1): 1–25.

——(2003) *Islam under Siege: Living Dangerously in a Post-honor World*, Cambridge: Polity.

——(2004) *Postmodernism and Islam: Predicament and Promise*, London: Routledge.

Ahmed, A.S. and B. Frost (2005) (eds) *After Terror*, Cambridge: Polity.

Ahmed, A.S. and D. Hastings (1994) (eds) *Islam, Globalisation and Postmodernity*, London: Routledge.

Ahmed, N.M. (2006) *The London Bombings: An Independent Inquiry*, London: Gerald Duckworth.

Ahmed, R. (2009) 'British Muslim Masculinities and Cultural Resistance: Kenny Glenaan and Simon Beaufoy's *Yasmin*', *Journal of Postcolonial Writing*, 4(3): 285–96.

Akhtar, S. (1989) *Be Careful with Muhammad: The Salman Rushdie Affair*, London: Bedlow.

Al-Ali, N., R. Black and K. Koser (2001) 'The Limits to "Transnationalism": Bosnian and Eritrean Refugees in Europe as Emerging Transnational Communities', *Ethnic and Racial Studies*, 24(4): 578–600.

Al-Azmeh, A. (1993) *Islams and Modernities*, London: Verso.

Al-Daffa, A.A. (1977) *Muslim Contribution to Mathematics*, London: Croom Helm.

Al-Hassani, S.T.S., E. Woodcock and R. Saoud (2007) (eds) *1001 Inventions: Muslim Heritage in Our World*, Manchester: 1001 Inventions.

Al-Nabhani, T.A. (1953) *Mafahim Hizb al-Tahrir*, n.p.: The Liberation Party.

Al-Sayyed, N. and M. Castells (2002) *Muslim Europe or Euro-Islam: Politics, Culture and Citizenship in the Age of Globalization*, Lanham, MD: Lexington.

Aldrich, H., C. Zimmer and D. McEvoy (1989) 'Continuities in the Study of Ecological Succession: Asian Businesses in Three English Cities', *Social Forces*, 67(4): 920–44.

Alexander, C.E. (2000) *The Asian Gang: Ethnicity, Identity, Masculinity*, Oxford: Berg.

Ali, M. (2002) (ed.) *Islam Encountering Globalization*, London and New York: Routledge-Curzon.

Ali, N., V.S. Kalra and S. Sayyid (2005) (eds) *A Postcolonial People: South Asians in Britain*, London: Hurst.

Ali, T. (2003) *The Clash of Fundamentalisms: Crusades, Jihads and Modernity*, London: Verso.

——(2005) *Rough Music: Blair, Bombs, Baghdad, London, Terror*, London: Verso.

——(2006) 'Tortured Civilisations: Islam and the West', in C. Moores (ed.), *The New Imperialists: Ideologies of Empire*, Oxford: Oneworld, pp. 45–60.

Allawi, A.A. (2009) *The Crisis of Islamic Civilisation*, New Haven, CT: Yale University Press.

Allen, C. and J.S. Nielsen (2001) *Summary Report on Islamophobia in the EU15 after 11 September 2001*, Vienna: European Monitoring Centre for Racism and Xenophobia.

Ameli, S.R., B. Faridi, K. Lindahl and A. Merali (2006) *Law and British Muslims: Domination of the Majority or Process of Balance?*, London: IHRC.

Ameli, S.R., M. Elahi and A. Merali (2004) *British Muslims' Expectations of the Government Social Discrimination: Across the Muslim Divide*, London: IHRC.

Amghar, S., A. Boubekeur and M. Emerson (2007) *Islam: Challenges for Society and Public Policy*, Brussels: Centre for European Policy Studies.

Amin, A. (2002) 'Ethnicity and the Multicultural City: Living with Diversity', *Environment and Planning A*, 34(6): 959–80.

——(2003) 'Unruly Strangers? The 2001 Urban Riots in Britain', *International Journal of Urban and Regional Research*, 27(2): 460–3.

——(2004) 'Multi-ethnicity and the Idea of Europe', *Theory Culture and Society*, 21(2): 1–24.

Amis, M. (2008) *The Second Plane: September 11, 2001–2007*, London: Jonathan Cape.

Amnesty International (2005) *UK: The Prevention of Terrorism Bill Is a Grave Threat to Human Rights and the Rule of Law*, EUR 45/006/2005, London: AI.

Ansari, F. (2006) *British Anti-terrorism: A Modern Day Witch-hunt*, London: Islamic Human Rights Commission.

Ansari, H. (2004) *The 'Infidel' Within: The History of Muslims in Britain, 1800 to the Present*, London: Hurst.

——(2005) 'Attitudes to Jihad, Martyrdom and Terrorism among British Muslims', in T. Abbas (ed.), *Muslim Britain: Communities under Pressure*, London and New York: Zed, pp. 144–64.

Anwar, M. (1979) *The 'Myth of Return': Pakistanis in Britain*, London: Heinemann.

——(1993) *Muslims in Britain: 1991 Census and Other Statistical Sources*, University of Birmingham: Centre for the Study of Islam and Christian–Muslim Relations.

——(1996) *British Pakistanis: Demographic, Social and Economic Position*, University of Warwick: Centre for Research in Ethnic Relations.

——(1998) *Between Cultures: Continuity and Change in the Lives of Young Asians*, London: Routledge.

——(2001) 'Participation of Ethnic Minorities in British Politics', *Journal of Ethnic and Migration Studies*, 27(3): 533–49.

Anwar, M. and Q. Bahksh (2003) *British Muslims and State Policies*, Coventry: Centre for Research in Ethnic Relations University of Warwick.

Armstrong, K. (2001) *Islam: A Short History*, London: Weidenfeld & Nicolson.

Asad, T. (1990) 'Multiculturalism and British Identity in the Wake of the Rushdie Affair', *Politics and Society*, 18(4): 455–80.

——(1999) 'Religion, Nation-state, Secularism', in P. van der Veer and H. Lehman (eds) *Nation and Religion: Perspectives on Europe and Asia*, Princeton, NJ: Princeton University Press, pp. 178–96.

——(2002) 'Muslims and European Identity: Can Europe Represent Islam?', in A. Pagden (ed.), *The Idea of Europe: From Antiquity to the European Union*, Cambridge: Cambridge University Press, pp. 209–27.

Asari, F. (1989) 'Iran in the British Media', *Index on Censorship*, 18(5): 9–13.

Aziz, S. (2007) *In the Land of the Ayatollahs Tupac Shakur Is King: Reflections from Iran and the Arab World*, Bristol: Amal Press.

Babb, P., H. Butcher, J. Church and L. Zealey (2006) (eds) *Social Trends, no. 36*, London: Office for National Statistics.

Bach, M. (1984) *Major Religions of the World*, London: DeVorss.

Back, L. and J. Solomos, J. (1992) 'Black Politics and Social Change in Birmingham, UK: An Analysis of Recent Trends', *Ethnic and Racial Studies*, 15(2): 327–51.

Back, L., M. Keith, A. Khan, K. Shukra and J. Solomos (2002a) 'New Labour's White Heart: Politics, Multiculturalism and the Return of Assimilation', *Political Quarterly*, 73(4): 445–54.

——(2002b) 'The Return of Assimilationism: Race, Multiculturalism and New Labour', *Sociological Research Online* 7(2). Available at <http://www.socresonline. org.uk/7/2/back.html>. Accessed 6 April 2010.

Bader, V. (2004) 'Multiculturalism: Finding or Losing Our Way?' Panel discussant at the Multicultural Futures conference. Convened by Monash University, Australian Multicultural Foundation and the Metropolis Project, Canada, held at Monash University Centre, Prato, Italy, 22–3 September.

——(2007) 'The Governance of Islam in Europe: The Perils of Modelling', *Journal of Ethnic and Migration Studies*, 33(6): 871–86.

Bagguley, P. and Y. Hussain (2006) 'Conflict and Cohesion: Official Constructions of "Community" Around the 2001 Riots in Britain', *Critical Studies*, 28: 347–65.

——(2008) *Riotous Citizens: Ethnic Conflict in Multicultural Britain*, Aldershot: Ashgate.

Ballard, R. (1990) 'Migration and Kinship: The Differential Effect of Marriage Rules on the Processes of Punjabi Migration to Britain', in C. Clarke, C. Peach and S. Vertovec (eds) *South Asian Overseas: Migration and Ethnicity*, Cambridge: Cambridge University Press, pp. 219–49.

——(1994) (ed.) *Desh Pardesh: The South Asian Presence in Britain*, London: Hurst.

Barber, B. (1996) *Jihad vs. McWorld: Terrorism's Challenge to Democracy*, New York: Balantine.

——(2003) *Fear's Empire*, New York; Norton.

——(2004) 'Jihad vs. McWorld', in F. Lechner and J. Boli (eds), *The Globalization Reader*, second edition, Oxford: Blackwell, pp. 29–36.

Barker, M. (1984) 'Het nieuwe racisme [The New Racism]', in A. Bleich and P. Schumacher (eds) *Nederlands Racisme* [Dutch Racism], Amsterdam: Van Gennep, pp. 62–85.

Barrett, G., T. Jones and D. McEvoy (1996) 'Ethnic Minority Business: Theoretical Discourse in Britain and North America', *Urban Studies*, 33(4/5): 783–809.

Barry, B. (2002) 'Second Thoughts: Some First Thoughts Revisited', in P. Kelly (ed.), *Multiculturalism Reconsidered*, Cambridge: Polity, pp. 204–38.

Bartels, E. (2000) ' "Dutch Islam": Young People, Learning and Integration', *Current Sociology*, 48(4): 59–73.

Basit, T.N. (1997) *Eastern Values; Western Milieu: Identities and Aspirations of Adolescent British Muslim Girls*, Aldershot: Ashgate.

Battutah, I. (2002) *The Travels of Ibn Battutah*, edited by Tim Mackintosh-Smith, London: Picador.

BBC News Online (2005a) 'Terror Arrest Conviction Rate 13%'. Available at <http:// news.bbc.co.uk/1/hi/uk/8047477.stm>. Accessed 25 July 2009.

——(2005b) 'London Bomber: Text in Full'. Available at <news.bbc.co.uk/2/hi/ uk_news/4206800.stm>. Accessed 21 July 2009.

——(2005c) 'Muslim Police Stops "more likely"'. Available at <http://news.bbc.co. uk/1/hi/uk/4309961.stm>. Accessed 25 July 2009.

Beckford, J. and S. Gilliat (1998) *Religion in Prison: Equal Rites in a Multi-faith Society*, Cambridge: Cambridge University Press.

Beckford, J.A., D. Joly and F. Khosrokhavar (2005) *Muslims in Prison: Challenge and Change in Britain and France*, Basingstoke: Palgrave-Macmillan.

Benjamin, D. and S. Simon (2002) *The Age of Sacred Terror: Radical Islam's War Against America*, New York: Random House.

Bennett, C. (1992) *Victorian Images of Islam*, London: Grey Seal.

Bergen, P. (2006) *The Osama bin Laden I Know: An Oral History of al Qaeda's Leader*, New York: Free Press.

Berggren, L. (2004) *Episodes in the Mathematics of Medieval Islam*, New York: Springer-Verlag.

Betts, G. (2001) *The Twilight of Britain: Cultural Nationalism, Multiculturalism and the Politics of Toleration*, London: Transaction.

Bhachu, P. (1985) *Twice Migrants: East African Sikh Settlers in Britain*, London: Tavistock.

Birmingham City Council (2003) *Population Census in Birmingham: Religious Group Profiles*, Birmingham: BCC.

Birt, J. (2005) 'Lobbying and Marching: British Muslims and the State', in T. Abbas (ed.), *Muslim Britain: Communities under Pressure*, London and New York: Zed, pp. 92–106.

Blair, A. (2005) 'Muslim School Offers Best Added Value', *The Times*, 13 January.

Blair, A. and W. Aps (2005) 'What Not to Wear and Other Stories: Addressing Religious Diversity in Schools', *Education and the Law*, 17(1–2): 1–22.

Boston, A.G. (2007) (ed.) *The Legacy of Jihad: Islamic Holy War and the Fate of Non-Muslims*, New York: Prometheus.

Bowen, J.R. (2004) 'Beyond Migration: Islam as a Transnational Public Space', *Journal of Ethnic and Migration Studies*, 30(5): 879–94.

——(2007) *Why the French Don't Like Headscarves: Islam, the State and the Public Space*, Princeton, NJ: Princeton University Press.

Bowling, B. and C. Phillips (2002a) 'Racism, Ethnicity, Crime, and Criminal Justice', in M. Maguire, R. Morgan and R. Reiner (eds), *The Oxford Criminological Handbook*, Oxford: Oxford University Press, pp. 579–619.

——(2002b) *Racism, Crime and Justice*, London: Longman.

——(2003) 'Racial Victimization in England and Wales', in D.F. Hawkins (ed.), *Violent Crime: Assessing Race and Ethnic Differences*, Cambridge: Cambridge University Press, pp. 154–70.

Bradford Vision (2001) *Community Pride, Not Prejudice: Making Diversity Work in Bradford*, Bradford: Bradford City Council.

Brah, A. (1996) *Cartographies of Diaspora: Contesting Identities*, London and New York: Routledge.

Brah, A. and S. Shaw (1992) *Working Choices: South Asian Young Muslim Women and the Labour Market*, London: Department of Employment Research Paper No. 91.

Briggs, R., C. Fieschi and H. Lownsbrough (2006) *Bringing It Home: Community-based Approaches to Counter-terrorism*, London: DEMOS.

Brighton, S. (2007) 'British Muslims, Multiculturalism and UK Foreign Policy: "Integration" and "Cohesion" in and Beyond the State', *International Affairs*, 83(1): 1–17.

Brown, M.S. (2000) 'Religion and Economic Activity in the South Asian Population', *Ethnic and Racial Studies*, 23(6): 1035–61.

Bruegal, I. and S. Warren (2003) 'Family Resources and Community Social Capital as Routes to Valued Employment in the UK?', *Social Policy and Society*, 2(4): 319–28.

Buaras, E.A. (2009) 'Terror Conviction Shows BNP True Colours, Says Anti-fascist Group', *Muslim News*, Issue 249, Friday 29 January 2010. Available at <http://www.muslimnews.co.uk/paper/index.php?article=4478>. Accessed 9 April 2010.

Bulmer, M. and J. Solomos (2004) *Researching Race and Racism*, London: Routledge.

Bunt, G.R. (2003) *Islam in the Digital Age: E-Jihad, Online Fatwas and Cyber Islamic Environments*, London: Pluto.

Burgat, F. (1999) *Face to Face with Political Islam*, London: I.B. Tauris.

Burgess, A. (1981) 'Islam in the Dark', *The Observer*, 27 September.

Burke, J. (1994) *Al-Qaeda: The True Story of Radical Islam*, London: Penguin.

Busse, H. (1973) 'The Revival of Persian Kingship under the Buyids', in D.S. Richards (ed.), *Islamic Civilisation 950–1150*, Oxford: Bruno Cassirer, pp. 47–69.

Calder, N., J.A. Mojaddedi and A. Rippin (eds) (2003) *Classical Islam: A Sourcebook of Religious Literature*, London and New York: Routledge.

Caldwell, C. (2009) *Reflections on the Revolution in Europe: Immigration, Islam, and the West*, London: Allen Lane.

Campbell, C. and C. McLean (2003) 'Social Capital, Local Community Participation and the Construction of Pakistani Identities in England: Implications for Health Inequalities Policies', *Journal of Health Psychology*, 8(2): 247–62.

Campbell, D. (2007) '21/7 Bomb Plotters Sentenced to Life as Judge Says They Were under Control of al-Qaida', *The Guardian*, 12 July.

Carney, D. and A. Sinclair (2006) 'School Uniform Revisited: Procedure, Pressure and Equality', *Education and the Law*, 18 (2/3): 131–48.

Carter, B. and S. Joshi (1984) 'The Role of Labour in the Creation of a Racist Britain', *Race and Class*, 25(3): 53–70.

Castells, M. (1997) *The Power of Identity: The Information Age – Economy, Society and Culture*, Oxford: Blackwell.

Castles, S. (2000) *Ethnicity and Globalization: From Migrant Worker to Transnational Citizen*, London and New York: Sage.

Castles, S. and G. Kosack (1973) *Immigrant Workers in Western Europe and Class Structure*, London: Oxford University Press.

Cavadino, M. (1999) *Criminal Justice 2000: Strategies for a New Century*, Hampshire: Waterside Press.

Cavaliero, R. (2002) *Strangers in the Land: The Rise and Decline of the British Indian Empire*, London: I.B. Tauris.

Cemal, K. (2007) *Turkey: Islam and Laicism Between the Interests of State, Politics, and Society*, Frankfurt: Peace Research Institute Frankfurt Report 78.

Cesari, J. (2003) 'Muslim Minorities in Europe: The Silent Revolution', in J.L. Esposito and F. Burgat (eds) *Modernizing Islam: Religion in the Public Sphere in the Middle East and in Europe*, New Brunswick, NJ: Rutgers University Press, pp. 251–69.

——(2005) 'Mosque Conflicts in European Cities: Introduction', *Journal of Ethnic and Migration Studies*, 31(6): 1015–24.

Cesari, J. and S. McLoughlin (2005) (eds) *European Muslims and the Secular State*, Aldershot: Ashgate.

Charsley, K. (2005) 'Unhappy Husbands: Masculinity and Migration in Transnational Pakistani Marriage', *Journal of the Royal Anthropological Institute*, 11(1): 85–105.

Cheng, Y. and A. Heath (1993) 'Ethnic Origins and Class Destinations', *Oxford Review of Education*, 19(2): 151–66.

Choudhury, G.W. (1968) *Pakistan's Relations with India 1947–1966*, London: Pall Mall.

Choueiri, Y.M. (1997) *Islamic Fundamentalism*, London: Cassell.

Clark, K. and S. Drinkwater (2007) *Ethnic Minorities in the Labour Market: Dynamics and Diversity*, London: Joseph Rowntree Foundation.

Clot, A. and J. Howe (2005) *Harun Al-Rashid and the World of the Thousand and One Nights*, London: Saqi.

Cohen, S. (1972) *Folk Devils and Moral Panics: The Creation of the Mods and the Rockers*, London: MacGibbon & Kee.

——(2000) 'Some Thoroughly Modern Monsters', *Index on Censorship*, 29(5): 36–42.

Cohn, B. (1995) *Colonialism and Its Forms of Knowledge: The British in India*, Princeton, NJ: Princeton University Press.

Commission for Racial Equality (1996) *Roots of the Future: Ethnic Diversity in the Making of Britain*, London: CRE.

Commission on British Muslims and Islamophobia (2004) *Islamophobia: Issues, Challenges and Action*, Stoke-on-Trent: Trentham.

Conner, H., C. Tyers and T. Modood (2004) *Why the Difference? A Closer Look at Higher Education Minority Ethnic Students and Graduates*, London: Department for Education and Skills Research Report RR552.

Conner, K. (2005) '"Islamism" in the West? The Life-span of Al-Muhajiroun in the United Kingdom', *Journal of Muslim Minority Affairs*, 25(1): 117–34.

Corbin, J. (2002) *The Base: In Search of Al-Qaeda*, London: Simon & Schuster.

Cottle, S. (2000) (ed.) *Ethnic Minorities and the Media: Changing Cultural Boundaries*, Buckingham: Open University Press.

Crick, B. (2000) *Essays on Citizenship*, London: Continuum.

Crone, P. (1987) *Meccan Trade and the Rise of Islam*, Princeton, NJ: Princeton University Press.

——(2004) *God's Rule: Government and Islam*, New York: Columbia University Press.

Crone, P. and M. Cook (1977) *Hagarism: The Making of the Islamic World*, Cambridge: Cambridge University Press.

Crone, P. and M. Hinds (2003) *God's Caliph: Religious Authority in the First Centuries of Islam*, Cambridge: Cambridge University Press.

Curran, J. (1988) 'Whig Press History as Political Myth', in J. Curran and J. Seaton (eds), *Power Without Responsibility: The Press and Broadcasting in Britain*, London: Routledge, pp. 7–10.

Dale, A. and C. Holdsworth (1997) 'Issues in the Analysis of Ethnicity in the 1991 British Census', *Ethnic and Racial Studies*, 20(1): 160–80.

Dale, A., N. Shaheen, E. Fieldhouse and V. Kalra (2002) 'Routes into Education and Employment for Young Pakistani and Bangladeshi Women in the UK', *Ethnic and Racial Studies*, 25(6): 942–68.

Dalrymple, W. (2003) *White Mughals: Love and Betrayal in Eighteenth-century India*, London: Harper-Perennial.

——(2007) *The Last Mughal: The Fall of a Dynasty, Delhi, 1857*, London: Bloomsbury.

Davidson, L. (2003) *Islamic Fundamentalism: An Introduction*, Westport, CT: Greenwood Press.

Dawkins, R. (2006) *The God Delusion*, London: Banton.

Day, R.J.F. (2004) 'Dialogue and Differends: On the Limits of Liberal Multiculturalism', *Canadian Diversity/Diversité Canadienne*, 3(2): 36–8.

Dayha, B. (1974) 'The Nature of Pakistani Ethnicity', in A. Cohen (ed.), *Urban Ethnicity*, London: Tavistock, pp. 97–125.

——(1988) 'South Asians as Economic Migrants in Britain', *Ethnic and Racial Studies*, 11(4): 439–56.

Deakin, N. (1970) *Colour Citizenship and British Society*, London: Panther.

DeLong Bas, N. (2004) *Wahhabi Islam: From Revival and Reform to Global Jihad*, New York: Oxford University Press.

Denman, S. (2001) *The Denham Report: Race Discrimination in the Crown Prosecution Service*, London: Crown Prosecution Service.

Desai, R. (1963) *Indian Immigrants in Britain*, London: Oxford University Press for the Institute of Race Relations.

Dreyfuss, R. (1980) *Hostage to Khomeini*, New York: New Benjamin Franklin House.

——(2005) *Devil's Game: How the United States Helped Unleash Fundamentalist Islam*, New York: Metropolitan.

Eade, J. (1989) *The Politics of Community: The Bangladeshi Community in East London*, Aldershot: Avebury.

Edwards, D.B. (2002) *Before Taliban: Genealogies of the Afghan Jihad*, California: University of California Press.

Edwards, R., J. Franklin and J. Holland (2003) *Families and Social Capital: Exploring the Issues*, South Bank University: Families and Social Capital ESRC Research Group.

Elliot, C. and F. Quinn (2009) *English Legal System*, tenth edition, London: Pearson.

Esposito, J.L. (1991) *Islam: The Straight Path*, Oxford: Oxford University Press.

——(1999) *The Islamic Threat: Myth or Reality?* New York: Oxford University Press.

——(2002) *Unholy War: Terror in the Name of Islam*, New York: Oxford University Press.

——(2003) (ed.) *The Oxford Dictionary of Islam*, Oxford: Oxford University Press.

——(2010) *The Future of Islam*, New York: Oxford University Press.

Esposito, J.L. and D. Mogahed (2008) *Who Speaks for Islam? What a Billion Muslims Really Think*, Washington: Gallup Press.

Ethnic Minority Employment Taskforce (2005) *Muslim Graduates in the Labour Market: Seminar Report*, London: Department of Work and Pensions.

Euben, R.L. (1999) *Enemy in the Mirror: Islamic Fundamentalism and the Limits of Modern Rationalism, a Work of Comparative Political Theory*, Princeton, NJ: Princeton University Press.

——(2002) 'Killing (for) Politics: Jihad, Martyrdom and Political Action', *Political Theory*, 30(1): 4–35.

Fakhry, M. (2004) *A History of Islamic Philosophy*, New York: Columbia University Press.

Faris, N.A. (1952) *The Book of Idols, Being a Translation from the Arabic of the Kitab Al-Asnam by Hisham Ibn-Al-Kalbi*, Princeton, NJ: Princeton University Press.

Federation of Student Islamic Societies (2005) *The Voice of Muslim Students: The FOSIS Muslim Student Survey 2005*, London: FOSIS.

Fekete, L. (2004) 'Anti-Muslim Racism and the European Security State', *Race and Class*, 46(1): 3–29.

——(2009) *A Suitable Enemy: Racism, Migration and Islamophobia in Europe*, London and New York: Pluto.

Ferguson, N. (2003) *Empire: The Rise and Demise of the British World Order and the Lessons for Global Power*, London: Basic.

Fieldhouse, E. and M. Gould (1998) 'Ethnic Minority Unemployment and Local Labour Market Conditions in Great Britain', *Environment and Planning A*, 30(5): 833–53.

Flood-Page, C. and A. Mackie (1998) *Sentencing Practice: An Examination of Decisions in Magistrates' Courts and the Crown Court in the mid-1990's*, London: Home Office Research Study 180.

Ford, R. (2009) 'Muslim Prison Gangs on the Rise as Inmates Seek Safety in Numbers', *The Times*, 13 January.

Fryer, P. (1984) *Staying Power: Black People in Britain since 1504*, London: Pluto.

Fukuyama, F. (1993) *The End of History and the Last Man*, New York: Penguin.

Furedi, F. (2006) *Culture of Fear*, London: Continuum.

——(2007) *Invitation to Terror: The Expanding Empire of the Unknown*, London: Continuum.

Geaves, R. (1996) *Sectarian Influences within Islam in Britain with Reference to the Concepts of 'Ummah' and 'Community'*, Leeds: University of Leeds.

——(2005) 'Negotiating British Citizenship and Muslim Identity', in T. Abbas (ed.), *Muslim Britain: Communities under Pressure*, London and New York: Zed, pp. 66–7.

Gibb, H.A. and J.H. Kramers (1965) *Shorter Encyclopaedia of Islam*, Ithaca, NY: Cornell University Press.

Giddens, A. (1989) *Sociology*, Cambridge: Polity.

Gies, L. (2007) 'What Not To Wear: Islamic Dress and School Uniforms', *Feminist Legal Studies*, 14(3): 377–89.

Gilroy, P. (1987) 'The Myth of Black Criminality', in P. Scraton (ed.) *Law, Order and the Authoritarian State: Readings in Critical Criminology*, Milton Keynes: Open University Press, pp. 107–20.

——(2000) *Between Camps: Nations, Cultures and the Allure of Race*, London: Penguin.

Glees, A. and C. Pope (2005) *When Students Turn to Terror: Terrorist and Extremist Activity on British Campuses*, London: Social Affairs Unit.

Goffman, E. (1990) *The Presentation of Self in Everyday Life*, London: Penguin.

Goody, J. (2004) *Capitalism and Modernity*, Cambridge: Polity.

Goulbourne, H. and J. Solomos (2003) 'Families, Ethnicity and Social Capital', *Social Policy and Society*, 2(4): 329–38.

Grare, F. (2001) *Anatomy of Islamism: Political Islam in the Indian Subcontinent*, New Delhi: Jamaat-e-Islami Manohar Publishers.

Grillo, R. (2004) 'Islam and Transnationalism', *Journal of Ethnic and Migration Studies*, 30(5): 861–78.

Grosvenor, I. (1997) *Assimilating Identities: Racism and Educational Policy in Post 1945 Britain*, London: Lawrence & Wishart.

Guardian Unlimited (2005) 'The Full Text of a Speech Made by David Bell, the Schools Inspector, to the Hansard Society in London Today', *The Guardian*, 17 January. Available at <www.guardian.co.uk/education/2005/jan/17/faithschools.schools>. Accessed 7 April 2010.

Gunaratna, R. (2002) *Inside the Al-Qaeda: Global Network of Terror*, London: Hurst.

Haddad, Y.Y. (1982) *Contemporary Islam and the Challenge of History*, New York: State University of New York Press.

Haddawy, H. (2008) *The Arabian Nights: Based on the Text Edited by Muhsin Mahdi*, London: W.W. Norton & Co.

Hall, S. (2000) 'Conclusion: The Multi-cultural Question', in B. Hesse (ed.) *Un/settled Multiculturalisms*, London and New York: Zed, pp. 209–41.

——(2002) 'Political Belonging in a World of Multiple Identities', in S. Vertovec and R. Cohin (eds), *Conceiving Cosmopolitanism*, Oxford: Oxford University Press, pp. 25–31.

Hall, S., C. Critcher, T. Jefferson, J. Clark and B. Roberts (1978) *Policing the Crisis: Mugging the State, and Law and Order*, Basingstoke: Macmillan.

Hallam, E.M. (2000) (ed.) *Cultural Encounters: Representing 'Otherness'*, London: Routledge.

Halliday, F. (1992) *Arabs in Exile: Yemeni Migrants in Urban Britain*, London: I.B. Tauris.

——(1996) *Islam and the Myth of Confrontation: Religion and Politics in the Middle East*, London: I.B. Tauris.

——(2003) *Islam and the Myth of Confrontation: Religion and Politics in the Middle East*, London: I.B. Tauris, p. 107.

Halstead, M.J. (2004) 'Education', in Open Society Institute (ed.), *Muslims in the UK: Policies for Engaged Citizens*, London and Budapest: OSI, pp. 101–92.

Hamid, S. (2007) 'Islamic Political Radical Radicalism in Britain: The Case of Hizb-ut Tahrir', in T. Abbas (ed.) *Islamic Political Radicalism: A European Perspective*, Edinburgh: Edinburgh University Press, pp. 145–59.

Hashmi, S.H. (2006) 'Interpreting the Islamic Ethics of War and Peace', in W. Evan (ed.), *War and Peace in an Age of Terrorism: A Reader*, Boston, BA: Allyn & Bacon, pp. 64–9.

Heath, A.F., C. Rothon and E. Kilpi (2008) 'The Second Generation in Western Europe: Education, Unemployment, and Occupational Attainment, *Annual Review of Sociology*, 34: 211–35.

Heath, A.F., D. McMahon and J. Roberts (2000) 'Ethnic Differences in the Labour Market: A Comparison of the SARs and LFS', *Journal of the Royal Statistical Society A*, 163(3): 341–61.

Hennessy, P. and M. Kite (2006) 'Poll Reveals 40 per cent of Muslims Want Sharia Law in UK', *The Telegraph*, 19 February.

Hippler, J. and A. Lueg (1995) (eds) *The Next Threat: Western Perceptions of Islam*, London: Pluto Press.

Hiro, D. (2002) *Iraq: In the Eye of the Storm*, London: Nation.

Hitchens, C. (2007) *God Is Not Great: The Case against Religion*, London: Twelve Books.

Hitti, P.K. (2002) *History of the Arabs*, Basingstoke: Palgrave-Macmillan.

Hofmann, M. (1997) *Islam: The Alternative*, Beltsville: Amana Publications.

Home Office (2002) *Community Cohesion: Report of the Independent Review Team*, chaired by Ted Cantle, London: Home Office.

——(2003a) *2001 Home Office Citizenship Survey: People, Families and Communities*, London: Home Office Research Study 270.

——(2003b) *Statistics on Race and the Criminal-justice System: A Home Office Publication Under Section 95 of the Criminal Justice Act 1991*, London: Home Office.

——(2004) *2003 Home Office Citizenship Survey: People, Families and Communities*, London: Home Office Research Study 289.

——(2005) *'Preventing Extremism Together' Working Groups: August–October 2005*, London: Home Office.

Home Office and Department for Education and Skills (2005) *2003 Home Office Citizenship Survey: Top-level findings from the Children's and Young People's Survey*, London: Crown Copyright.

Hood, R. (1992) *Race and Sentencing: A Study in the Crown Court*, Oxford: Clarendon.

House of Commons (2006) *Report of the Official Account of the Bombings in London on 7th July 2005*, London, HC 1087, London: Stationery Office.

House of Lords (2004) *Opinions of The Lords of Appeal for Judgement in the Cause A (FC) and Others (FC) (Appellants) v. Secretary of State for the Home Department (Respondent) and X (FC) and another (FC) (Appellants) v. Secretary of State for the Home Department (Respondent), on Thursday 16 December*, Paragraph 97, London: UKHL 56.

Human Rights Watch (2004) *Neither Just Nor Effective: Indefinite Detention Without Trial in the United Kingdom Under Part 4 of the Anti-Terrorism, Crime and Security Act 2001*, London: HRW Briefing Paper, 24 June. <www.ihrc.org.uk/show.php?id=938>. Accessed 10 April 2010.

Hunter, S.H. (1998) *The Future of Islam and the West: Clash of Civilizations or Peaceful Coexistence?* Westport, CT: Greenwood.

Huntingdon, S. (2002) *The Clash of Civilizations and the Remaking of World Order*, New York: Free Press.

Husain, E. (2007) *The Islamist: Why I Joined Radical Islam in Britain, What I Saw Inside and Why I Left*, London: Penguin.

Hussain, A.M. and W.L. Miller (2006) *Multicultural Nationalism: Islamophobia, Anglophobia, and Devolution*, Oxford: Oxford University Press.

Hussain, S. (2008) *Muslims on the Map: A National Survey of Social Trends in Britain*, London: I.B. Tauris.

Hussain, Y. and P. Bagguley (2007) *Moving On Up: South Asian Women and Higher Education*, Stoke-on-Trent: Trentham.

Idriss, M.M. (2006a) 'The Defeat of Shabina Begum in the House of Lords', *Liverpool Law Review*, 27(3): 417–26.

——(2006b) 'Jilbaabs in Schools', *Nottingham Law Journal*, 15(1): 19–27.

——(2006c) 'The House of Lords, Shabina Begum and Proportionality', *Judicial Review*, 11(3): 239–45.

Idriss, M.M. and T. Abbas (2010) (eds) *Honour, Violence, Women and Islam*, London and New York: Routledge.

Ijaz, I. and T. Abbas (2010) 'The Impact of Intergenerational Change on the Attitudes of Working-class South Asian Muslim Parents on the Education of Their Daughters', *Gender and Education*, first published 4 February 2010 (iFirst).

Islamic Human Rights Commission (2002) *The Hidden Victims of September 11: Prisoners of UK Law*, London: IHRC.

Jackson, R. (2003) 'Should the State Fund Faith Based Schools? A Review of the Arguments', *British Journal of Religious Education*, 25(2): 89–102.

Jacobson, J. (1998) *Islam in Transition: Religion and Identity Among British Pakistani Youth*, London: Routledge.

James, L. (1997) *Raj: The Making and Unmaking of British India*, New York: St Martin's Press.

Johns, A.H. and N. Lahoud (2005) 'The World of Islam and the Challenge of Islamism', in N. Lahoud and A.H. Johns (eds), *Islam in World Politics*, New York: Routledge, pp. 7–28.

Jonson, R. (2002) *Them: Adventures with Extremists*, London: Picador.

Kabbani, R. (1989) *A Letter to Christendom*, London: Virago.

Kahani-Hopkins, V. and N. Hopkins (2002) '"Representing" British Muslims: The Strategic Dimension to Identity Construction', *Ethnic and Racial Studies*, 25(2): 288–309.

Karagiannis, E. and C. McCauley (2006) 'Hizb ut-Tahrir al-Islami: Evaluating the Threat Posed by a Radical Islamic Group That Remains Nonviolent', *Terrorism and Political Violence, 1556–1836*, 18(2): 315–34.

Keddie, N.R. (1972) *Sayyid Jamal al-Din al-Afghani: A Political Biography*, Berkeley: University of California Press.

Keith, M. (2005) *After the Cosmopolitan? Multicultural Cities and the Future of Racism*, London: Routledge.

Kelly, P. (2002) 'Defending Some Dodos: Equality and/or Liberty', in P. Kelly (ed.), *Multiculturalism Reconsidered*, Cambridge: Polity, pp. 62–80.

——(2003) 'Identity, Equality and Power: Tensions in Parekh's Theory of Multiculturalism', in B. Haddock and P. Sutch (eds), *Multiculturalism, Identity and Rights*, London: Routledge, pp. 94–110.

Kepel, G. (2005) *The Roots of Radical Islam*, London: Saqi.

Klausen, J. (2005) *The Islamic Challenge: Politics and Religion in Western Europe*, New York: Oxford University Press.

Kohlman, E.F. (2004) *Al-Qaida's Jihad in Europe: The Afghan-Bosnian Network*, Oxford: Berg.

Koyaleski, S.F. (2006) 'For Britain's Young Muslims, Forks in the Road', *International Herald Tribune*, 30 August.

Küçükcan, T. (1999) *Politics of Ethnicity, Identity and Religion: Turkish Muslims in Britain*, Aldershot: Ashgate.

——(2004) 'The Making of Turkish-Muslim Diaspora in Britain: Religious Collective Identity in a Multicultural Public Sphere', *Journal of Muslim Minority Affairs*, 24(2): 243–58.

Kundnani, A. (2001) 'From Oldham to Bradford: The Violence of the Violated', in *The Three Faces of British Racism: Race and Class*, 43(3): 41–60.

——(2004) 'Analysis: The War on Terror Leads to Racial Profiling', *Institute of Race Relations News*. Available at <www.irr.org.uk/2004/july/ak000006.html>. Accessed 24 July 2009.

——(2007) *The End of Tolerance: Racism in 21st Century Britain*, London: Pluto.

——(2009) *Spooked! How Not to Prevent Violent Extremism*, London: Institute of Race Relations.

Kurzman, C. (1998) 'Liberal Islam and Its Islamic Context', in C. Kurzman (ed.), *Liberal Islam: A Sourcebook*, Oxford: Oxford University Press, pp. 3–28.

Kymlicka, W. (2002) *Contemporary Political Philosophy: An Introduction*, Oxford: Oxford University Press.

——(2004) 'Multiculturalism: Finding or Losing Our Way?' Panel discussant at the Multicultural Futures conference. Convened by Monash University, Australian Multicultural Foundation and the Metropolis Project, Canada, held at Monash University Centre, Prato, Italy, 22–3 September.

Lahiri, S. (2001) 'South Asians in Post-imperial Britain: Decolonisation and Imperial Legacy', in S. Ward (ed.), *British Culture and the End of Empire*, Manchester: Manchester University Press, pp. 200–16.

Lahoud, N. (2005) *Political Thought in Islam: A Study in Intellectual Boundaries*, London and New York: Routledge-Curzon.

Lahoud, N. and A.H. Johns (2005) (eds), *Islam in World Politics*, New York: Routledge.

Laoust, H. (1979) *The Encyclopedia of Islam*, Leiden: Brill.

Lapidus, I.M. (1997) 'Islamic Revival and Modernity: The Contemporary Movements and the Historical Paradigms', *Journal of the Economic and Social History of the Orient*, 40(4): 444–60.

Laville, S., R. Norton-Taylor and S. Bates (2009) 'All 12 Men Arrested During Anti-terror Raids Released Without Charge', *The Guardian*, 22 April.

Lawrence, B.B. (2000) *Shattering the Myth: Islam Beyond Violence*, Princeton, NJ: Princeton University Press.

Layton-Henry, Z. (1984) *The Politics of Race in Britain*, London: Harper-Collins.

Lewis, B. (1968) *The Assassins*, New York: Basic Books.

——(2003) *The Crisis of Islam: Holy War and Unholy Terror*, London: Weidenfeld & Nicolson.

Lewis, P. (2002) *Islamic Britain: Religion, Politics and Identity Among British Muslims*, London: I.B. Tauris.

——(2007) *Young, British and Muslim*, London: Continuum.

Lindley, J. (2002) 'Race or Religion? The Impact of Religion on the Employment and Earnings of Britain's Ethnic Communities', *Journal of Ethnic and Migration Studies*, 28(3): 427–42.

Lloyd, S. (1988) *English Society and the Crusade, 1216–1307*, Oxford: Clarendon Press.

Lockhart, L. (1930) *Hasan-i-Sabah and the Assassins*, London: School of Oriental Studies.

Lowin, S.L. (2006) *The Making of a Forefather: Abraham in Islamic and Jewish Exegetical Narratives*, Leiden: Brill.

Mac an Ghaill, M. (1999) *Contemporary Racisms and Ethnicities: Social and Cultural Transformations*, Milton Keynes: Open University Press.

Mac an Ghaill, M., M.J. Hickman and A. Brah (1999) (eds) *Thinking Identities: Ethnicity, Racism and Culture*, Basingstoke: Palgrave-Macmillan.

McDonald, K. (2006) *Global Movements: Action and Culture*, Oxford: Blackwell.

MacDonald, M. (2003) *Exploring Media Discourse*, London: Hodder Arnold.

McGhee, D. (2008) *The End of Multiculturalism? Terrorism, Integration and Human Rights*, Milton Keynes: Open University Press.

McRoy, A. (2005) *From Rushdie to 7/7: The Radicalisation of Islam in Britain*, London: Social Affairs Unit.

Macey, M. (1999) 'Class, Gender and Religious Influences on Changing Patterns of Pakistani Muslim Male Violence in Bradford', *Ethnic and Racial Studies*, 22(5): 847–9.

——(2002) 'Interpreting Islam: Young Muslim Men's Involvement in Criminal Activity in Bradford', in B. Spalek (ed.), *Islam, Crime and Criminal Justice*, Uffculme: Willan, pp. 19–49.

——(2007) 'Islamic Political Radicalism in Britain: Muslim Men in Bradford', in T. Abbas (ed.), *Islamic Political Radicalism: A European Perspective*, Edinburgh: Edinburgh University Press, pp. 160–72.

MacPherson, W. (1999) *The Stephen Lawrence Inquiry*, London: Stationery Office.

Mahmood, J. (2009) personal communication, 22 August.

Mahmud, S.F. (1989) *A Concise History of Indo-Pakistan*, Karachi: Oxford University Press.

Malik, A.A. (2006) (ed.) *The State We Are In: Identity, Terror and the Law of Jihad*, Bristol: Amal Press.

Malik, K. (2005) 'The Islamophobia Myth', *Prospect*, 107, February.

Manzoor, S. (2007) *Greetings from Bury Park: Race, Religion and Rock'n'Roll*, London: Bloomsbury.

Marranci, G. (2004) 'Multiculturalism, Islam and the Clash of Civilisations Theory: Rethinking Islamophobia', *Culture and Religion*, 5(1): 105–17.

Martín-Muñoz, G. (1999) (ed.) *Islam, Modernism and the West: Cultural and Political Relations at the End of the Millennium*, London and New York: I.B. Tauris.

Masood, E. (2006) *British Muslims: Media Guide*, London: British Council.

Massey, D. and R. Meegan (1982) *The Anatomy of Job Loss*, London: Routledge.

Masud, M.M., A. Salvatore and M.V. Bruinessen (2009) (eds) *Islam and Modernity: Key Issues and Debates*, Edinburgh: Edinburgh University Press.

Matar, N. (1998) *Islam in Britain, 1558–1685*, Cambridge: Cambridge University Press.

Mattausch, J. (1998) 'From Subjects to Citizens: British "East African Asians"', *Journal of Ethnic and Migration Studies*, 24(1): 121–41.

Maudidi, S.A.A. (1955) *Islamic Law and Its Introduction*, Lahore: Islamic Publications.

Maussen, M. (2007) *The Governance of Islam in Western Europe: A State of the Art Report*, Amsterdam: International Migration, Integration and Social Cohesion in Europe working paper 16.

May, T., T. Gyateng and M. Hough, with the assistance of B. Bhardwa, I. Boyce and J.C. Oyanedel (2010) *Differential Treatment in the Youth Justice System*, London: Equality and Human Rights Commission.

Meer, N. (2007) Muslim Schools in Britain: Challenging Mobilisations or Logical Developments? *Asia-Pacific Journal of Education*, 27(1): 55–71.

Mhlanga, B. (1999) *The Colour of English Justice: A Multivariate Analysis*, Aldershot: Avebury.

Michaels, W.B. (2006) *The Trouble with Diversity: How We Learned to Love Identity and Ignore Inequality*, New York: Metropolitan Books.

Migration Watch UK (2004) *Immigration and Marriage: The Problem of Continuous Migration*, Briefing Paper 10.8, Guildford: MWUK. Available at <http://migration-watchuk.org/pdfs/10_8_immigration_marriage.pdf>. Accessed 10 April 2010.

Miles, R. (1989) *Racism*, London: Routledge.

Milne, S. (2005) 'This Law Won't Fight Terror – It Is an Incitement to Terrorism', *The Guardian*, 13 October.

Milton-Edwards, B. (2004) *Islam and Politics in the Contemporary World*, Cambridge: Polity.

Modood, T. (1990) 'British Asian Muslims and the Rushdie Affair', *Political Quarterly*, 61(2): 143–60.

——(1998) 'Anti-Essentialism, Multiculturalism and the "Recognition" of Religious Groups', *Journal of Political Philosophy*, 6(4): 378–99.

——(2004a) 'Capitals, Ethnic Identity and Educational Qualifications', *Cultural Trends*, 13(2): 87–105.

——(2004b) 'The Muslims in Britain: An Emerging Community', paper presented to conference 'Muslims in Britain: The Making of a New Underclass?' One-day workshop organised by the Centre for the Study of Democracy, University of Westminster with the Leverhulme Programme on Migration and Citizenship at Bristol University and University College London, 18 November.

——(2005) *Multicultural Politics: Racism, Ethnicity and Muslims in Britain*, Edinburgh: Edinburgh University Press.

——(2006) 'Ethnicity, Muslims and Higher Education Entry in Britain', *Teaching in Higher Education*, 11(2): 247–50.

——(2007) *Multiculturalism: A Civic Idea*, Cambridge: Polity.

Modood, T. and F. Ahmad (2007) 'British Muslim Perspectives on Multiculturalism', *Theory Culture Society*, 24(2): 187–213.

Modood, T., R. Zapata-Barrero and A. Triandafyllidou (2005) (eds) *Multiculturalism, Muslims and Citizenship: A European Approach*, London: Routledge.

Modood, T., R. Berthoud, J. Lakey, J. Nazroo, P. Smith, S. Virdee and S. Beishon (1997) *Ethnic Minorities in Britain: Diversity and Disadvantage*, London: Policy Studies Institute.

Morris, N. (2007) 'Less Than One in 20 Held under Anti-Terror Laws is Charged', *The Independent*, 6 March.

Motha, S. (2007) 'Veiled Women and the Affect of Religion in Democracy', *Journal of Law and Society*, 34(1): 139–62.

Mukherjee, R. (1990) '"Satan Let Loose Upon Earth": The Kanpur Massacres in India in the Revolt of 1857', *Past and Present*, 128(1): 92–116.

Mukhopadhyay, A.R. (2007) 'Radical Islamic Organisations in Europe: South Asia in Their Discourse', *Strategic Analysis*, 31(2): 267–85.

Munton, T. and A. Zurawan (2004) *Active Communities: Headline Findings from the 2003 Home Office Citizenship Survey*, London: Home Office Research Development and Statistics.

Murata, S. and W.C. Chittick (1996) *The Vision of Islam*, London: I.B. Tauris.

Negrine, R. (1989) (ed.) *Politics and the Mass Media in Britain*, London: Routledge.

Nellis, M. and R. North (2005) 'Electronic Monitoring and the Creation of Control Orders for Terrorists Suspects in Britain', unpublished paper, University of Birmingham.

Newburn, T. and S. Hayman (2001) *Policing, Surveillance and Social Control: CCTV and Police Monitoring of Suspects*, Uffculme: Willan.

Nielsen, J.S. (2005) *Muslims in Western Europe*, Edinburgh: Edinburgh University Press.

Office for National Statistics (2003) *Prison Statistics: England and Wales 2002*, Home Office Cmd 5996, London: Home Office.

——(2004) *Education: One in Three Muslims Has No Qualifications*. Available at <http://www.statistics.gov.uk/cci/nugget.asp?id=963>. Accessed 15 July 2009.

——(2006) *Employment Patterns: Pakistanis Most Likely to Be Self-employed*. Available at <http://www.statistics.gov.uk/cci/nugget.asp?id=463>. Accessed 12 July 2009.

——(2008) *Census 2001: Ethnicity and Religion in England and Wales.* Available at <http://www.statistics.gov.uk/census2001/profiles/commentaries/ethnicity.asp>. Accessed 12 July 2009.

O'Hara, M. (2005) 'Fatal Flaws', *The Guardian*, 15 June.

Oliver, H.J. (2002) *The 'Wahhabi' Myth: Dispelling Prevalent Fallacies and the Fictitious Link*, Oxford: Trafford.

Omaar, R. (2007) *Only Half of Me: Being a Muslim in Britain*, London: Penguin.

Onfray, M. (2008) *Atheist Manifesto: The Case Against Christianity, Judaism and Islam*, London: Arcade.

Open Society Institute (2004a) *Muslims in the UK: Policies for Engaged Citizens*, New York: OSI.

——(2004b) *Aspirations and Reality: British Muslims and the Labour Market*, New York: OSI.

——(2009) *Muslims in Europe: A Report on 11 EU Cities*, Hungary: OSI.

Osler, A. and Z. Hussain (2005) 'Educating Muslim Girls: Do Mothers Have Faith in the State System?', in T. Abbas (ed.), *Muslims in Britain: Communities Under Pressure*, London and New York: Zed, pp. 127–43.

Owen, D. and M. Johnson (1996) 'Ethnic Minorities in the Midlands', in P. Ratcliffe (ed.), *Ethnicity in the 1991 Census, Vol. III: Social Geography and Ethnicity in Britain: Geographical Spread, Spatial Concentration and Internal Migration*, London: HMSO, pp. 227–70.

Pape, R.A. (2006) *Dying to Win: Why Suicide Terrorists Do It*, London and New York: Random House.

Parekh, B. (1990) 'The Rushdie Affair: Research Agenda for Political Philosophy', *Political Studies*, 38(4): 695–709.

——(1992) *The Concept of Fundamentalism*, University of Warwick: Centre for Research in Asian Migration and Pepal Tree Press.

——(2002) 'Barry and the Dangers of Liberalism', in P. Kelly (ed.), *Multiculturalism Reconsidered*, Cambridge: Polity, pp. 133–50.

——(2003) 'Muslims in Britain', *Prospect*, 88, July.

——(2004) 'The Future of Multiculturalism', inaugural address at the launch of the Centre for Research on Nationalism, Ethnicity and Multiculturalism, University of Surrey, 9 June.

——(2006) *Rethinking Multiculturalism: Cultural Diversity and Political Theory*, Basingstoke: Palgrave-Macmillan.

Parekh Report (2000) *The Future of Multi-ethnic Britain*, London: Profile Books.

Parker-Jenkins, M. (2002) 'Equal Access to State Funding: The Case of Muslim Schools in Britain', *Race Ethnicity and Education*, 5(3): 273–89.

Parker-Jenkins, M. and K.F. Haw (1998) 'Educational Needs of Muslim Children in Britain: Accommodation or Neglect?', in S. Vertovec and A. Rogers (eds), *Muslim European Youth: Reproducing Ethnicity, Religion, Culture*, Aldershot: Ashgate, pp. 193–215.

Pauly, R.J. (2004) *Islam in Europe: Integration or Marginalization?* Aldershot: Ashgate.

Peach, C. (1996) (ed.) *The Ethnic Minority Populations of Great Britain, Vol. II: Ethnicity in the 1991 Census*, London: ONS and HMSO.

——(1997) 'Estimates of the 1991 Muslim Population of Great Britain', *Oxford Plural Societies and Multicultural Cities Research Group Working Paper 1*, Oxford University: School of Geography.

——(2005) 'Muslims in the UK', in T. Abbas (ed.), *Muslim Britain: Communities under Pressure*, London and New York: Zed, pp. 18–30.

——(2006a) 'Muslims in the 2001 Census of England and Wales: Gender and Economic Disadvantage', *Ethnic and Racial Studies*, 8(4): 629–55.

——(2006b) 'Islam, Ethnicity and South Asian Religions in the London 2001 Census', *Transactions of the Institute of British Geographers*, 31(3): 353–70.

——(2006c) 'South Asian Migration and Settlement in Great Britain, 1951–2001', *Contemporary South Asia*, 15(2): 133–46.

Peach, C. and G. Glebe (1995) 'Muslim Minorities in Western Europe', *Ethnic and Racial Studies*, 18(1): 26–45.

Perusek, D. (1992) 'Subaltern Consciousness and the Historiography of the Indian Rebellion of 1857', *Novel: A Forum on Fiction*, 25(3): 286–301.

Peters, R. (1996) *Jihad in Classical and Modern Islam*, Princeton, NJ: Markus Wiener.

Pew Research Center (2006) *The Great Divide: How Westerners and Muslims View Each Other*, Washington, DC: Pew Global Attitude Project.

Philips, R.S. (2008) 'Standing Together: The Muslim Association of Britain and the Anti-war Movement', *Race & Class*, 50(2): 101–13.

Phillips, C. and D. Brown (1998) *Entry into the Criminal-justice System: A Survey of Police Arrests and Their Outcomes*, London: Home Office Research Study 185.

Phillips, D. (1998) 'Black Minority Ethnic Concentration, Segregation and Dispersal in Britain', *Urban Studies*, 35(10): 1681–702.

——(2006) 'Parallel Lives? Challenging Discourses of British Muslim Self-Segregation', *Environment and Planning D: Society and Space*, 24(1): 25–40.

Phillips, M. (2008) *Londonistan: How Britain Is Creating a Terror State Within*, London: Gibson.

Phillips, T. (2005) 'After 7/7: Sleepwalking to Segregation', speech delivered to the Manchester Council for Community Relations, 22 September.

Polo, M. (1903) *The Book of Ser Marco Polo the Venetian, Concerning the Kingdoms and Marvels of the East*, trans. and ed. Sir Henry Yule, third edition, revised by Henri Cordier, Vol. I, Chapters 23 and 24, pp. 139–43, quoted in Lockhart (1930), op. cit., pp. 680–1.

Poole, E. (2002) *Reporting Islam: Media Representations and British Muslims*, London: I.B. Tauris.

Portes, A. and M. Zhou (1992) 'Gaining the Upper Hand: Economic Mobility Among Immigrant and Domestic Minorities', *Ethnic and Racial Studies*, 15(4): 491–522.

Portes, A. and P. Landolt (1996) 'The Downside of Social Capital', *The American Prospect*, 26 (May–June): 18–23.

Putnam, R. (2001) Bowling Alone: The Collapse and Revival of American Community, New York: Simon & Schuster.

Qur'ān, 'The Embryo' (Al-' Alaq), 96: 1–5.

Quraishi, M. (2005) *Muslims and Crime*, Aldershot: Ashgate.

Rafiq, M. (1992) 'Ethnicity and Enterprise: A Comparison of Muslim and Non-Muslim Owned Asian Businesses in Britain', *New Community*, 19(1): 43–60.

Rahman, H.U. (1989) *A Chronology of Islamic History, 570–1000 CE*, London: Mansell.

Ram, M. and T. Jones (1998) *Ethnic Minorities in Business*, Open University, Milton Keynes: Small Business Research Trust.

Ram, M. T. Jones, T. Abbas and B. Sanghera (2002) 'Ethnic Enterprise in Its Urban Context: South Asian Restaurants in Birmingham', *International Journal of Urban and Regional Research*, 26(1): 26–40.

Ram, M., T. Abbas, B. Sanghera, G. Barlow and T. Jones (2001a) '"Apprentice Entrepreneurs"? Ethnic Minority Workers in the Independent Restaurant Sector', *Work, Employment and Society*, 15(2): 353–72.

——(2001b) 'Making the Link: Households and Ethnic Minority Business Activity', *Community Work and Family*, 4(3): 327–48.

Ramadan, T. (2005) *Western Muslims and the Future of Islam*, Oxford: Oxford University Press.

——(2009) *What I Believe*, Oxford: Oxford University Press.

Rampton, S. and J. Stauber (2003) *Weapons of Mass Deception: The Uses of Propaganda in Bush's War on Iraq*, New York: Penguin.

Ratcliffe, P. (1999) 'Housing Inequality and "Race": Some Critical Reflections on the Concept of "Social Exclusion"', *Ethnic and Racial Studies*, 22(1): 1–22.

Rawnsley, A. (2000) *Servants of the People: The Inside Story of New Labour*, London: Hamish Hamilton.

——(2010) *The End of the Party: The Rise and Fall of New Labour*, London: Viking.

Reeves, F. and E. Seward (2006) *From BUF to BNP*, Birmingham: Race Equality West Midlands.

Reuter, C. (2002) *My Life as a Weapon: A Modern History of Suicide Bombing*, Princeton, NJ: Princeton University Press.

Rex, J. (2005) 'An Afterword on the Situation of British Muslims in a World Context', in T. Abbas (ed.) *Muslim Britain: Communities under Pressure*, London and New York, pp. 235–43.

Rex, J. and R. Moore (1967) *Race, Community and Conflict: A Study of Sparkbrook*, London: Institute of Race Relations and Oxford University Press.

Rex, J. and S. Tomlinson (1979) *Colonial Immigrants in a British City: A Class Analysis*, London: Routledge.

Richardson, R. (2004) (ed.) *Islamophobia: Issues, Challenges and Action: A Report by the Commission on British Muslims and Islamophobia*, Stoke-on-Trent: Trentham.

Riley-Smith, J. (2002a) *The Oxford History of the Crusades*, Oxford: Oxford University Press.

——(2002b) *What Were the Crusades?* Basingstoke: Palgrave-Macmillan.

Rippon, A. (1990) *Muslims: Their Religious Beliefs and Practices, Vol. I: The Formative Period*, London: Routledge.

——(1993) *Muslims: Their Religious and Practices, Vol. II: The Contemporary Period*, London: Routledge.

——(2008) (ed.) *The Blackwell Companion to the Qur'an*, new edition, Oxford: Wiley-Blackwell.

Robinson, F. (1988) *Varieties of South Asian Islam*, University of Warwick: Centre for Research in Ethnic Relations.

——(1989) (ed.) *The Cambridge Illustrated History of the Islamic World*, Cambridge: Cambridge University Press.

Robinson, N. (1997) 'Sectarian and Ideological Bias in Muslim Translations of the Qur'an', *Islam and Christian–Muslim Relations*, 8(3): 261–78.

Robinson, V. (1996) 'Inter-generational Differences in Ethnic Settlement Patterns in Britain', in P. Ratcliffe (ed.), *Ethnicity in the 1991 Census, Vol. III: Social Geography and Ethnicity in Britain: Geographical Spread, Spatial Concentration and Internal Migration*, London: HMSO, pp. 175–99.

Rodinson, M. (2002) *Muhammad*, London: New Press.

Rogerson, B. (2004) *The Prophet Muhammad: A Biography*, London: Abacus.

——(2006) *The Heirs of the Prophet Muhammad and the Roots of the Sunni–Shia Schism*, London: Abacus.

Rose, E.J.B. in association with N. Deakin, M. Abrams, V. Jackson, A.H. Vanags, B. Cohen, J. Gaitskill and P. Ward (1969) *Colour and Citizenship: A Report on British Race Relations*, London: Institute of Race Relations and Oxford University Press.

Roy, O. (2004) *Globalised Islam: The Search for a New Ummah*, London: Hurst.

Runnymede Trust (1997) *Islamophobia: A Challenge for Us All: Report of the Runnymede Trust Commission on British Muslims and Islamophobia*, London: Runnymede Trust.

Ruthven, M. (1991) *A Satanic Affair: Salman Rushdie and the Rage of Islam*, London: Hogarth Press.

Saeed, A. (2007) 'Media, Racism and Islamophobia: The Representation of Islam and Muslims in the Media', *Sociology Compass*, 1(2): 443–62.

Safi, O. (2003) (ed.) *Progressive Muslims: On Justice, Gender and Pluralism*, Oxford: Oneworld.

Sageman, M. (2008) *Leaderless Jihad: Terror Networks in the Twenty-first Century*, Philadelphia: University of Pennsylvania Press.

Saghal, G. (2002) 'Blair's Jihad, Blunkett's Crusade: The Battle for the Hearts and Minds of Britain's Muslims', *Radical Philosophy*, 112 (March/April): 2–5.

Sagiv, D. (1995) *Fundamentalism and Intellectuals in Egypt, 1973–1993*, London: Frank Cass.

Said, E. (1978) *Orientalism*, London: Routledge & Kegan Paul.

——(1981) *Covering Islam: How the Media and the Experts Determine How We See the Rest of the World*, London: Routledge & Kegan Paul.

——(1993) *Culture and Imperialism*, New York: Vintage.

——(1997) *Covering Islam: How the Media and the Experts Determine How We See the Rest of the World*, London: Vintage.

Saifullah-Khan, V. (1976) 'Pakistanis in Britain: Perceptions of a Population', *New Community*, 5(3): 222–9.

Saikul, A. (2003) *Islam and the West: Conflict or Cooperation?* Basingstoke: Palgrave-Macmillan.

Sajoo, A.B. (2008) (ed.) *Muslim Modernities: Expressions of the Civil Imagination*, London and New York: I.B. Tauris.

Salvatore, A. (2004) 'Making Public Space: Opportunities and Limits of Collective Action Among Muslims in Europe', *Journal of Ethnic and Migration Studies*, 30(5): 1013–31.

Samad, Y. and J. Eade (2003) *Community Perceptions of Forced Marriage*, London: Foreign and Commonwealth Office.

Sanghera, G. and S. Thapar-Bjorkert (2007) '"Because I am Pakistani … and I am Muslim … I am Political": Gendering Political Radicalism – Young Masculinities and Femininities in Bradford', in T. Abbas (ed.), *Islamic Political Radicalism: A European Perspective*, Edinburgh: Edinburgh University Press, pp. 173–91.

Sardar, Z. (1978) *Muhammad: Aspects of his Biography*, Leicester: Islamic Foundation.
——(2004) *Desperately Seeking Paradise: Journeys of a Sceptical Muslim*, London: Granta.
——(2006) *What Do Muslims Believe?* London: Granta.
Sardar, Z. and Z.A. Malik (1999) *Introducing Muhammad*, Cambridge: Icon.
Sardar, Z. and M. Wyn-Davies (1990) *Distorted Imagination: Lessons from the Rushdie Affair*, London: Grey Seal.
——(2004) *Introducing Islam: A Graphic Guide*, second revised edition, Cambridge: Icon.
Sarup, M. (1991) *Education and the Ideologies of Racism*, Stoke-on-Trent: Trentham.
Sarwar, G. (1991) *British Muslims and Schools*, London: Muslim Educational Trust.
Sayyid, B.S. (2003) *A Fundamental Fear: Eurocentrism and the Emergence of Islamism*, London and New York: Zed.
Scarman, Lord (1982) *The Scarman Report: The Brixton Disorders, 10–12 April 1981*, London: Penguin.
Schuster, L. and J. Solomos (2001) 'Asylum, Refuge and Public Policy: Current Trends and Future Dilemmas', *Sociological Research Online*, 6(1). Available at <www.socresonline.org.uk/6/1/schuster.html>. Accessed 6 April 2010.
——(2004) 'Race, Immigration and Asylum: New Labour's Agenda and Its Consequences', *Ethnicities*, 4(2): 267–300.
Scruton, R. (2003) *The West and the Rest: Globalization and the Terrorist Threat*, London: Continuum.
Secretary of State for Work and Pensions Rt Hon. John Hutton (2007) 'Ethnic Minority Employment in Britain: Recognising Women's Potential, Women's Enterprise Project – Bethnal Green', speech delivered 28 February. Avalible at <www.dwp.gov.uk/newsroom/ministers-speeches/2007/28-02-07.shtml>. Accessed 10 April 2010.
Sellick, P. (2004) *Muslim Housing Experiences*, London: Housing Corporation and Oxford Centre for Islamic Studies.
Shaban, M.A. (1979) *Islamic History: A New Interpretation: AD 600–750 (AH 132), Vol. I*, Cambridge: Cambridge University Press.
——(1979) *The Abbasid Revolution*, Cambridge: Cambridge University Press.
Shah, S.G.M. (1993) *The British in the Subcontinent*, Lahore: Ferozans.
Shaheen, J. (1980) 'The Arab Stereotype on Television', *Americans for Middle East Understanding*, 13(2): 1–16.
——(2001) *Reel Bad Arabs: How Hollywood Vilifies a People*, Northam: Roundhouse.
——(2003) '"Reel Bad Arabs": How Hollywood Vilifies a People', *The Annals of the American Academy of Political and Social Science*, 588(1): 171–93.
Shaw, A. (1988) *A Pakistani Community in Britain*, Oxford: Basil Blackwell.
——(2000) *Kinship and Continuity: Pakistani Families in Britain*, London: Routledge.
——(2001) 'Kinship, Cultural Preference and Immigration: Consanguineous Marriage Among British Pakistanis', *Journal of the Royal Anthropological Institute*, 7(2): 315–34.
Shayegan, D. (1997) *Cultural Schizophrenia: Islamic Societies Confronting the West*, New York: Syracuse University Press.
Sheridan, L.P. (2006) 'Islamophobia Pre- and Post-September 11th, 2001', *Journal of Interpersonal Violence*, 21(3): 317–36.

Sherif, M.A. (2004) *Searching for Solace: Biography of Yusuf Ali, Interpreter of the Qur'an*, Kuala Lumpar: Islamic Book Trust.

Shukra, K., L. Back, M. Keith and J. Solomos (2004) 'Black Politics and the Web of Joined-up Governance: Compromise, Ethnic Minority Mobilisation and the Transitional Public Sphere', *Social Movement Studies*, 3(1): 31–50.

Siddiqui, M. (2004) 'The Doctrines of Hizb ut-Tahrir', in Z. Baran (ed.), *The Challenge of Hizb ut-Tahrir: Deciphering and Combating Radical Islamist Ideology*, Washington, DC: The Nixon Centre. Available at <www.nixoncenter.org/Program %20Briefs/PB%202004/confrephiztahrir.pdf>. Accessed 10 April 2010.

Sikand, Y. (1994) 'Muslims and the Mass Media', *Economic and Political Weekly*, 29(33): 2134–5.

Silverman, M. (2007) 'The French Republic Unveiled', *Ethnic and Racial Studies*, 30(4): 628–42.

Simpson, L. (2004) 'Statistics of Racial Segregation: Measures, Evidence and Policy', *Urban Studies*, 41(3): 661–81.

Sinno, A.H. (2009) *Muslims in Western Politics*, Bloomington: Indiana University Press.

Sivan, E. (1985) *Radical Islam*, New Haven, CT: Yale University Press.

Sivanandan, A. (1982) *A Different Hunger: Writings on Black Resistance*, London: Pluto.

Skeggs, B. (2004) *Class, Self, Culture*, London: Routledge.

Small, S. and J. Solomos (2006) 'Race, Immigration and Politics in Britain Changing Policy Agendas and Conceptual Paradigms: 1940s–2000s', *International Journal of Comparative Sociology*, 47(3–4): 235–57.

Smith, C.D. (2007) *Palestine and the Arab–Israeli Conflict: A History with Documents*, Basingstoke: Palgrave-Macmillan.

Smith, D. and S. Tomlinson (1989) *The School Effect: A Study of Multi-racial Comprehensives*, London: Policy Studies Institute.

Smith, G. and S. Stephenson (2005) 'The Theory and Practice of Group Representation: Reflections on the Politics of Race Equality in Birmingham', *Public Administration*, 83(2): 323–43.

Smith, S.J. (1993) 'Residential Segregation and the Politics of Racialisation', in M. Cross and M. Keith (eds), *Racism, the City and the State*, London: Routledge, pp. 128–43.

Smithies, B. and P. Fiddick (1969) *Enoch Powell on Immigration*, London: Sphere.

Solomos, J. (2003) *Race and Racism in Britain*, Basingstoke: Palgrave-Macmillan.

Song, M. (2003) *Choosing Ethnic Identity*, Cambridge: Polity.

Spalek, B. (2002) 'Conclusion: Religious Diversity and Criminal Justice Policy', in B. Spalek (ed.), *Islam, Crime and Criminal Justice*, Uffculme: Willan, pp. 133–40.

——(n.d.) *Muslims in British Prisons: Pen Picture*, Article 496. Available at <www. hmprisonservice.gov.uk/assets/documents/100011E4496_muslims_in_- british_prisons.doc>. Accessed 6 March 2010.

Spalek, B. and S. El-Hassan (2007) 'Muslim Converts in Prison', *Howard Journal of Criminal Justice*, 46(2): 99–114.

Spalek, B. and D. Wilson (2001) 'Not Just "Visitors" to Prisons: The Experiences of Imams Who Work Inside the Penal System', *Howard Journal of Criminal Justice*, 40(1): 3–13.

Sulieman, Y. (2009) *Contextualising Islam in Britain: Exploratory Perspectives*, Cambridge: University of Cambridge in Association with the Universities of Exeter and Westminster.

Surty, M.I.H. (1996) *Muslim Contribution to the Development of Hospitals*, Birmingham: Qur'anic Arabic Foundation.

Sutton, P. and S. Vertigans (2005) *Resurgent Islam: A Sociological Approach*, London: Polity.

Taji-Farouki, S. (1996) *A Fundamental Quest: Hizb ut-Tahrir and the Search for the Islamic Caliphate*, London: Grey Seal.

Taylor, C. (1994) *Multiculturalism: Examining the Politics of Recognition*, Princeton, NJ: Princeton University Press.

Terrorism Act 2000, Section 1(1).

The 1990 Trust (2006) *Muslim Views: Foreign Policy and Its Effects*, London: The 1990 Trust.

Tibi, B. (1990) *Islam and the Cultural Accommodation of Social Change*, trans. C. Krojzl, Oxford: Westview.

——(2001) *Islam Between Culture and Politics*, Basingstoke: Palgrave-Macmillan.

Tomlinson, S. (2005) *Education in a Post-welfare Society*, Milton Keynes: Open University Press and McGraw-Hill.

Townsend, M. (2006) 'Leak Reveals Official Story of London Bombings', *The Observer*, 9 April.

Toynbee, P. (2001) 'Last Chance to Speak Out', *The Guardian*, 5 October.

Travis, A. (2010) 'Stop and Search Powers Illegal, European Court Rules', *The Guardian*, 12 January.

Troyna, B. and J. Williams (1986) *Racism, Education and the State: The Racialization of Educational Policy*, Beckenham: Croom Helm.

Tryer, D. and F. Ahmed (2006) *Muslim Women and Higher Education: Identities, Experiences and Prospects: A Summary Report*, Liverpool: Liverpool John Moores University and European Social Fund.

United Nations (1948) *Universal Declaration of Human Rights*, New York: UN.

van Dijk, T. (1993) *Elite Discourse and Racism*, London: Sage.

——(2000) 'New(s) Racism: A Discourse Analytical Approach', in S. Cottle (ed.), *Ethnic Minorities and the Media: Changing Cultural Boundaries*, Buckingham: Open University Press, pp. 33–49.

Versteegh, K. (2001) *The Arabic Language*, Edinburgh: Edinburgh University Press.

Vertovec, S. (2001) 'Transnational Challenges to the "New" Multiculturalism', paper presented to the Association of Social Anthropologists Conference', held at the University of Sussex, 30 March–2 April. Available at <www.transcomm.ox.ac.uk/working papers/WPTC-2K-06 Vertovec.pdf>. Accessed 10 April.

——(2002) 'Islamophobia and Muslim Recognition in Britain', in Y. Haddad (ed.), *Muslims in the West: From Sojourners to Citizens*, New York: Oxford University Press, pp. 19–35.

Vertovec, S. and C. Peach (1997) 'Introduction: Islam in Europe and the Politics of Religion and Community', in S. Vertovec and C. Peach (eds), *Islam in Europe: The Politics of Religion and Community*, Basingstoke: Macmillan, pp. 3–47.

Vishram, R. (1986) *Ayahs, Lascars and Princes: Indians in Britain 1700–1947*, London: Pluto.

von Hirsch, A. and J.V. Roberts (1997) 'Racial Disparity in Sentencing: Reflections on the Hood Study', *Howard Journal of Criminal Justice*, 36(3): 227–36.

vorn Bruck, G. (2008) 'Naturalising, Neutralising Women's Bodies: The "Headscarf Affair" and the Politics of Representation', *Identities*, 15(1): 51–79.

Wainright, M. (2006) 'Tribunal Dismisses Case of Muslim Woman Ordered Not to Teach in Veil', *The Guardian*, 20 October.

Waldinger, R. (1995) 'The "Other Side" of Embeddedness: A Case Study of the Interplay of Economy and Ethnicity', *Ethnic and Racial Studies*, 18(3): 555–80.

Waldinger, R., R. Ward and H. Aldrich (1985) 'Ethnic Business and Occupational Mobility in Advanced Societies', *Sociology*, 19(4): 586–97.

Waldinger, R., H. Aldrich and R. Ward (1990) (eds) *Ethnic Entrepreneurs: Immigrants Business in Industrial Societies*, Thousand Oaks, CA: Sage.

Waldinger, R., I. Light, G. Sabagh, M. Bozorgmehr and C. Der-Martirosian (1993) 'Internal Ethnicity in the Ethnic Economy', *Ethnic and Racial Studies*, 16(4): 581–97.

Walford, G. (1998) *Doing Research about Education*, London: Routledge.

——(2003) 'Separate Schools for Religious Minorities in England and the Netherlands: Using a Framework for the Comparison and Evaluation of Policy', *Research Papers in Education*, 18(3): 281–99.

——(2004) 'English Education and Immigration Policies and Muslim Schools', in H. Daun and G. Walford (eds), *Educational Strategies among Muslims in the Context of Globalization: Some National Case Studies*, Leiden: Brill, pp. 209–28.

Walker, C. (2002) *Blackstone's Guide to the Anti-Terrorism Legislation*, Oxford: Oxford University Press.

Wallace-Murhpy, T. (2007) *What Islam Did For Us: Understanding Islam's Contribution to Western Civilization*, London: Watkins.

Ward, I. (2006) 'Shabina Begum and the Headscarf Girls', *Journal of Gender Studies*, 15(2): 119–31.

Waters, R. (1990) *Ethnic Minorities and the Criminal-justice System*, Aldershot: Avebury.

Watt, W.M. (1999) *Islam: A Short History*, second edition, Oxford: Oneworld.

Weller, P. (2009) *A Mirror for our Times: 'The Rushdie Affair' and the Future of Multiculturalism*, London: Continuum.

Weller, P., A. Feldman and K. Purdam, with contributions from A. Andrews, A. Doswell, J. Hinnells, M. Parker-Jenkins, S. Parmar and M. Wolfe of the University of Derby (2001) *Religious Discrimination in England and Wales*, London: Home Office Research Study 220.

Werbner, P. (2000) 'Divided Loyalties, Empowered Citizenship? Muslims in Britain', *Citizenship Studies*, 4(3): 307–24.

——(2002) *The Migration Process: Capital, Gifts and Offerings Among British Pakistanis*, Oxford: Berg.

——(2004a) 'Theorising Complex Diasporas: Purity and Hybridity in the South Asian Public Sphere in Britain', *Journal of Ethnic and Migration Studies*, 30(5): 895–911.

——(2004b) personal communication, 15 July.

Whelan, E. (1998) 'Forgotten Witness: Evidence for the Early Codification of the Qur'an', *Journal of the American Oriental Society*, 118(1): 1–14.

White, A. (2002) (ed.) *Social Focus in Brief: Ethnicity 2002*, London: Office for National Statistics.

Wiktorowicz, Q. (2004a) 'Joining the Cause: Al-Muhajiroun and Radical Islam', paper presented to the conference, The Roots of Radicalism, Yale University, 8–9 May. Available at <http://insct.syr.edu/Projects/islam-ihl/research/Wiktorowicz. Joining%20the%20Cause.pdf>. Accessed 10 April 2010.

——(2004b) *Islamic Activism: A Social Movement Theory Approach*, Bloomington: Indiana University Press.

Wolton, S. (2006) 'Immigration Policy and the "Crisis of British Values"', *Citizenship Studies*, 10(4): 453–67.

Wylde, H. (1932) (ed.) *Universal Dictionary of the English Language*, London: Routledge.

Yuval-Davis, N. (1992) 'Fundamentalism, Multiculturalism and Women in Britain', in J. Donald and A. Rattansi (eds), *Race, Culture and Difference*, London and New York: Sage, pp. 278–91.

Zaidi, A.H. (2006) 'Muslim Reconstructions of Knowledge and the Re-enchantment of Modernity', *Theory Culture Society*, 23(5): 69–91.

Zaman, M.Q. (1999) 'Religious Education and the Rhetoric of Reform: The Madrasa in British India and Pakistan', *Comparative Studies in Society and History*, 41(2): 294–323.

Zimmer, C. and H. Aldrich (1987) 'Resource Mobilization through Ethnic Networks: Kinship and Friendship Ties of Shopkeepers in England', *Sociological Perspectives*, 30(4): 422–55.

Index

Lightning Source UK Ltd.
Milton Keynes UK
UKOW06f1802280915

259415UK00003B/143/P